LEGENDARY LOCALS

OF

IDAHO FALLS

IDAHO

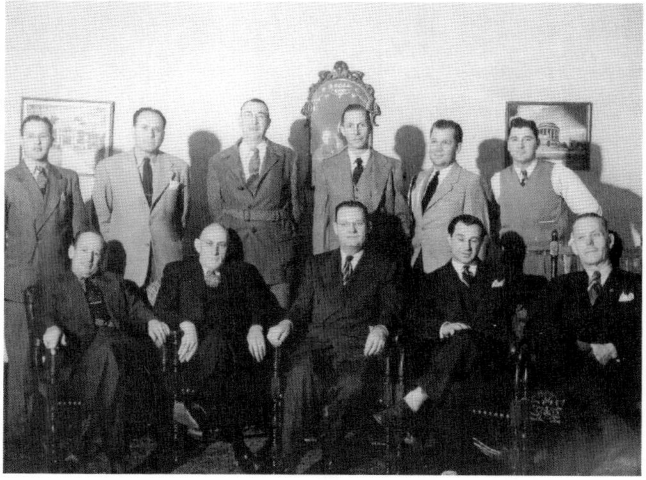

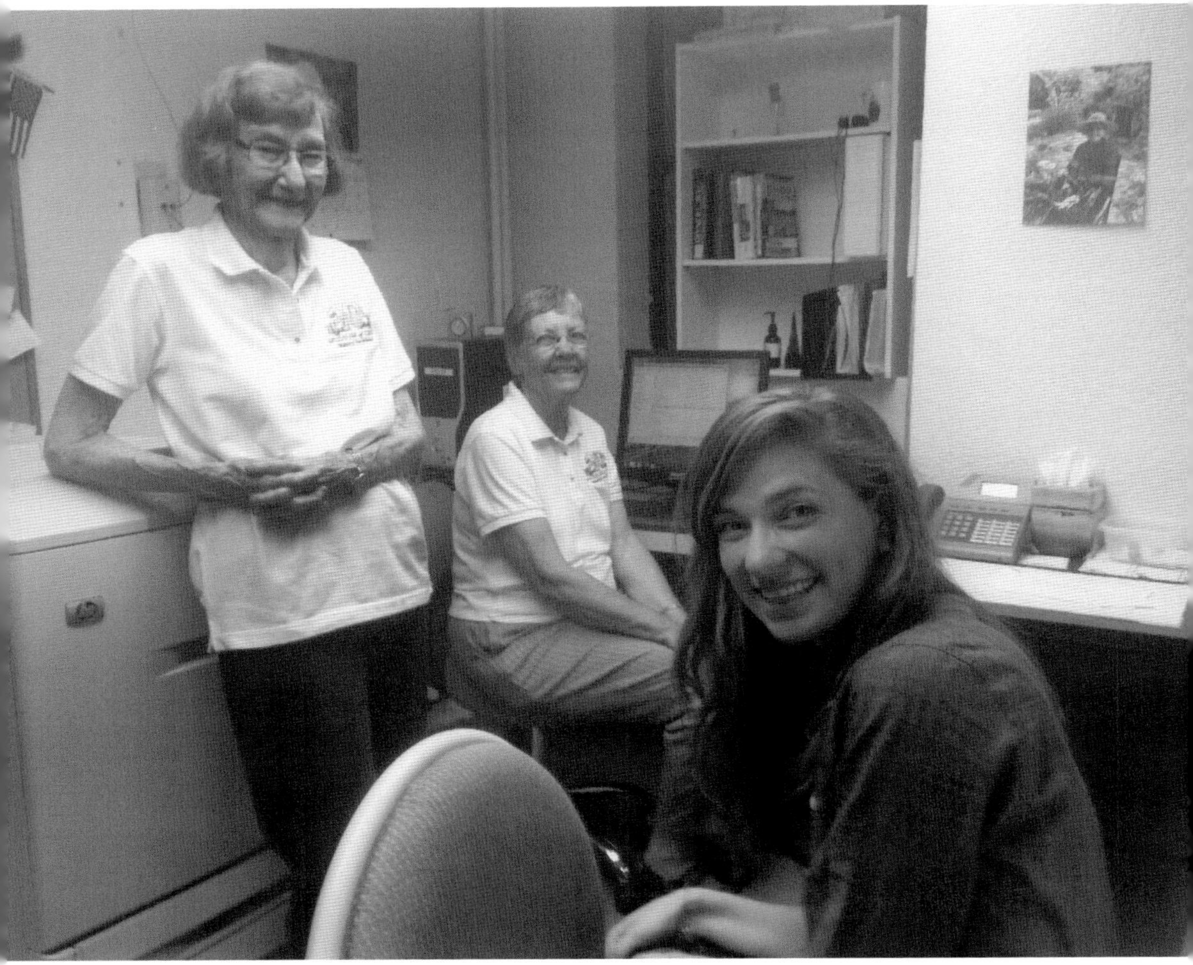

History Central

Pictured here is the Reading Room at the Museum of Idaho (MOI), owned by the Bonneville County Historical Society, and the two women who staff it, LaDean Harmston (left) and Judy House (center). In the foreground at right is MOI curator Claire Smith, whose great-grandfather David Smith is one of the legendary locals featured in this book (see page 44). The museum is a top repository of historical information and photographs of Eagle Rock and Idaho Falls. The imposing Carr Atrium was built in 2002 to join two buildings from the early 20th century: the old Public Library, which had been built with a grant from Andrew Carnegie in 1916, and the Masonic Lodge, which was remodeled in 2002, one hundred years after its construction. (Author photograph.)

Page 1: In the Clubhouse

Idaho Falls Golf Association members pictured in 1948 are, from left to right, (first row) Spike Ballard, Bill Gourley, B.L. Harris, George Orullian, and Russ Freeman; (second row) Jack Couch, A.M. Smith, Ross Corbett, N.O. Anderson, S. Eddie Pedersen, and J. Robb Brady. (Courtesy of Idaho Falls Parks and Recreation.)

LEGENDARY LOCALS

OF

IDAHO FALLS

IDAHO

PAUL MENSER

LEGENDARY LOCALS

ISBN 978-1-4671-0168-4

Legendary Locals is an imprint of Arcadia Publishing
Charleston, South Carolina

Printed in the United States of America

Library of Congress Control Number: 2014933838

For all general information, please contact Arcadia Publishing:
Telephone 843-853-2070
Fax 843-853-0044
E-mail sales@arcadiapublishing.com
For customer service and orders:
Toll-Free 1-888-313-2665

Visit us on the Internet at www.arcadiapublishing.com

Dedication
To my father, David Menser, who believed in the ideals of democracy and the possibilities of community.

On the Front Cover: Clockwise from top left:
Rachel Martin (courtesy of National Public Radio, see page 117), Gilbert G. Wright (courtesy of the Museum of Idaho, see page 25), Joe Marmo (courtesy of the Idaho Falls *Post Register*, see page 79), E.W. Fanning (courtesy of the City of Idaho Falls, see page 59), Minnie Gibson Hitt (courtesy of the Museum of Idaho, see page 20), Joe L. Marker (courtesy of the Museum of Idaho, see page 72), Joseph A. Clark (courtesy of the Museum of Idaho, see page 14), Helen Hoff Aupperle (courtesy of the Museum of Idaho, see page 68), Dr. Thomas C. Willson (courtesy of the Museum of Idaho, see page 26).

On the Back Cover: From left to right:
Ed F. Winn (courtesy of the Museum of Idaho, see page 13), and Jared Gold (courtesy of Jared Gold, see page 120).

CONTENTS

ACKNOWLEDGMENTS

I believe any person has an epic story to tell if he or she is willing to see it that way. Trying to condense any person's story down to a few hundred words is a huge challenge, yet I have discovered that the cumulative impact of all these short sketches is a picture of our community that might shed new light on who we are.

This project has been a deep dip into Idaho Falls's history, yet my greatest worry is that I neglected someone who ought to be included; for that, I apologize. I have lived here 32 years and written a weekly history column for more than a decade, yet there are still people I either don't know about or whose significance I don't fully recognize.

The greatest pleasure I received from this project has been the conversations I had with the children and grandchildren of many of the people in this book. Likewise, I am grateful for the help I received from the Museum of Idaho and the Idaho Falls *Post Register.* Individually, I wish to credit Monte LaOrange at the newspaper and LaDean Harmston and Judy House at the museum. Their assistance and good humor were invaluable. From the *Post Register*'s past, I wish to credit Robert Bower, Randy Hayes, and Bob Schwieger, three photographers with whom I worked in my newsroom days and whose images appear in this book.

My reading in the Idaho Room of the Idaho Falls Public Library was enlightening. A few books were essential to the profiles of the people in this book, and I encourage anyone with a deeper interest in local history to read them:

Second Stories Revisited: Historical Narratives of Idaho Falls Women by Cheryl A. Cox and Lexie French
Idaho Falls, City of Destiny by Mary Jane Fritzen
Idaho Falls by William Hathaway
Bonneville County in the Making by Barzilla W. Clark
Unsung Heroes and Settlers of Bonneville County, Idaho by Connie Otteson
Beautiful Bonneville, County of Contrasts by Alice Horton, Afton Bitton, and Patti Sherlock

The information on the Bonneville County Heritage Association's website was essential, and without the historical record provided by the *Post Register*—all on microfilm at the Idaho Falls Public Library—there would be huge gaps in the story. However imperfect they may sometimes be, news accounts and obituaries are vital to our comprehension and understanding of the past.

I am very grateful for old Polk City Directories, which don't have much in the way of plot but offer valuable information about where people worked and lived and who was related to whom.

Last of all, my hat is off to two newsmen now gone on to greater glory: Joe L. Marker, my old friend and colleague at the *Post Register*, and Perry Swisher, the public utilities commissioner who was always good for an interesting story. It is a privilege to have known them.

—Paul Menser
July 2014

INTRODUCTION

At its most romantic, the past is a place full of barn dances, front porches, and lodge meetings. People had time for other people. There was no television, so families gathered in the kitchen or living room to listen to Jack Benny on the radio and sing around the piano. Wives stayed home to take care of the children, because a husband could earn enough to support a family by himself.

The story of Idaho Falls over the past 150 years is a story common to thousands of American towns. Roads were paved. Men went to war. Indoor plumbing replaced the outhouse.

What sets Idaho Falls apart? One thing would be water. Due to the city's hydroelectric power projects, Idaho Falls enjoys some of the lowest electricity rates in the nation. Because of irrigation, the Snake River Valley is one of the world's largest unbroken pieces of irrigated farmland.

Idaho Falls changed its name from Eagle Rock in 1891 on the recommendation of businessmen who thought the new name had less of a frontier ring. The people who built the town live on in the names of roads, streets, parks, schools, and businesses.

Longtime newsman and local historian Joe Marker remembered Ethel Boyes, his teacher at Emerson Elementary School. "She had the gall to be herself," he said. As for O.E. Bell, the namesake of a junior high school (now an office building), Marker mused, "robust fellow . . . strict as all get out."

Was life better? The late Perry Swisher, another newsman, remembered the 1930s, when his father managed a farm cooperative and nobody had any money. The entire economy was based on a bartering system. Services were traded for items such as quilts, canned goods, and firewood. "The Mormon culture made it less tough for people," he said.

During the Great Depression, nearly one quarter of the working people of the United States did not have jobs. In eastern Idaho, that was tempered somewhat by the area's farms. No one who wanted to work had to stand around for lack of a job. But the work—digging beets and potatoes by hand—was monotonous and grueling.

Methods of healing and relief from pain taken for granted today were unthinkable as recently as 75 years ago. Before antibiotics, even an infected cut could kill. "Your medical help was your neighbor," said Sharon Bennett, whose grandparents built a landmark house on Sunnyside Road. She recalled the story of an aunt who died in the influenza epidemic of 1918. "The funeral was held on the front porch," she said. "Nothing was held inside, because people were so deathly afraid."

After World War II ended, the world was not the same. Swisher, who moved to Pocatello in the 1940s, remembered Idaho Falls at that time as a rowdy place where he and his friends would come to party. "It was our fun town," he said. Clubs and dance halls like the Bon Villa and the Wandamere were thriving. Business and the city government worked together in Idaho Falls to enhance the town's appeal. "The competition was Pocatello, and Pocatello lost," Swisher said.

Tamer times lay ahead, however. In 1945, the Church of Jesus Christ of Latter-day Saints (LDS) dedicated its Idaho Falls temple, which helped bring about a more sober self-image for the community. In 1949, the US Atomic Energy Commission (AEC) announced it would locate its headquarters for the National Reactor Testing Station in Idaho Falls. "The AEC, and the euphoria when it came . . . it's definitely the biggest thing that's happened," Swisher said.

Linden Bateman, a history teacher and Idaho state legislator, agrees the AEC and the site changed Idaho Falls. He remembers an arrowhead-hunting trip he once took as a child with Lynn Crandall, the valley's water master for decades, in the desert near the Experimental Breeder Reactor as it was being built. Security was less stringent in 1950, and nobody kicked them off the land. "He [Crandall] went back later, and they kicked him off then," Bateman said.

He has memories of collecting frogs from Crow Creek, where the Idaho Falls Civic Auditorium now stands. "I remember hearing the news they were going to build the new high school, and wondering why they would want to put it so far away from town."

With the 21st century well underway, Idaho Falls continues to feel the effects of many 20th-century decisions, enjoying the benefits of some and paying the price for others. Is it possible that someone who is alive right now might be around in 2114 to explain these times to our children and great-grandchildren? Who in 1914 could have imagined the atomic bomb or the eradication of smallpox? Or that people would go to the moon, only to decide it wasn't that interesting?

In the people's stories lie the clues to who we are and what makes a community unique. Times may change, but if there's one thing history reveals, it is that human nature is a constant. The eastern Idahoans of 100, 50, or 25 years ago might as well be our neighbors.

CHAPTER ONE

Saloon Keepers and Sunday School Teachers

The exact date of the founding of Idaho Falls is unknown, but the town's beginning was James Madison "Matt" Taylor's toll bridge, which opened to traffic in the spring of 1865.

In the East, the Civil War was coming to an end. The war had been fought over a number of issues—slavery, state's rights, the growing economic power of the industrial North over the agrarian South—but it also concerned the future of the West. In 1863, the same year he signed the Emancipation Proclamation, Pres. Abraham Lincoln also signed the act that made Idaho a US territory.

Lincoln's body was on the train home to Illinois around the same time Taylor and his partners were finishing their toll bridge over the river at Black Rock Canyon. In the dust and sweat—or perhaps a blinding blizzard, as anyone who has experienced springtime in eastern Idaho can attest—it is a stretch to think they had more on their minds than getting the job done.

Still, as a Midwesterner who knew opportunity when he saw it, Taylor offers a textbook example of someone who was making a reality out of Lincoln's ideal for the West.

Because of his frontier background, Lincoln saw America as a place for people to pursue their dreams, govern themselves, and build community in the wilderness. From his experience as a railroad lawyer in the 1850s, he also recognized that vast sections of the country were going to be open to settlement.

Who were the people who would settle the land? People with a nose for opportunity and a sharp eye for business.

In his book *Bonneville County in the Making*, Barzilla W. Clark tells how Matt Taylor, recognizing Salt Lake City's large number of English immigrants, could get 40 pounds of butter for a pound of tea from Denver. He would then take butter, eggs, and salt pork north to the gold camps in Montana.

As for the women, they had to make the best of what they found. Taylor's wife, LeGrande Anderson Taylor, never got used to the smell of the hides at the trading post near the toll bridge. She was the first of many women who followed their husbands into the sagebrush determined that if they had to live in this place, they were going to do everything in their power to make it civilized for themselves and their children.

A running thread in Idaho Falls history is the push and pull between rough and genteel—Saturday night and Sunday morning. The Idaho Falls legacy of enterprise and initiative began when one man decided he would build something. The city that followed has always been about trade and commerce, creating a place where people can do more than simply survive; a place to live in community, if not always in harmony.

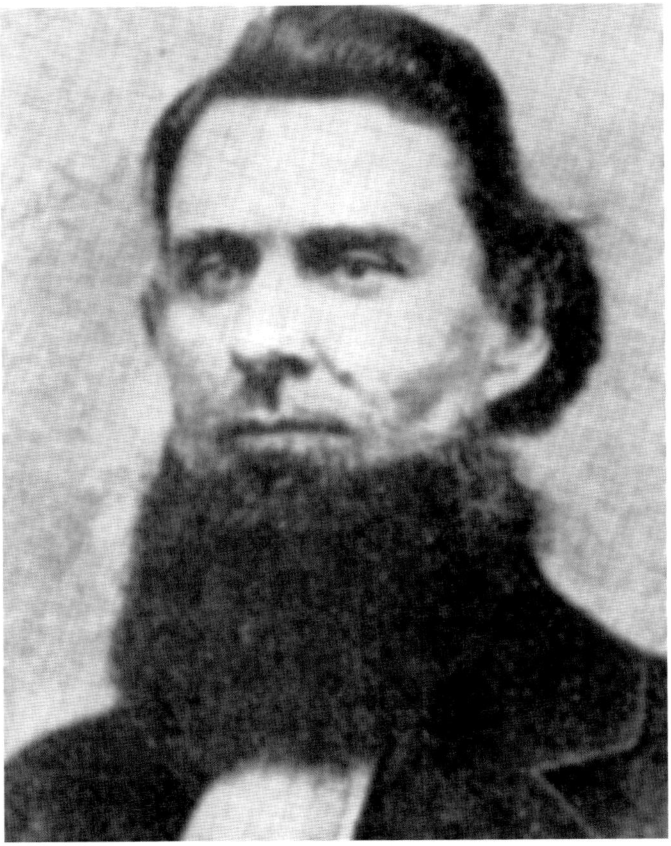

The Bridge Builder
This portrait of Matt Taylor is from *Bonneville County in the Making*. A Midwesterner, Taylor was hauling goods between Salt Lake City and Montana when it occurred to him that a toll bridge at Black Rock Canyon might be a good business opportunity. (Courtesy of Idaho Falls Public Library.)

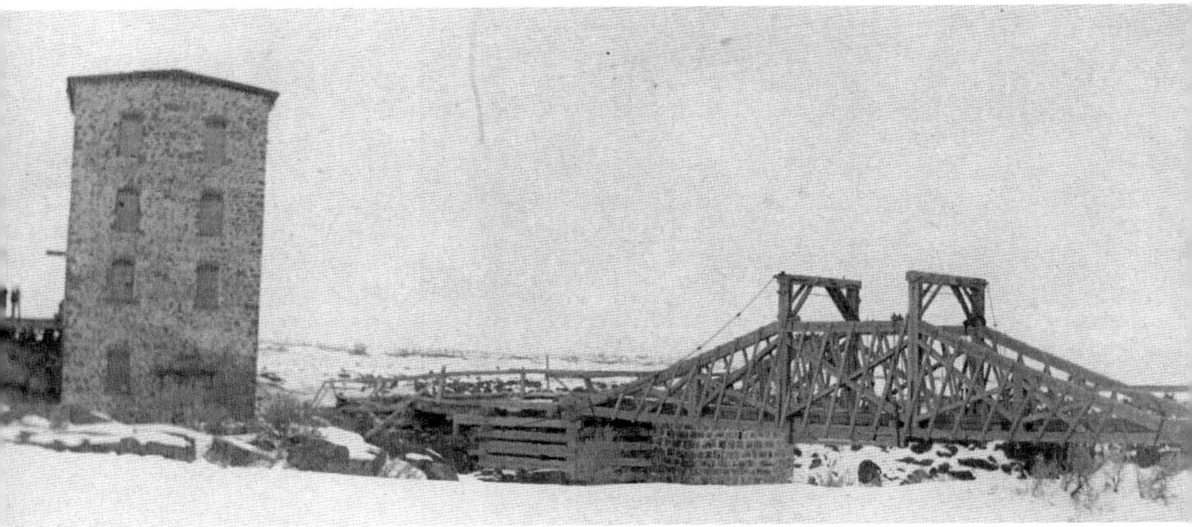

A Rough Place
Pictured here is the Taylor toll bridge soon after it opened, with a stone building and little else nearby. The bridge was washed out in an 1867 flood and rebuilt. While the telegraph and a post office would soon arrive, widespread settlement did not come until the Utah & Northern Railroad arrived in 1879. (Courtesy of the Museum of Idaho.)

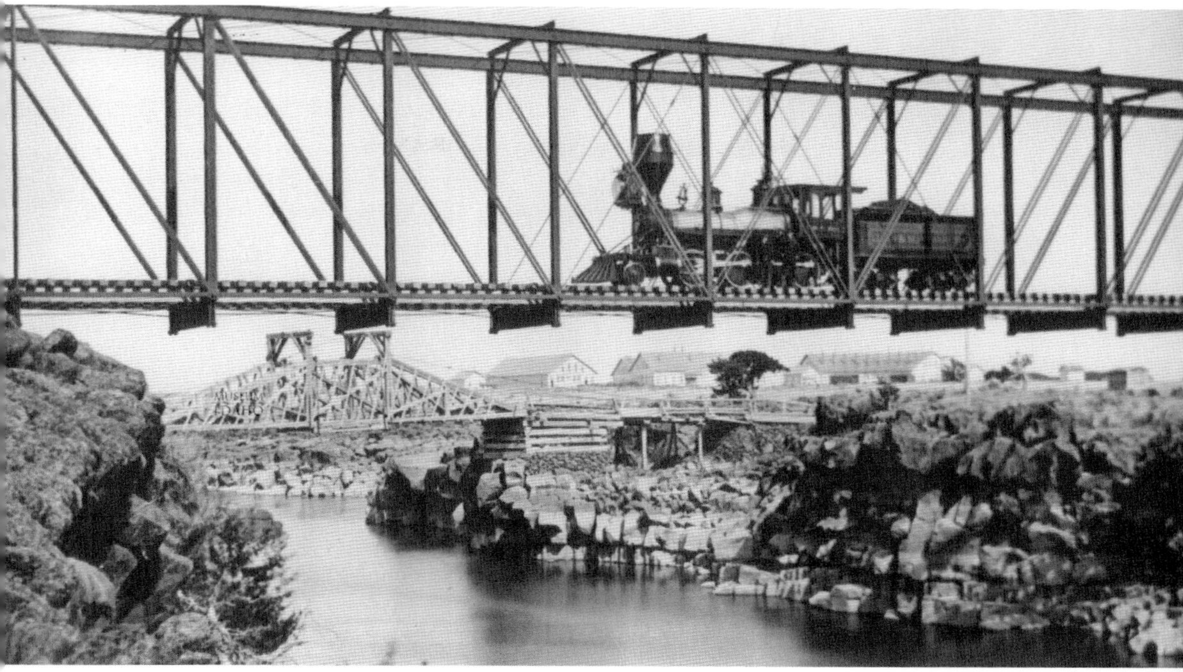

The Railroad Arrives
This view of Eagle Rock from the south shows the Utah & Northern Railroad bridge in the foreground with the Taylor toll bridge in back. Matt Taylor and his wife, LeGrande, returned to the Midwest in 1886, but left behind family members to manage the business interests they had established. (Courtesy of the Museum of Idaho.)

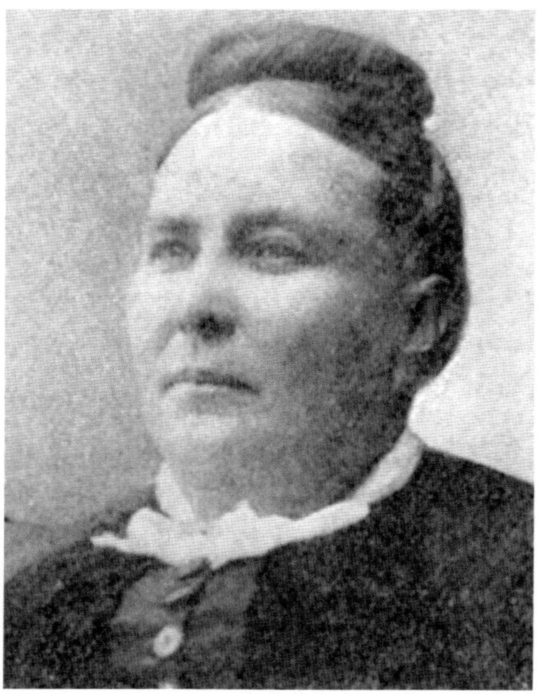

A Tough Customer
Emma Ott Corbett managed the stage stop at the Eagle Rock Ferry and reportedly weighed more than 400 pounds. She once knocked a cowboy out cold when she didn't like his tone, and threw a flatiron at legendary trapper Beaver Dick's head. She died in 1892. (Courtesy of Idaho Falls Public Library.)

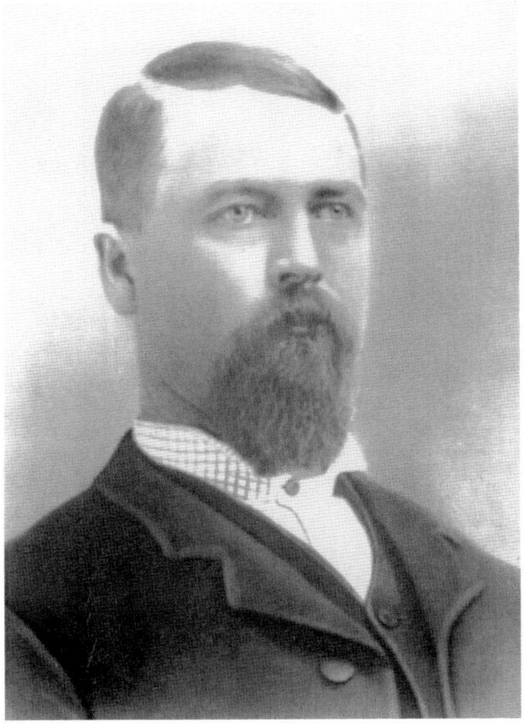

"Captain Dick"
Known as "Captain Dick" or "Uncle Dick," DeForest C. Chamberlain came to Eagle Rock with the railroad and, by 1882, owned Burgess House on Eagle Rock Street, a two-story building with a saloon, billiards, dancing, and rooms for rent. He was appointed to the village council in 1889 and co-founded Eagle Rock's first fire department. (Courtesy of the Museum of Idaho.)

Funeral Procession
When Dick Chamberlain died in 1909, businesses closed and the O.P. Thayer Military Band led mourners down Broadway. (Courtesy of the Museum of Idaho.)

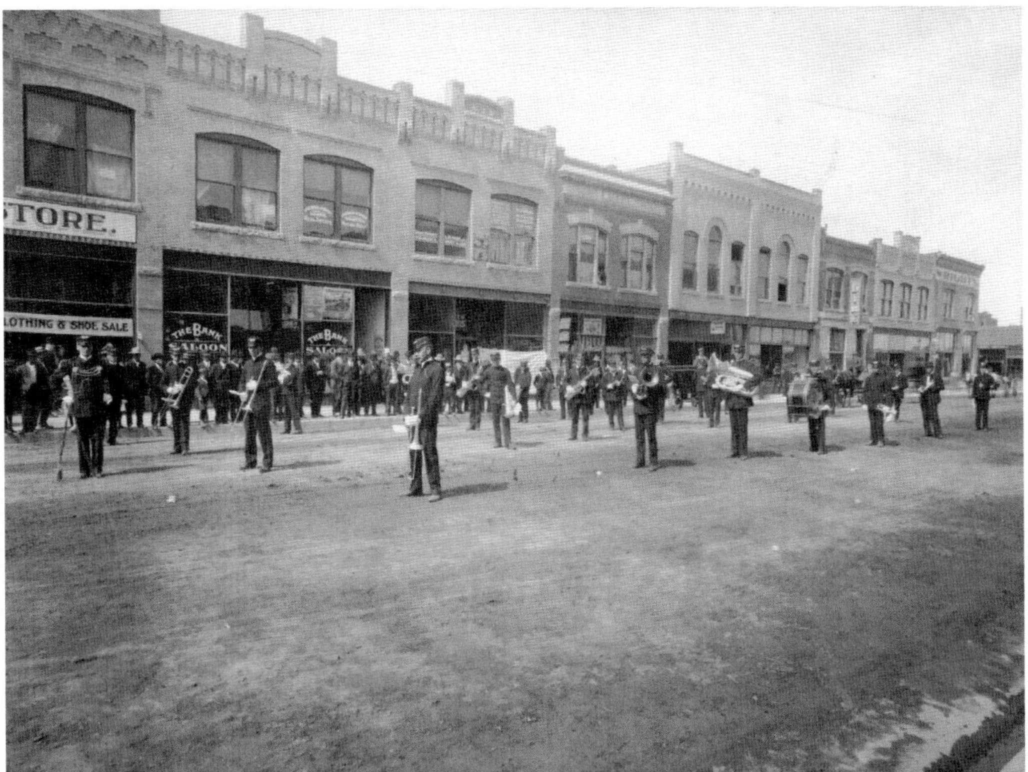

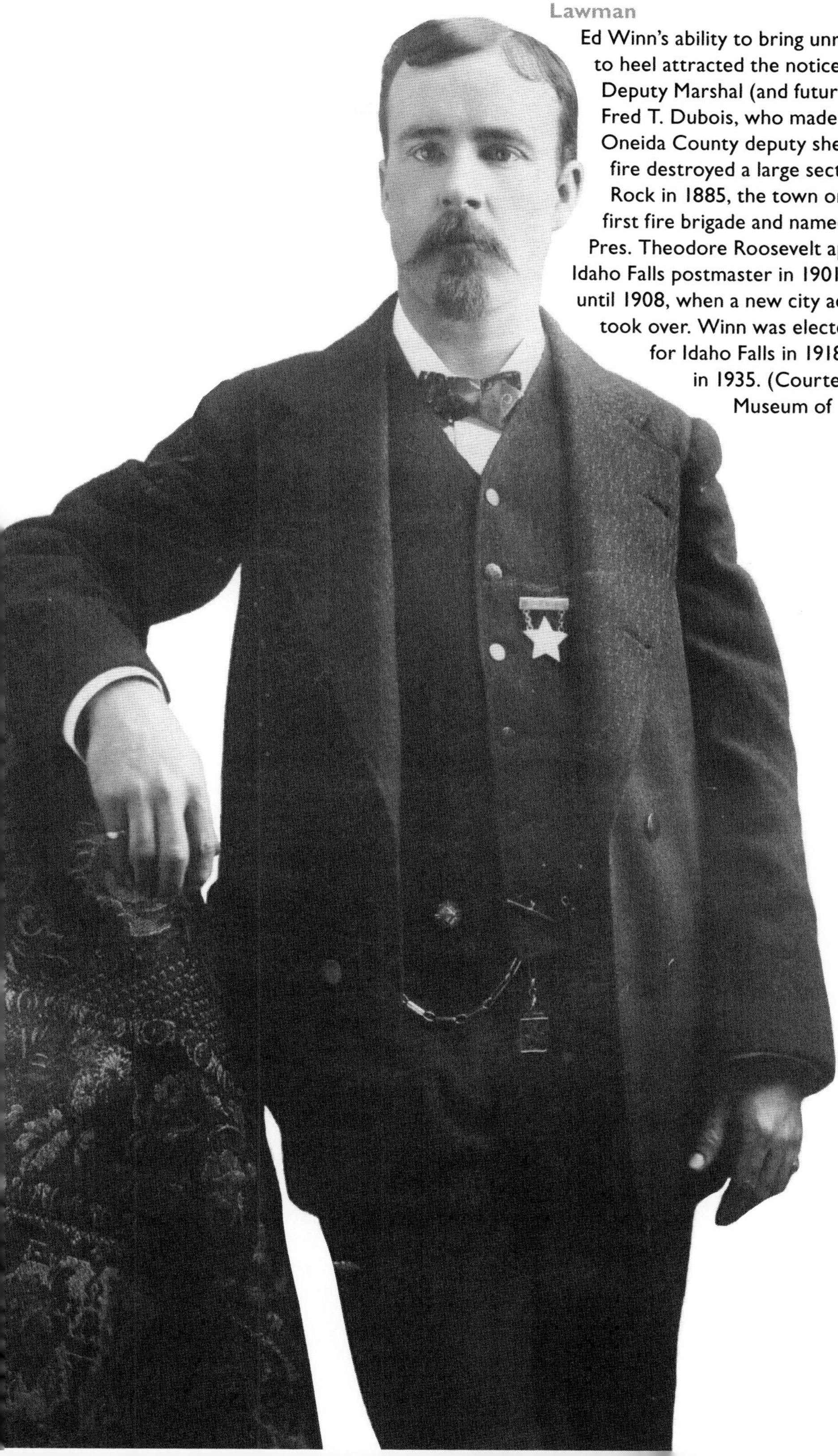

Lawman

Ed Winn's ability to bring unruly characters to heel attracted the notice of US Deputy Marshal (and future governor) Fred T. Dubois, who made him an Oneida County deputy sheriff. After a fire destroyed a large section of Eagle Rock in 1885, the town organized its first fire brigade and named Winn chief. Pres. Theodore Roosevelt appointed him Idaho Falls postmaster in 1901. He served until 1908, when a new city administration took over. Winn was elected a constable for Idaho Falls in 1918 and died in 1935. (Courtesy of the Museum of Idaho.)

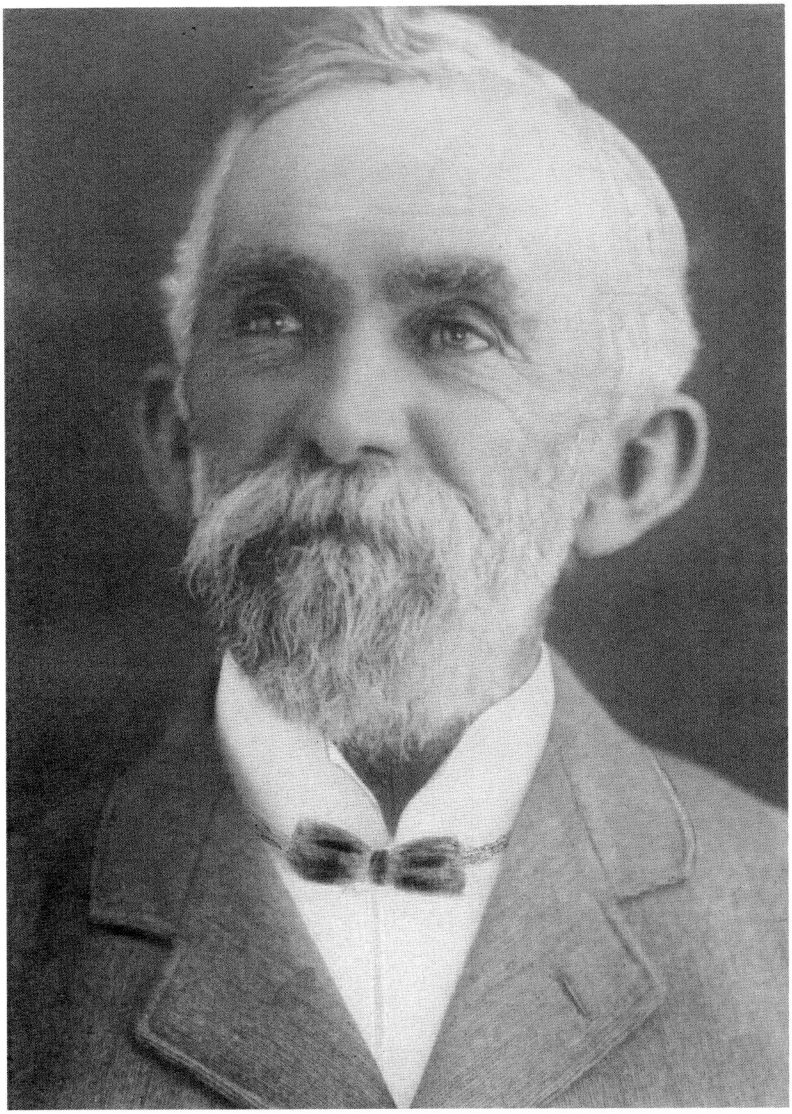

First Mayor
Joseph A. Clark came to Idaho from Indiana in 1881 to engineer an early canal on the Snake River. Settling in Eagle Rock, he served as president of the village council. In 1900, when Idaho Falls became a city of the second class and switched to a mayor-council system of government, he was elected its first mayor, a position two of his sons, Barzilla and Chase, would also hold. Clark's experience in the Midwest with publicly owned electrical power and his experience digging canals had a great influence on Idaho Falls. Though voters had rejected a bond issue twice, a 125-horsepower hydroelectric plant went into operation in October 1900, using water from Crow Creek and a Snake River diversion canal to drive its turbines. "Over 300 incandescent lights are now in use in the stores and dwellings, and about 200 more are already ordered," the *Idaho Falls Times* reported. By 1902, it was obvious that increased demand from commercial and residential customers meant the city would have to expand its generating capacity, but a dam-based power plant wasn't finished until 1912. Clark left office in 1902 and passed away in 1905. He lived long enough to see the Oregon Short Line Railroad build a new station, some city streets paved, two new banks open, and the city's schools expanded. (Courtesy of the Museum of Idaho.)

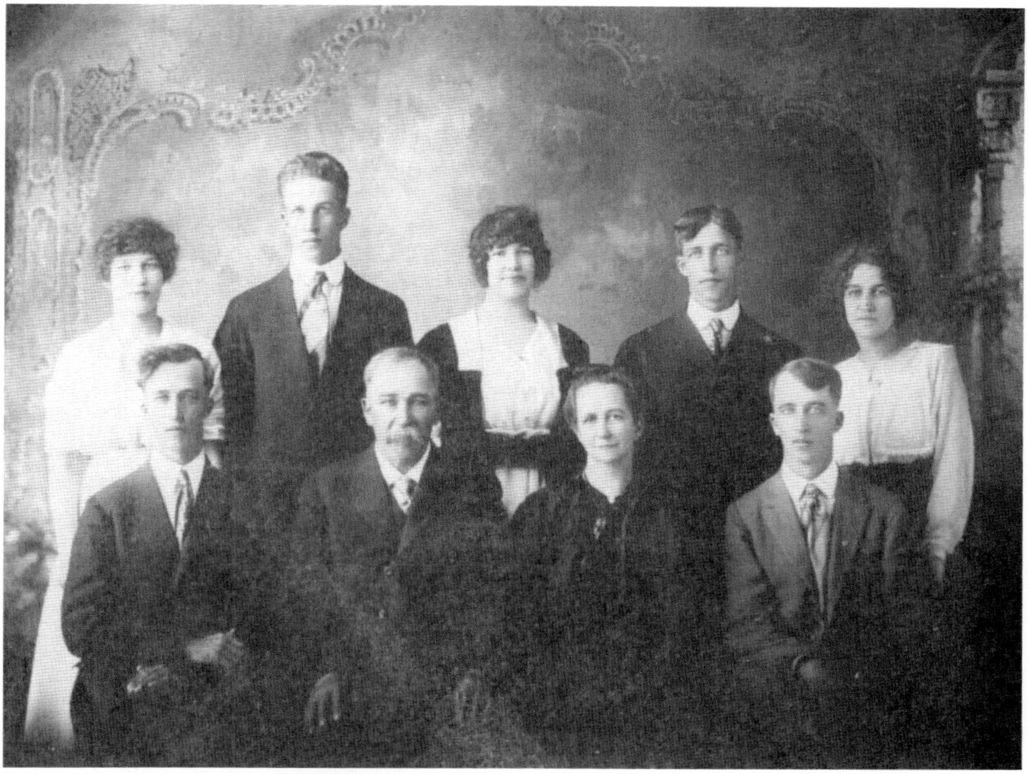

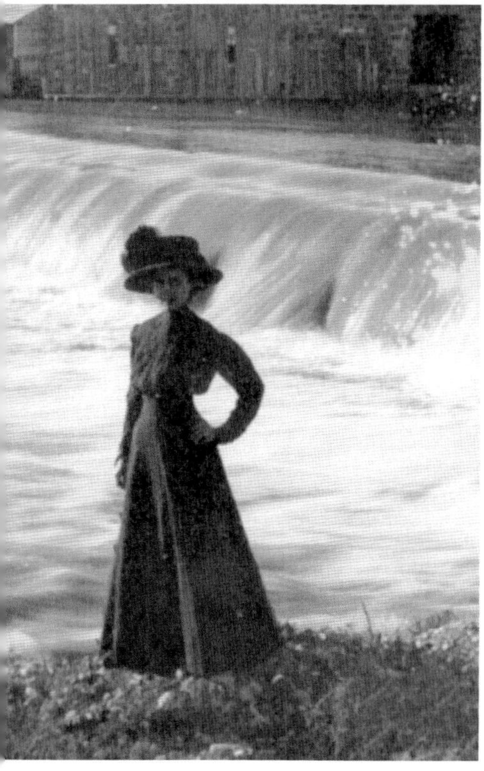

The Builder

Pictured here are William and Eldora Keefer with their seven children. When Eagle Rock was platted in 1884, Pennsylvania-born Keefer began buying real estate. A builder and a brewer, his most lasting impact may have been on the Snake River itself. In 1909, he directed construction of a dam and retaining wall north of Broadway. In 1912, the water from that dam flowed into a hydroelectric power plant. Keefer served two years as county coroner and two terms on the Idaho Falls city council before passing away in March 1940. (Courtesy of the Museum of Idaho.)

By the Falls

Eldora Keefer poses by the falls. Before her husband built the diversion dam in 1909, the falls were hardly more than a big set of rapids. (Courtesy of the Museum of Idaho.)

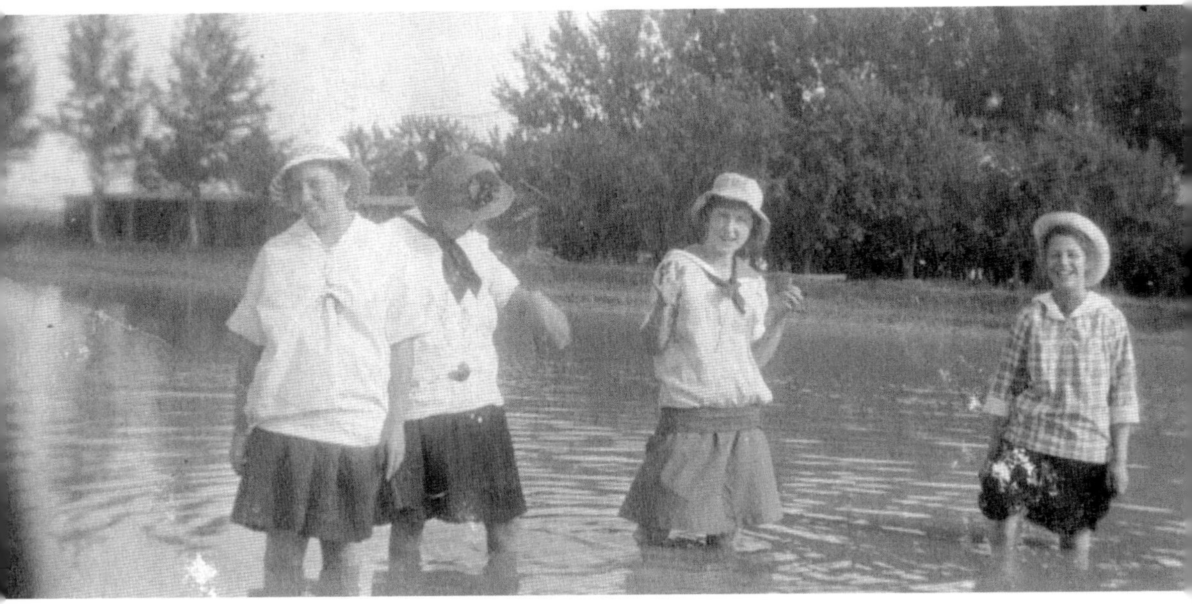

Oasis Maker

John Lingren (right) came to Eagle Rock in March 1879 to work at Anderson Brothers Store and Bank. In 1881, he bought 160 acres on Willow Creek and planted trees by the dozens, intending it as a place for city residents to escape the heat in summer and have fun year-round. Pictured above are bathers in the lake at Highland Park, which was also the city's source of ice in the winter. (Both, courtesy of the Museum of Idaho.)

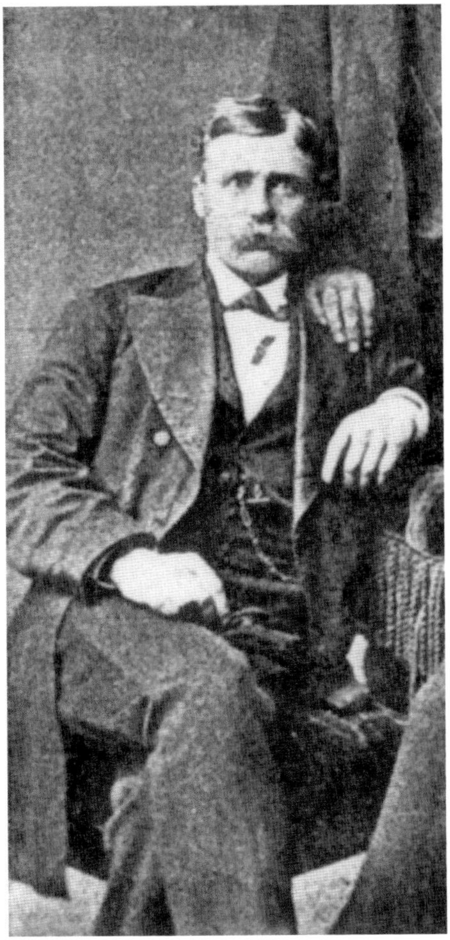

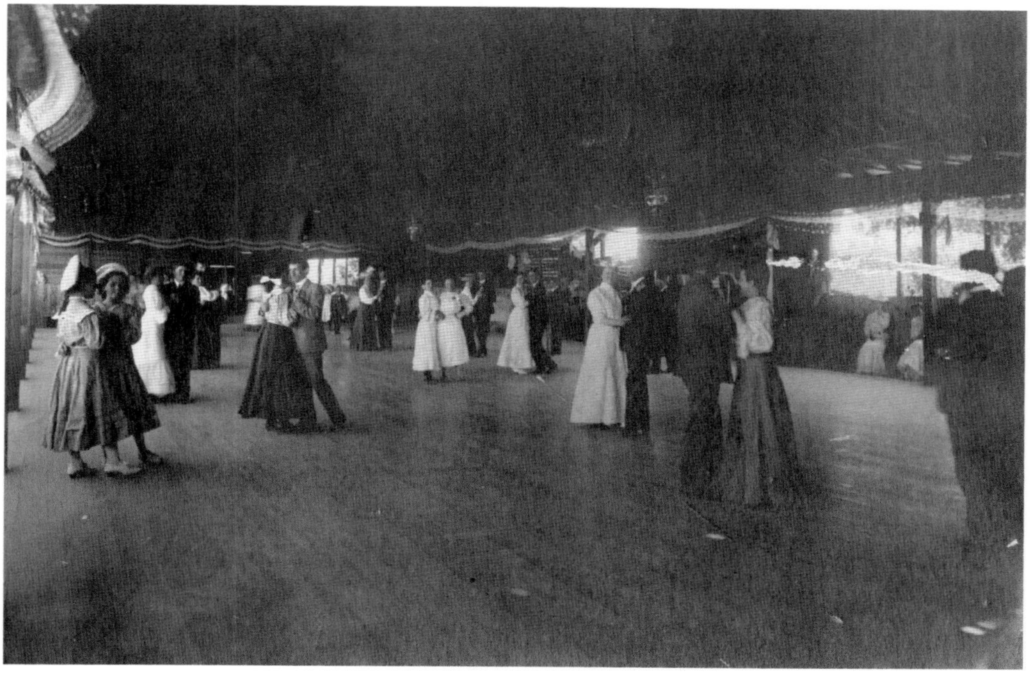

Highland Park

In its heyday, Highland Park had a dance pavilion (above) and a baseball diamond. The wooden grandstands pictured below were built by the Works Projects Administration in 1940 and burned down in the mid-1970s. Melaleuca Field, home of Pioneer League baseball, now occupies the grounds. (Both, courtesy of the Museum of Idaho.)

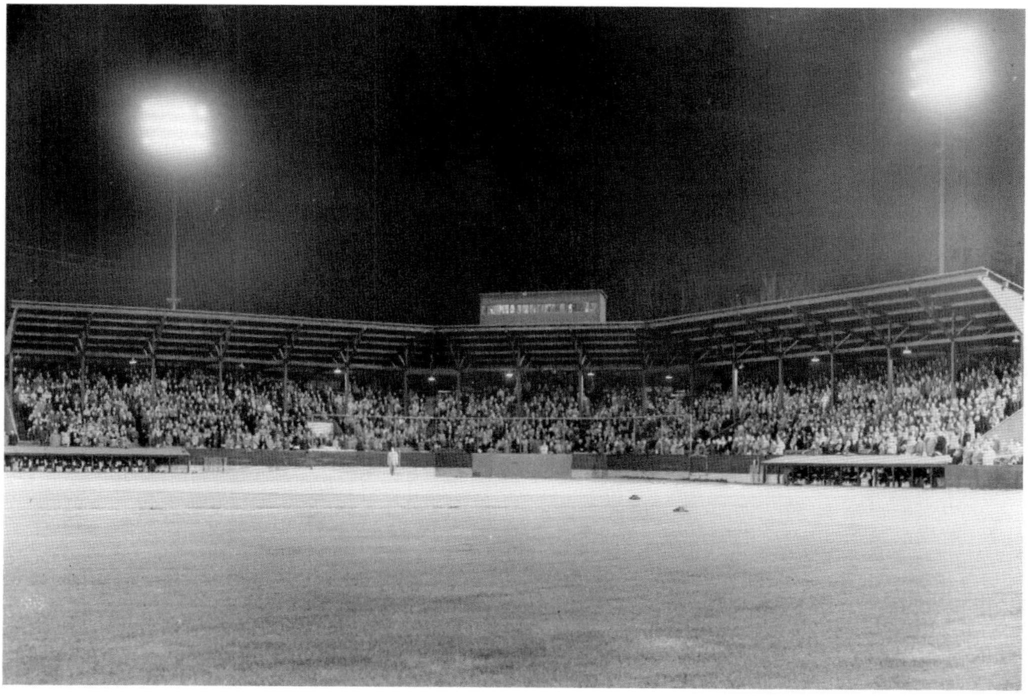

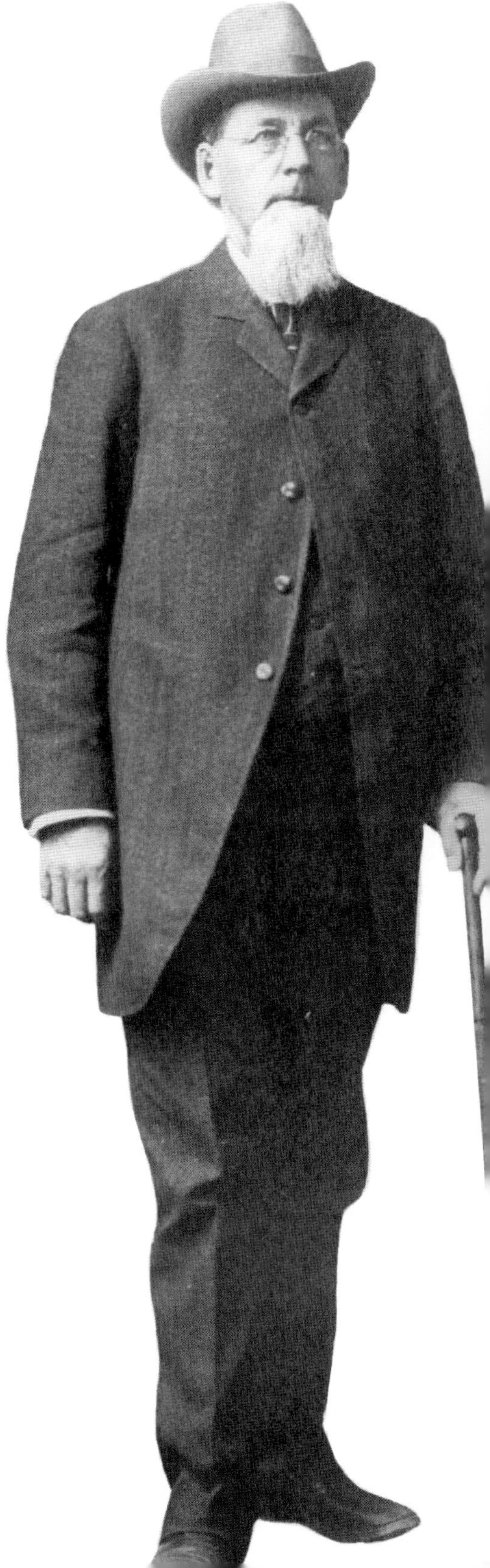

Republican Voice
Born in Vermont, William E. Wheeler started his newspaper, the *Register*, in Blackfoot in 1880. He moved to Eagle Rock in 1884. For decades, the *Register* was the Republican voice in the community, and the rival *Times* offered a more populist slant. A business booster of the first order, Wheeler believed the city's water system was the top priority. He died in 1919 after being hit by a truck while crossing Broadway on his customary evening stroll. "[Few] employers have more cause to be regretted and mourned," wrote rival publisher Sam Dennis. (Courtesy of the Idaho Falls *Post Register*.)

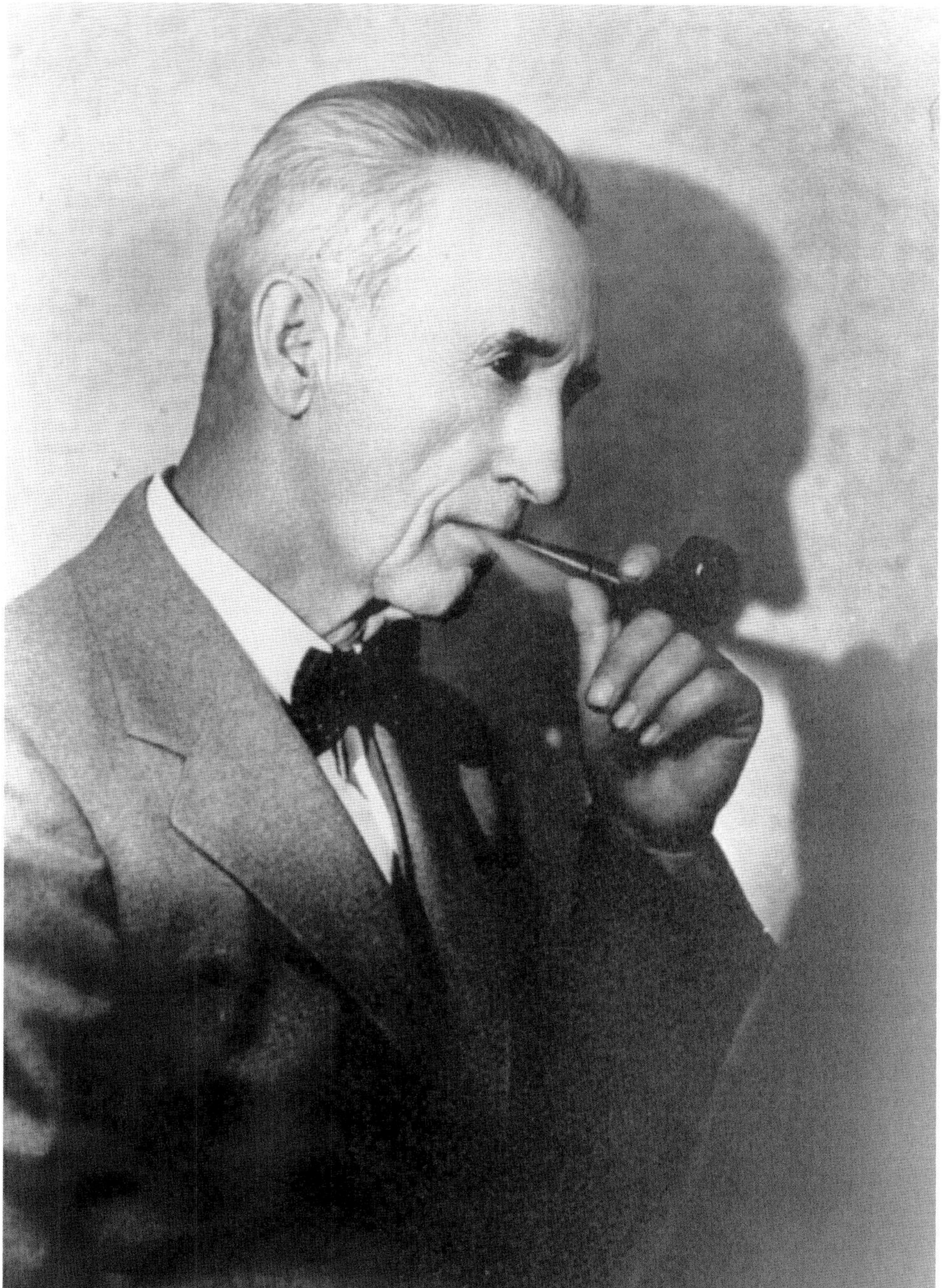

Progressive Rival
Sam Dennis started as a printer for the *Register*, but launched a rival paper, the *Idaho Falls Times*, in 1890 with Rufus Bonney. When it failed to do as well as he hoped, he sold his share and took up farming with his family. But there was ink in his blood. He returned to the *Times* as co-owner in 1915 and bought the *Register* in 1920, forming the *Times-Register*. Active in Democratic Party politics, Dennis retired from print when the *Times-Register* merged with the *Daily Post* in 1931. He was a probate judge when he died in May 1949. (Courtesy of the Idaho Falls *Post Register*.)

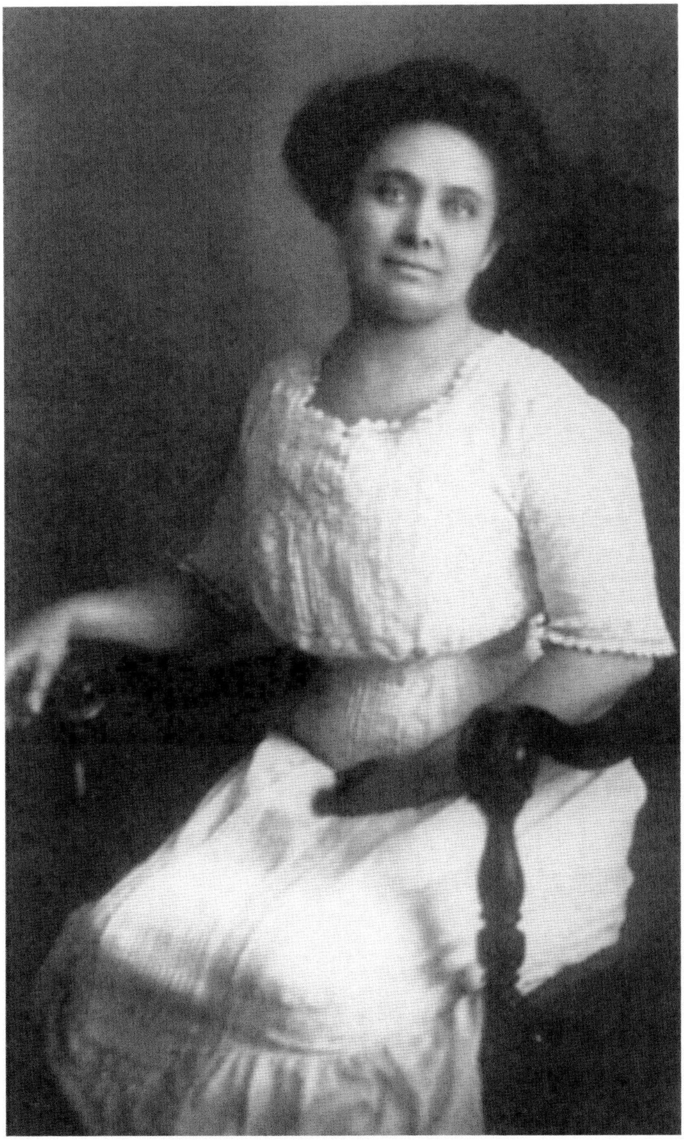

Lady Banker

Originally from Iowa, 17-year-old Minnie Gibson arrived in Eagle Rock in the fall of 1889 with her widowed mother and her younger sister. Soon after arriving, she began working at Anderson Brothers Store and Bank. She graduated to the position of banker and eventually held a seat on the board of directors. In a career that spanned nearly 50 years, she was renowned as a shrewd judge of both people and business opportunities. Throughout the 1920s and 1930s, she could be seen shopping downtown and rarely missing a picture at the movie theaters. After 27 years of widowhood, she met Raymond Burger, the physician in charge of health services at the Civilian Conservation Corps camp in Swan Valley, who was nearly 30 years her junior. The two were married in 1941, but Burger was unable to establish a practice in Idaho Falls and moved to Southern California. His wife remained at the bank, but each Christmas they would meet in Salt Lake City and travel by train to his home. She would return in the spring, in time for taxes. In 1946, Minnie Gibson Hitt Burger retired from banking and moved to California, where she died in 1959. (Courtesy of the Museum of Idaho.)

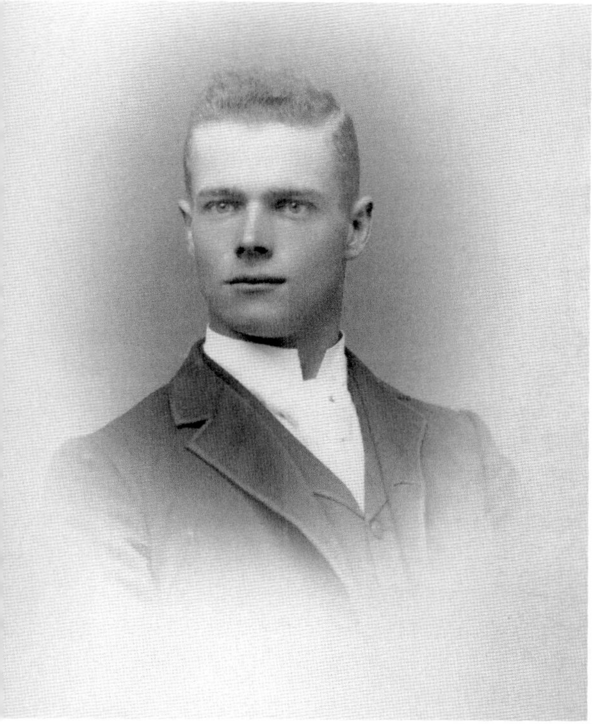

Ladies' Man

Minnie Gibson went into business with Frank Hitt, an outfitter and cattleman notorious for his way with the ladies. They were married in 1901; the following day, Frank was shot by a jealous husband. Many believe it was to protect Minnie's money in their partnership. Frank Hitt survived and lived another 13 years. (Courtesy of the Museum of Idaho.)

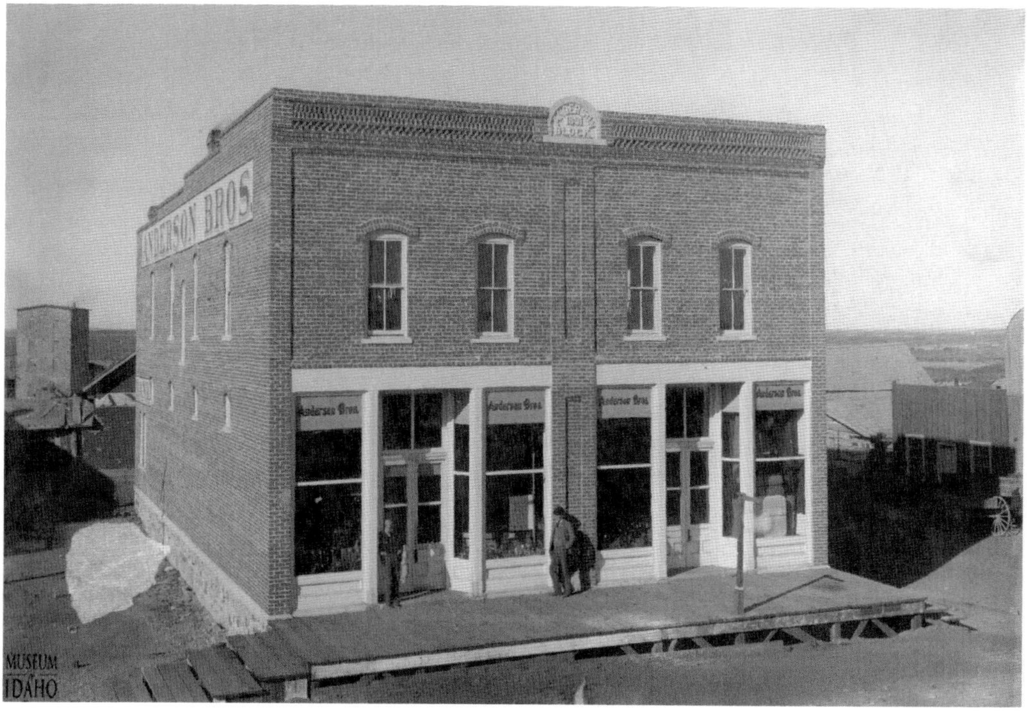

The First Bank

Minnie Gibson Hitt rarely sat behind a desk at Anderson Brothers Bank (pictured), preferring to meet people in the lobby and size them up as they spoke. (Courtesy of the Museum of Idaho.)

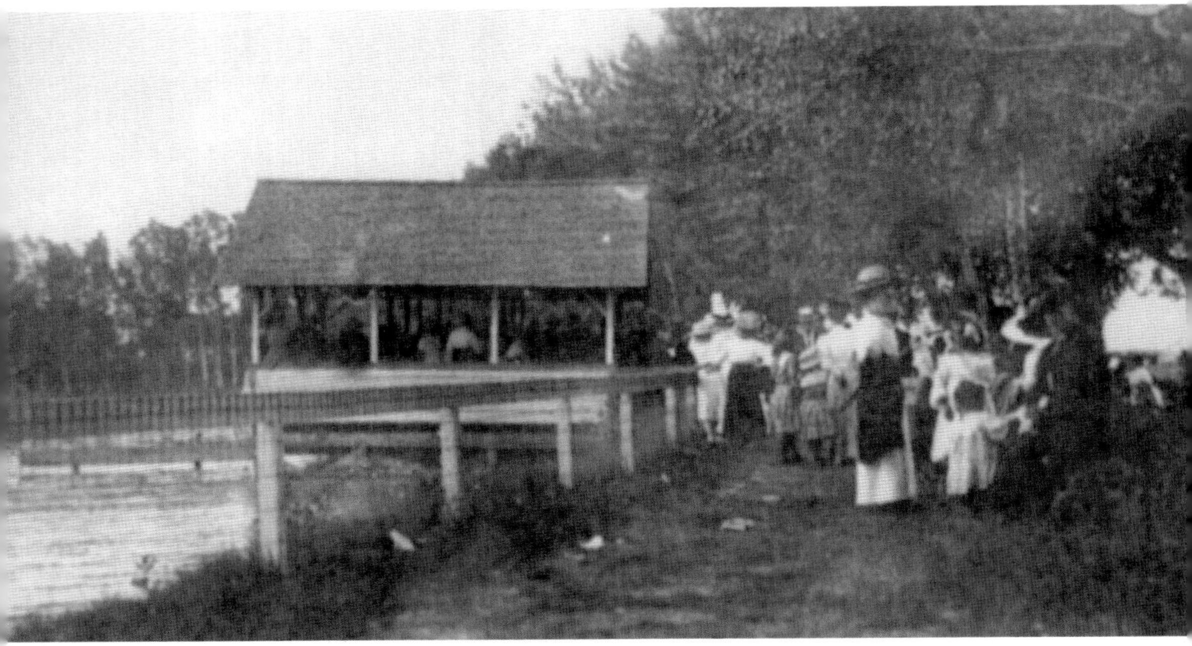

Old Tautphaus Park
The lake at Tautphaus Park was a popular place for picnics and swimming and remained in use until the middle of the 20th century, when the city of Idaho Falls built a public pool on Elm Street. (Courtesy of the Museum of Idaho.)

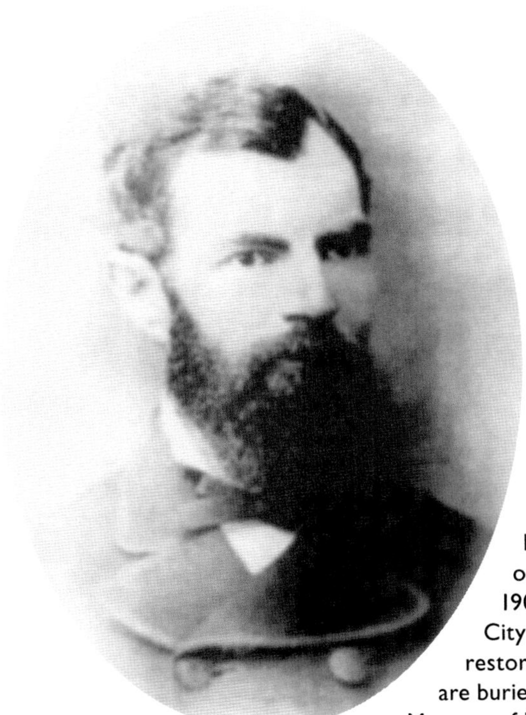

Taming the Wilderness
Charles C. Tautphaus came from Montana in the mid-1880s with a desire to transform the desert. Once his oasis was completed and became a popular picnic spot, Tautphaus moved on to Alaska and then Nevada, where he died in 1906. First called Tautphaus Park, it was known as City Park and Reno Park before the original name was restored in the mid-20th century. Tautphaus and his wife are buried in nearby Rose Hill Cemetery. (Courtesy of the Museum of Idaho.)

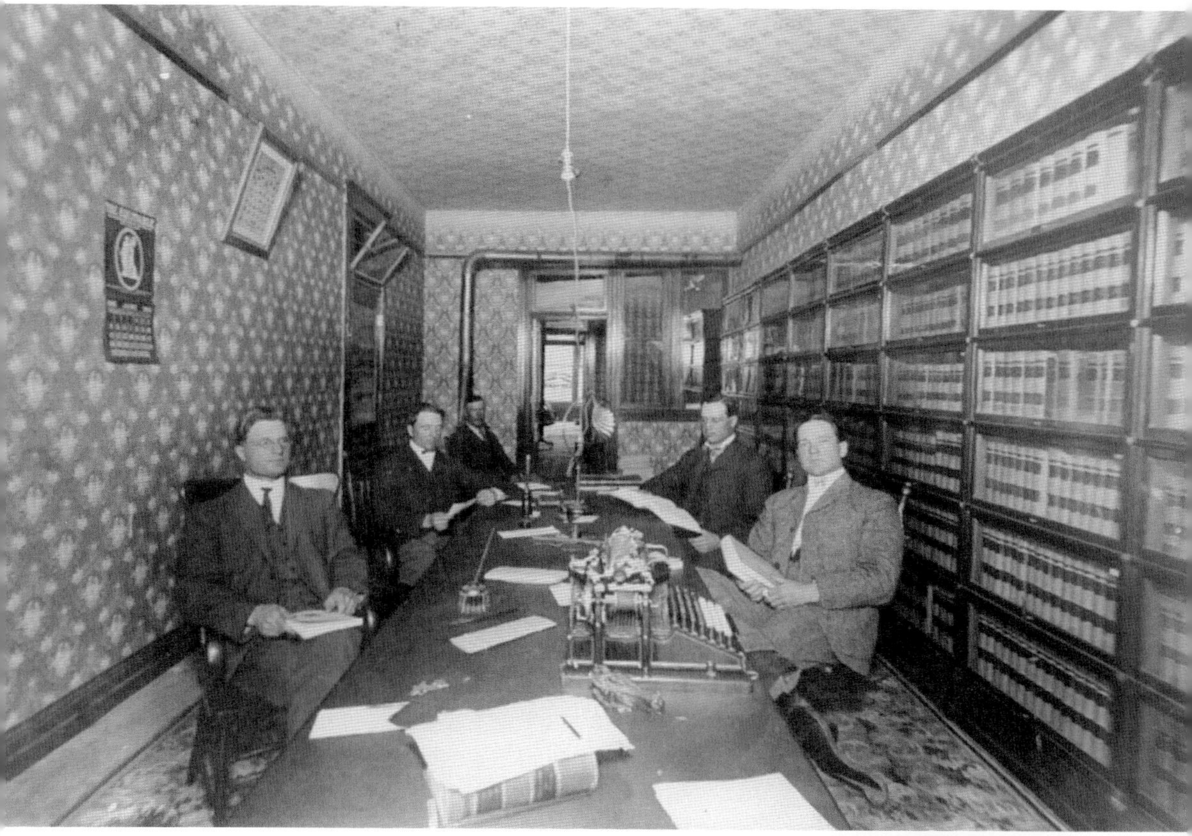

Brothers in Law

William Harry Holden came to Idaho Falls in 1895 to practice law. In 1902, he teamed up with his brothers, Edwin M. Holden, Arthur W. Holden, and J. Wesley Holden. The firm exists today as Holden, Kidwell, Hahn & Crapo and is one of the largest law practices in eastern Idaho. (Courtesy of the Holden family.)

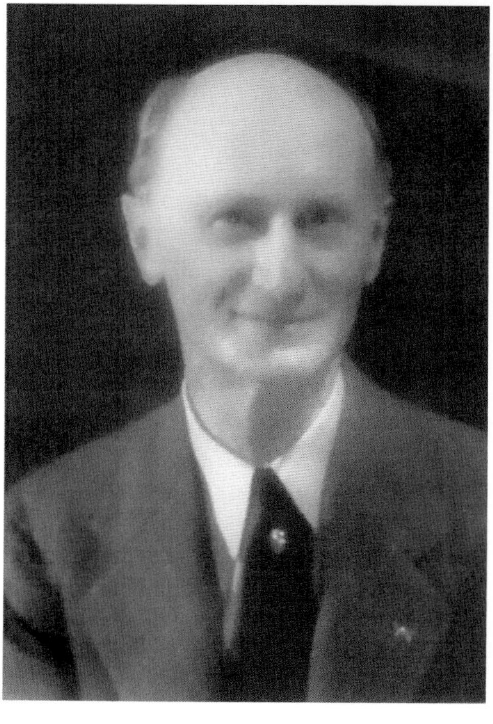

Lawyer, Lodge Leader

Along with the Holdens, Clency St. Clair was a leading lawyer in Idaho Falls's early years. A Midwesterner, he came to Idaho Falls in 1903. In addition to practicing law, he developed farming interests in Bonneville County, was elected to the Idaho State Senate in 1911, and served as a delegate to the Republican National Convention of 1912. He was associated with the Masons and Elks and presided over the Rotary Club of Idaho Falls. (Courtesy of John St. Clair.)

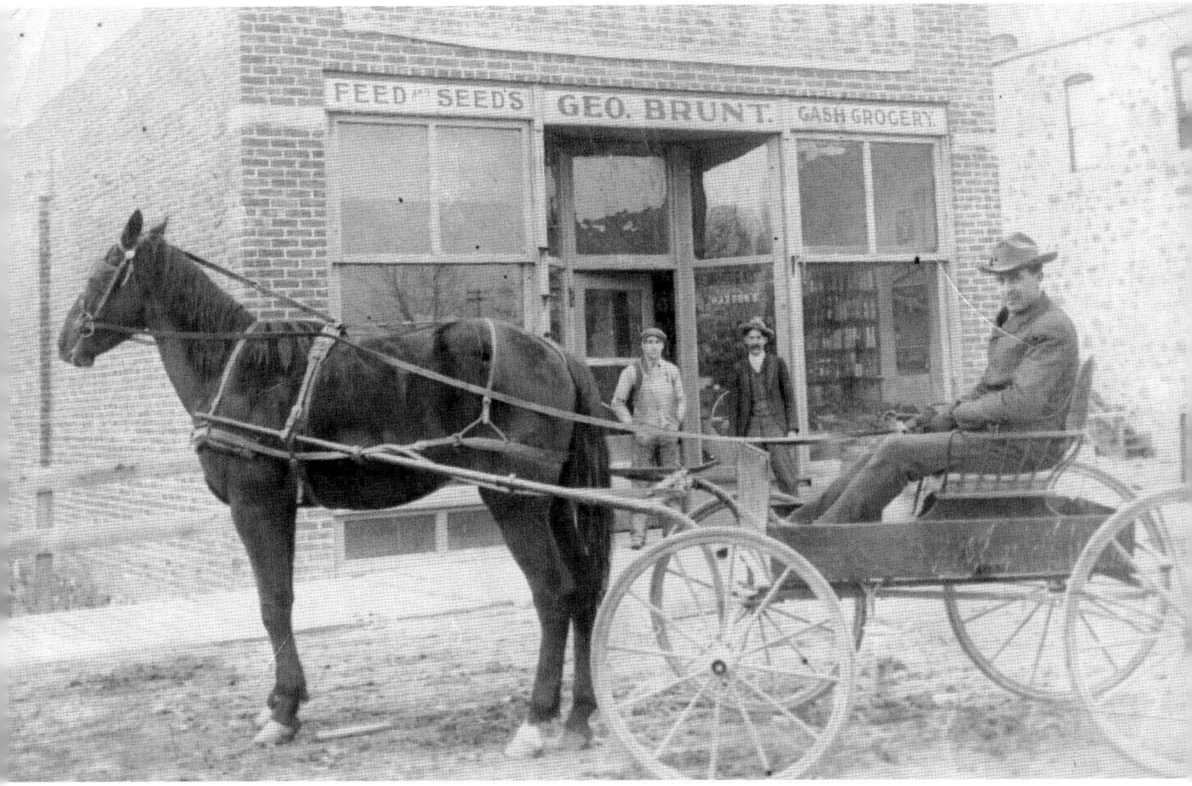

The Grocer

Born in 1876, George Brunt came to Eagle Rock with his Mormon pioneer family at the age of nine, gaining a foothold in business at an early age by helping his mother, a laundress. His first grocery store burned down in the great fire of 1904, which destroyed a large part of downtown. He moved into a store on A Street, which he operated until 1917 when he sold the business. He invested in land and agriculture and was elected twice to the Idaho legislature, which honored him in 1947 for his service. He died in 1956 at the age of 80. (Courtesy of the Museum of Idaho.)

Farmers' Friend

Gilbert George Wright arrived from Utah in 1889 to manage a branch of the Consolidated Wagon & Machine (CW&M) Company. Wright was regarded as a great friend to farmers, especially in New Sweden, where he was a member of the Pioneers Association. After he was promoted to a management position within CW&M, he moved to Salt Lake City but commuted to Idaho Falls each weekend. In 1933, en route from Salt Lake City, he was killed in a car accident. In Idaho Falls, stores and banks were closed on the day of his funeral. (Courtesy of the Museum of Idaho.)

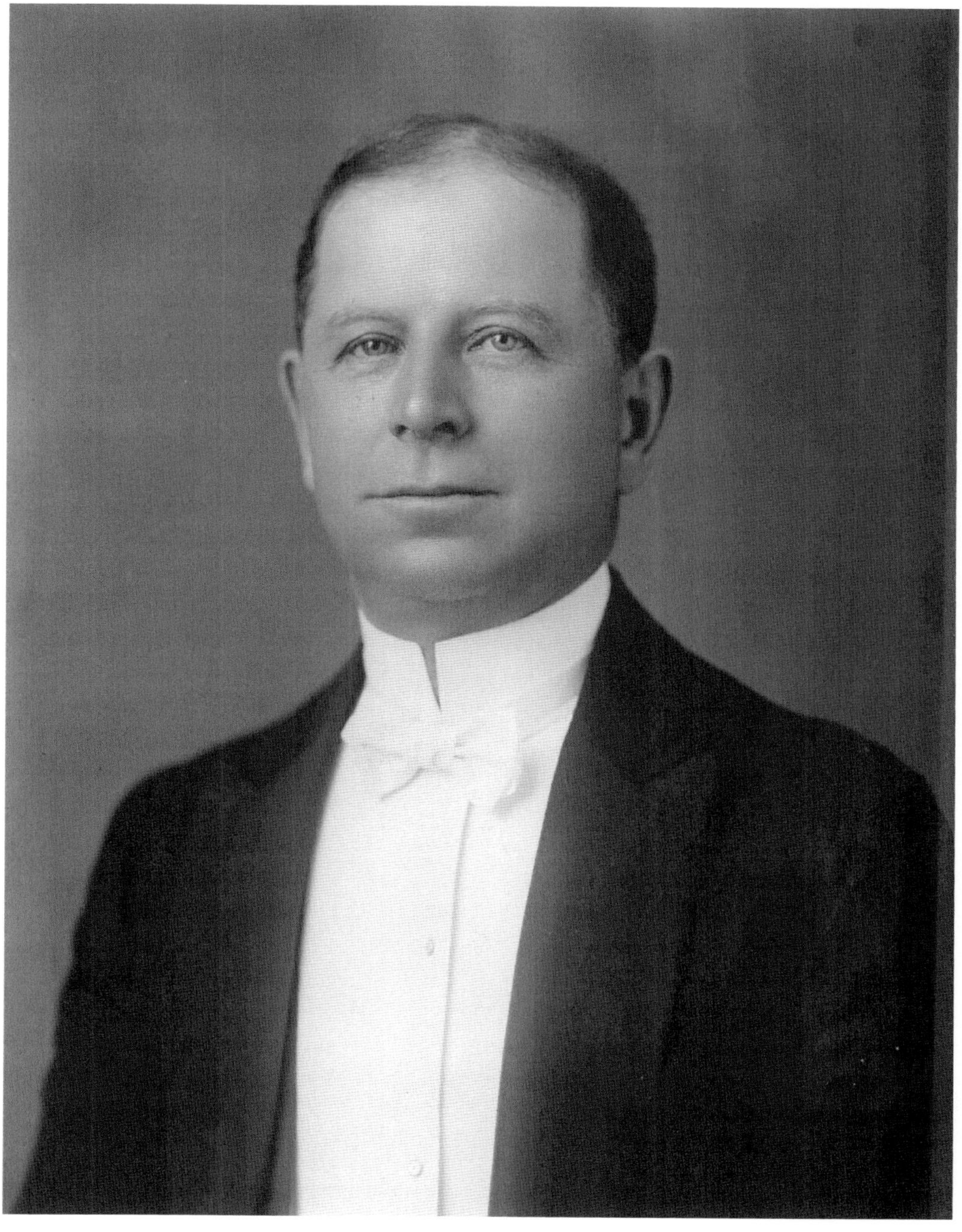

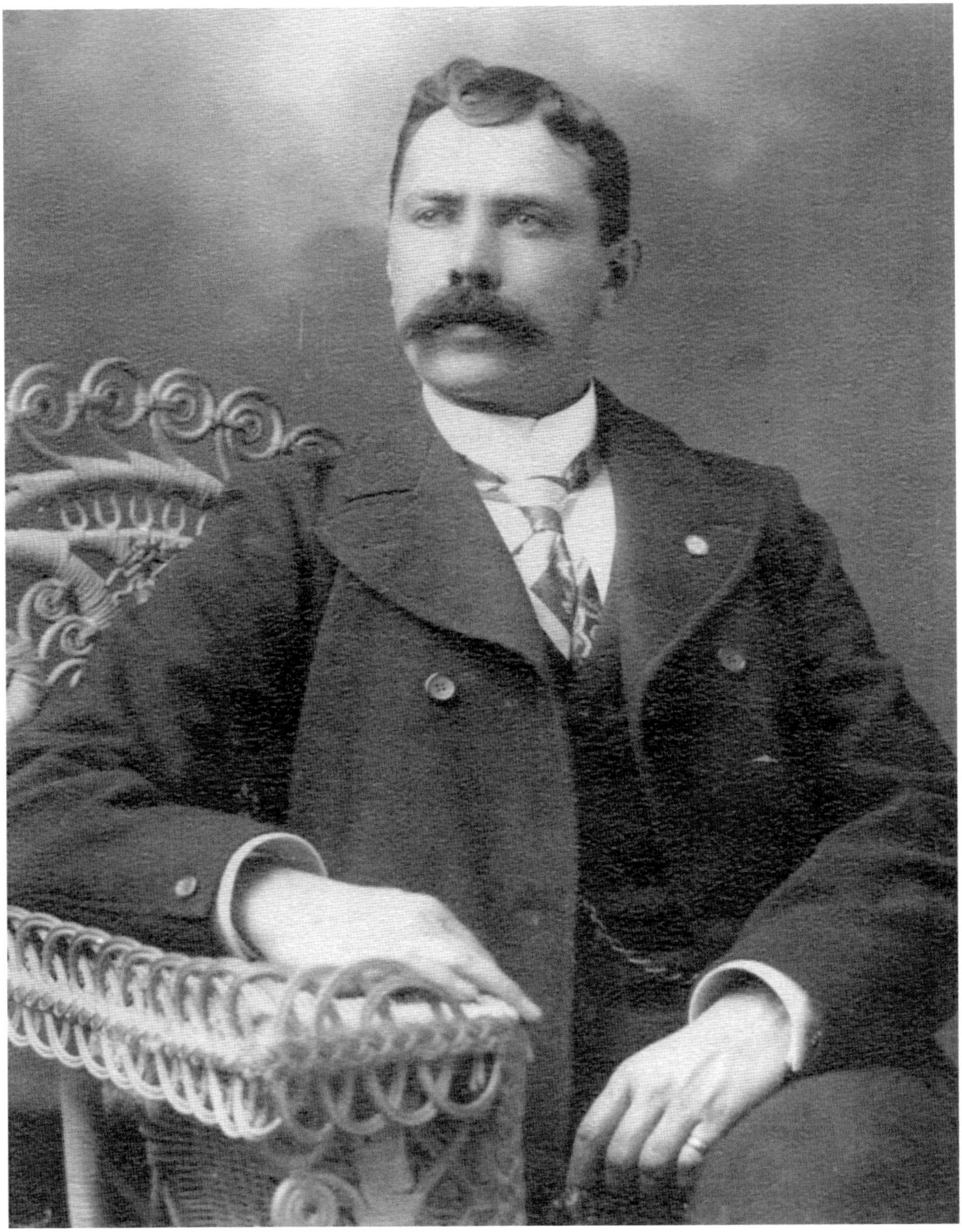

Country Doctor
Virginia native Dr. Thomas C. Willson arrived in Idaho Falls in 1890. He practiced medicine, owned extensive farming interests, was a pillar of the Masonic Lodge, and helped found the Order of the Eastern Star Henrietta Chapter. Turn-of-the-century editions of the *Idaho Register* feature many reports in which victims of horse bites, broken bones, and pneumonia were seen by Dr. Willson. In 1928, there is a report of him serving as city sanitary inspector and revising city health codes. His son, Harry, also became a local doctor. Dr. Thomas C. Willson died in 1940. (Courtesy of the Museum of Idaho.)

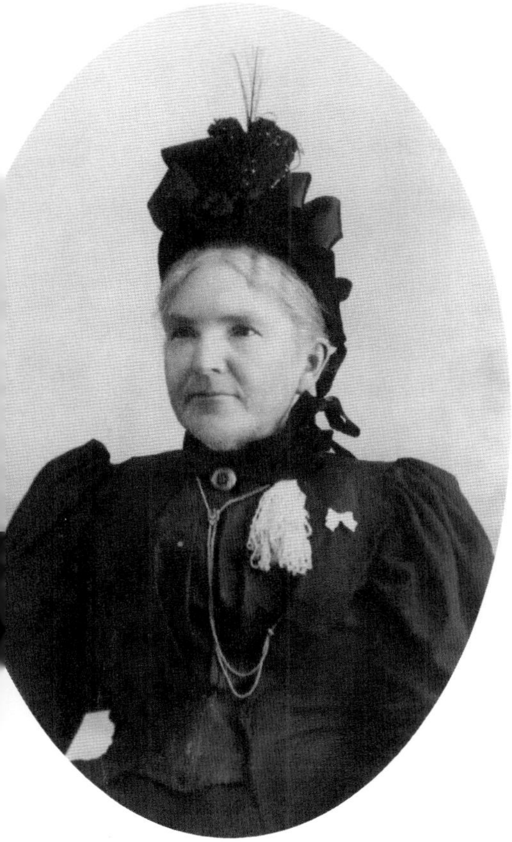

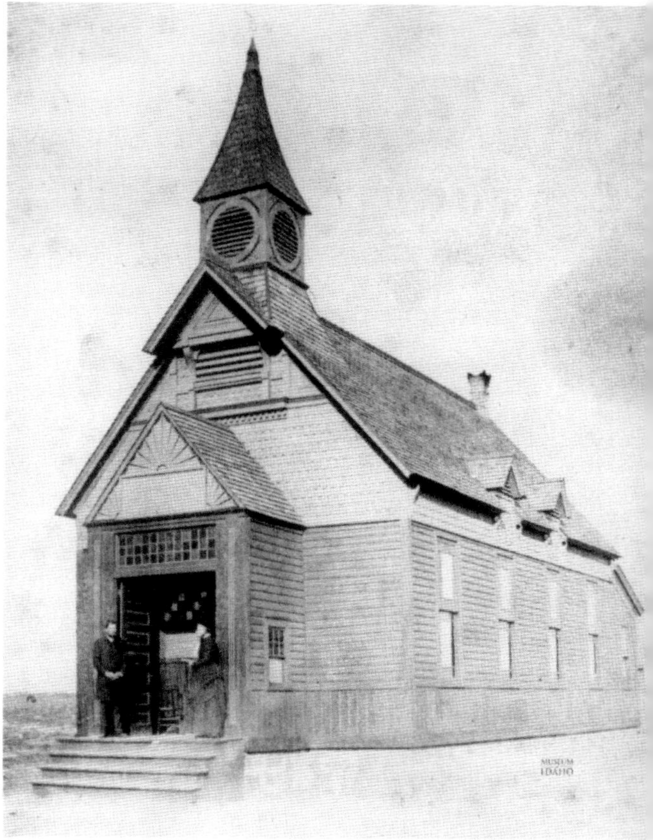

Temperance and Teaching
A widow in her 40s with a teenage daughter, Rebecca Mitchell stopped in Eagle Rock in June 1882 on her way to the mining town of Bellevue, where she intended to do Baptist missionary work. With money running short she decided that Eagle Rock—with one store and plenty of saloons but no schools or churches—was where God intended her to be after all. Within five days, she had visited every family in the community and on Sunday, June 11, 1882, she conducted the first Sunday School. The following morning, with the same 18 pupils, she organized a day school. Before long, she had acquired a lot on the corner of Eastern Avenue and Ash Street, and with help from the Baptist Mission Society and private gifts, First Baptist Church opened its doors in August 1885. Mitchell was active in the Women's Christian Temperance Union, serving as state superintendent of legislation and lobbying the Idaho legislature for women's voting rights, which were granted in 1896. From 1896 to 1899, she was chaplain of the Idaho House of Representatives. In Idaho Falls, she remained active in the Village Improvement Society and the Round Table Club. She died in 1908 and is buried in Rose Hill Cemetery. (Both, courtesy of the Museum of Idaho.)

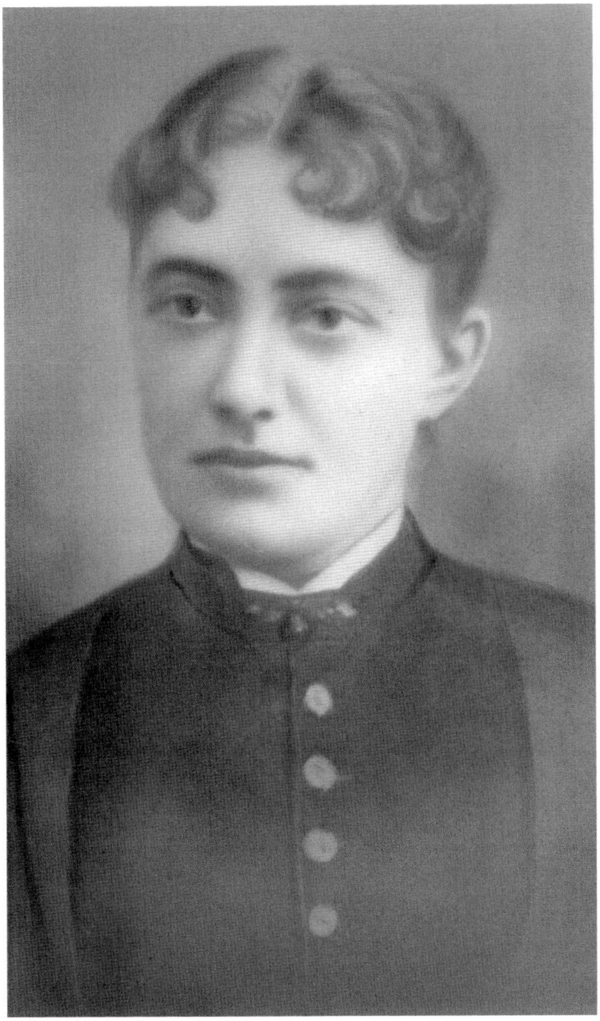

Civilizing Influence

Kate Baker Curley came to Idaho Falls with her husband, Bowen Curley, a banker and future mayor. Determined to uphold the ideals of culture and civic improvement, in January 1897 she helped organize the Nineteenth Century Club with the purpose to educate women in politics and literary work. Within 18 months, it had been reorganized into the Village Improvement Society (VIS). Its motto: "Slumber not in the tents of your fathers. The World is advancing. Advance with it." Kate Curley was appalled by the scarcity of trees and overabundance of trash in the streets of Idaho Falls. Gathering 50¢ from each of its 40 members, the society hired a carpenter to build 50 pine trash boxes, which they painted white with "V.I.S." in black block lettering and equipped with rope handles. Woe to anyone who did not use them. The Village Improvement Society lobbied the city council for an ordinance prohibiting livestock from roaming free in the streets. In time, the society swelled to almost 200 members who pooled their resources to buy 20,000 hardwood seedlings from Iowa, which were planted along the streets and in the parks. In spring 1903, stricken with cancer, Kate Curley gave the commencement address to the Idaho Falls High School graduating class. "Think not that the world owes you a living, but that you owe the world a life," she said. Kate Curley Park, a city block between Ninth and Tenth Streets, was named in her honor in 1908. The Idaho Falls Public Library, financed with a $10,000 Carnegie grant she helped secure, is now part of the Museum of Idaho. (Courtesy of the Museum of Idaho.)

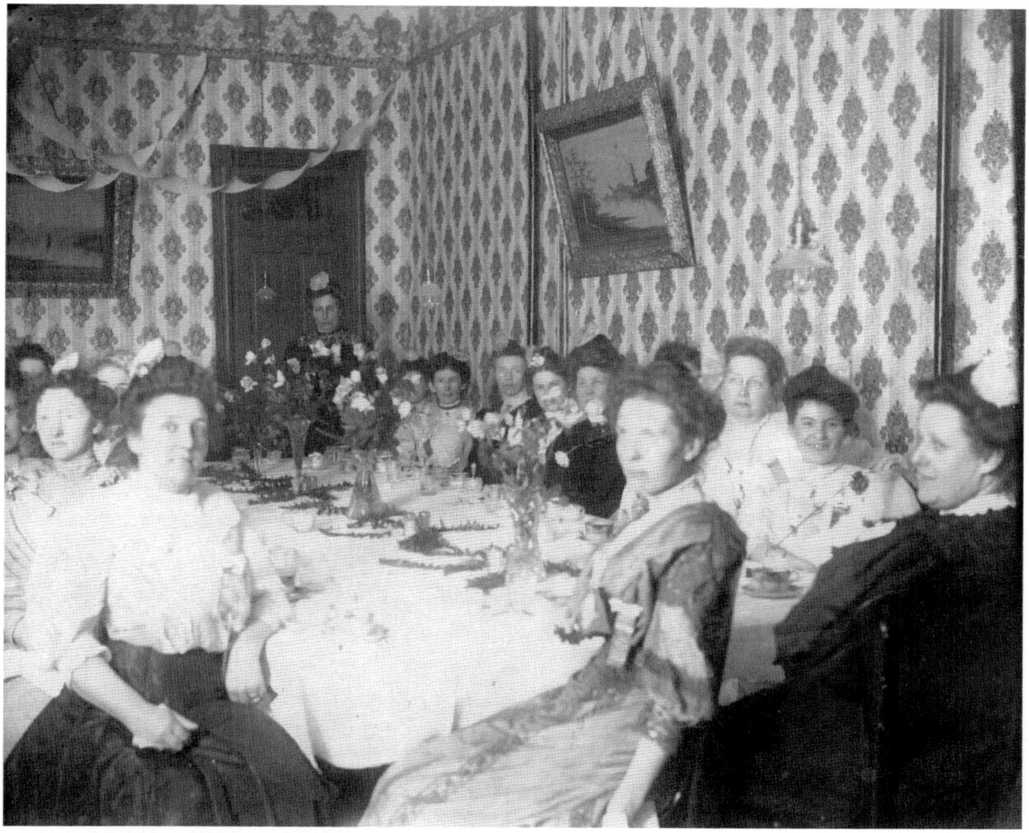

Village Improvement Society
After Kate Curley's death, Adelia Bridgett Duggan Scott took over the society's leadership. She was already a justice of the peace, having run in 1898 and won. By the end of her time on the bench, Mayor A.T. Shane was impressed enough with her that he named her the city's police magistrate. She served nine years on the Idaho Falls Board of Education, bringing newer, more modern schools to the community. The Village Improvement Society disbanded in 1918 after the city started municipal trash collection service. (Courtesy of the Museum of Idaho.)

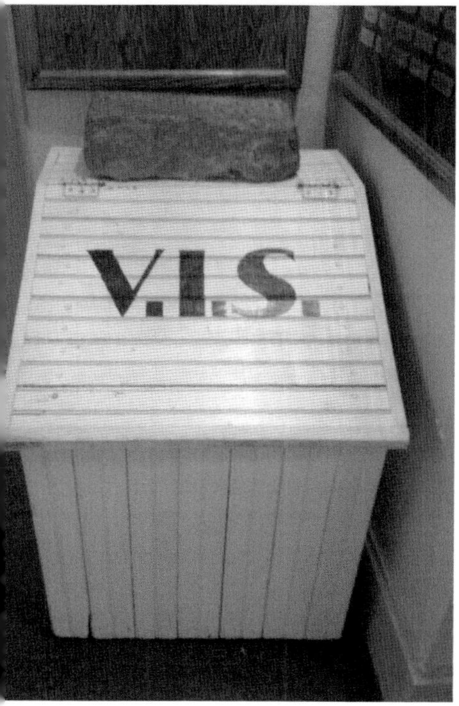

V.I.S. Litter Box
This replica of one of the Village Improvement Society's trash boxes is on display at the Museum of Idaho. (Author photograph.)

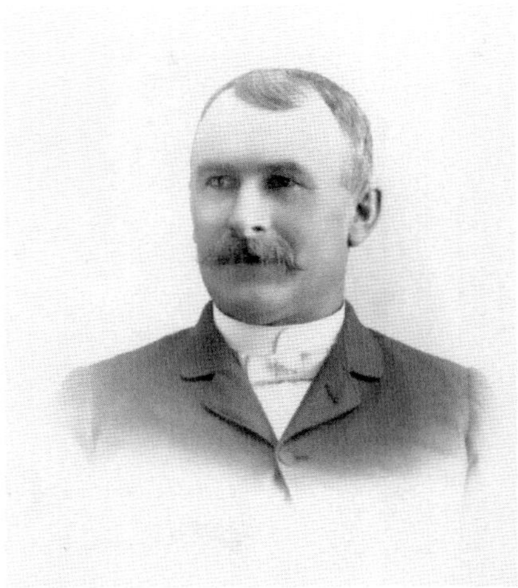

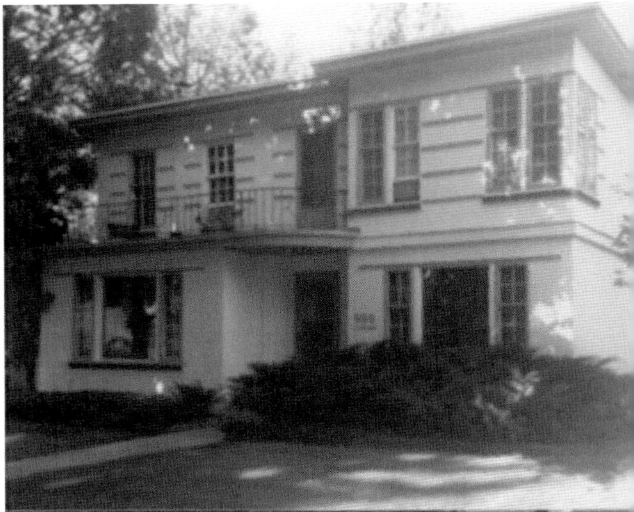

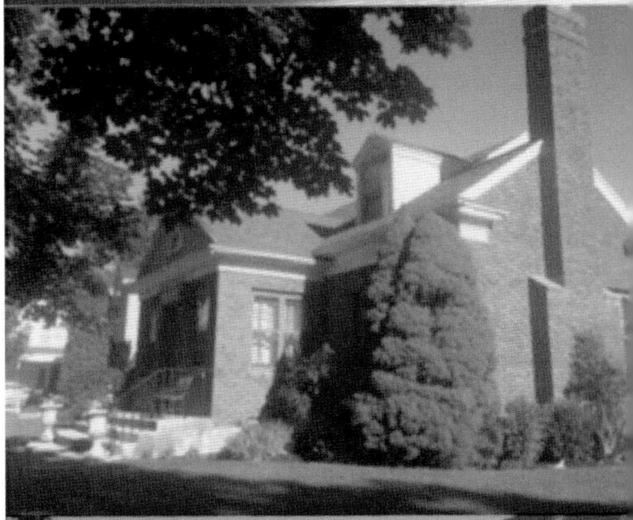

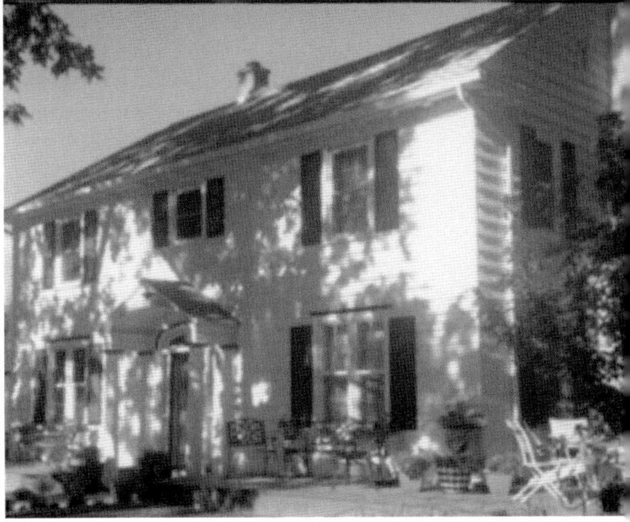

The Developer
Byron Crow came with the railroad and was appointed to supervise the town's water supply. In 1890, he platted a rectilinear grid of 64 blocks east of Eagle Rock. As Idaho Falls's population grew from 1,262 to 8,084 between 1900 and 1920, Crow's Addition became home to much of the city's most unique and interesting residential architecture, with styles ranging from Queen Anne to Art Moderne. Crow Creek, which originally ran through the neighborhood, is now completely underground. (Courtesy of the Museum of Idaho.)

Crow's Addition
Here are three very different homes in Crow's Addition, also commonly called the "Numbered Streets." (Author photograph.)

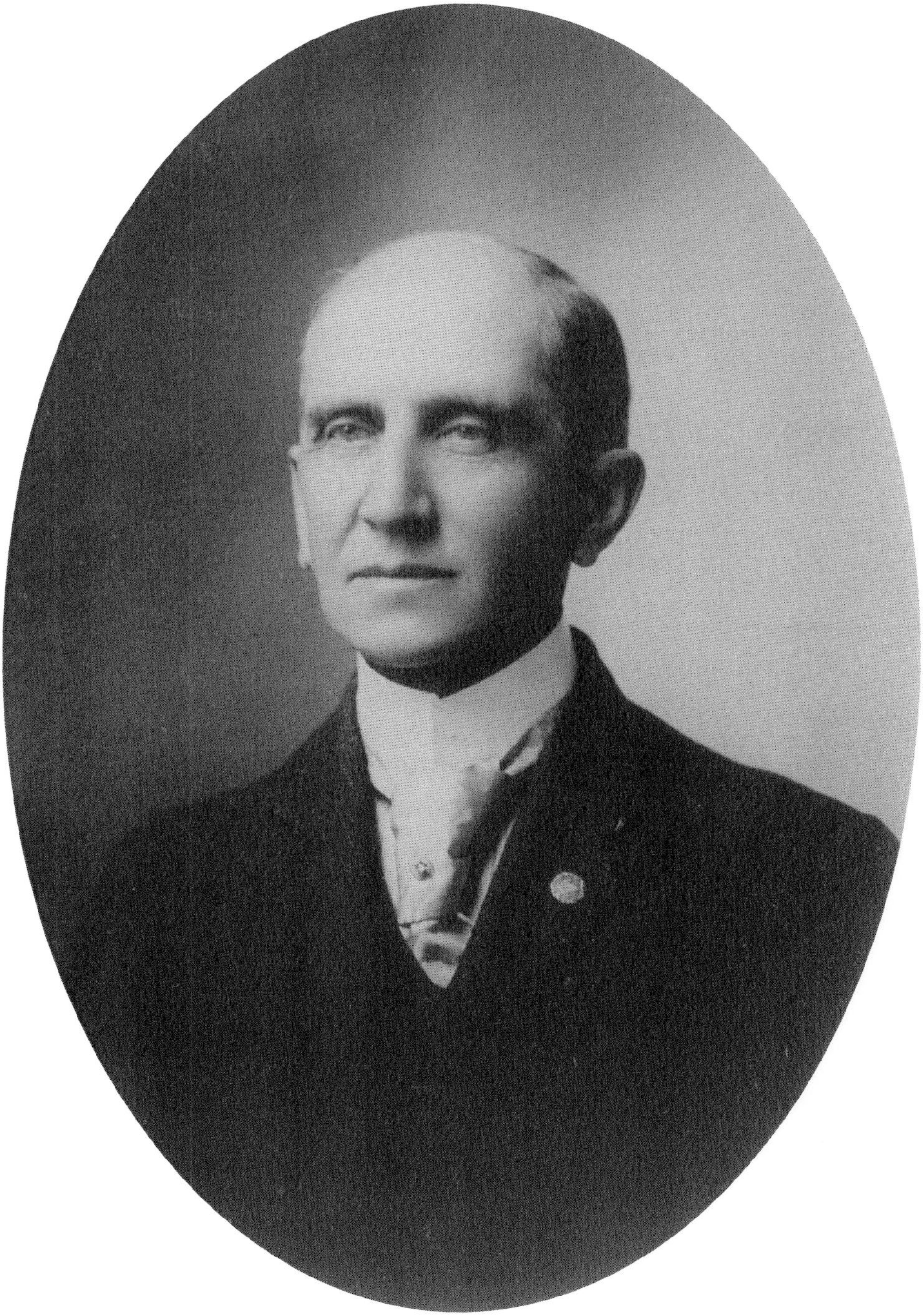

The Judge

Otis Eddy McCutcheon came to Idaho Falls in 1896 and was soon recognized as one of the leaders of the Republican Party. In 1906, he was elected to the Idaho State Senate and then appointed to the state university board of regents in 1907. He served in the Idaho House of Representatives, and in 1910, was appointed dean of the University of Idaho law school, serving until 1913. He retired in 1915, but maintained an interest in his family hardware business. (Courtesy of the Museum of Idaho.)

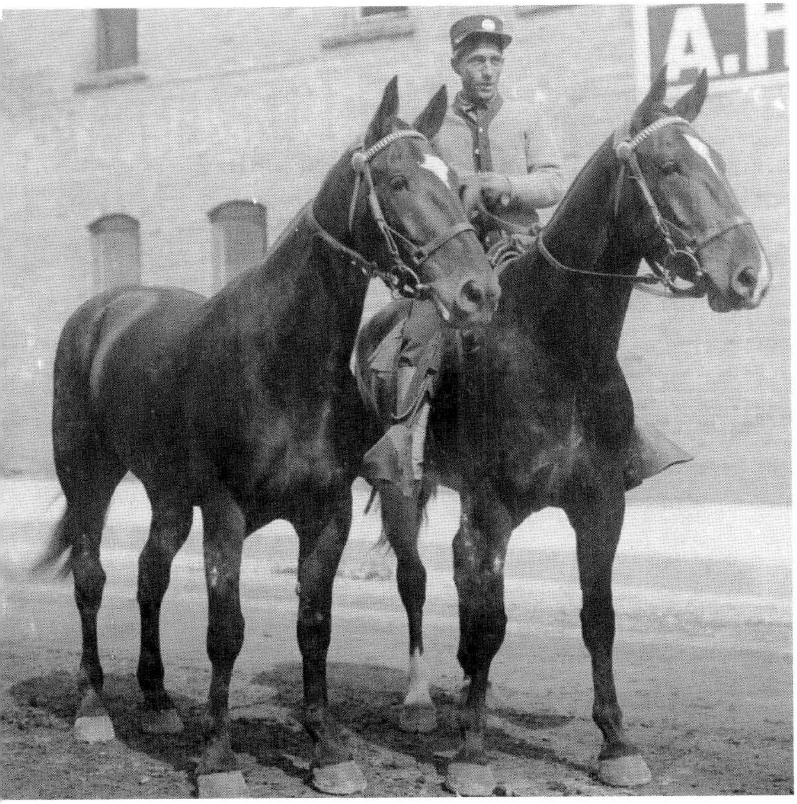

The Fire Chief

Idaho Falls's first driver of horse-drawn fire equipment, Julius Marker, was appointed chief in 1910 and served until his death in 1937. In 1916, the city acquired its first motorized equipment and saw significant expansion of the department's paid personnel. In 1929, Station No. 1 (pictured below) moved from Park Avenue to below city hall. The city's ladder-and-hose engine truck, a 1928 American LaFrance, is still housed there and used in parades and other public events. (Both, courtesy of the Museum of Idaho.)

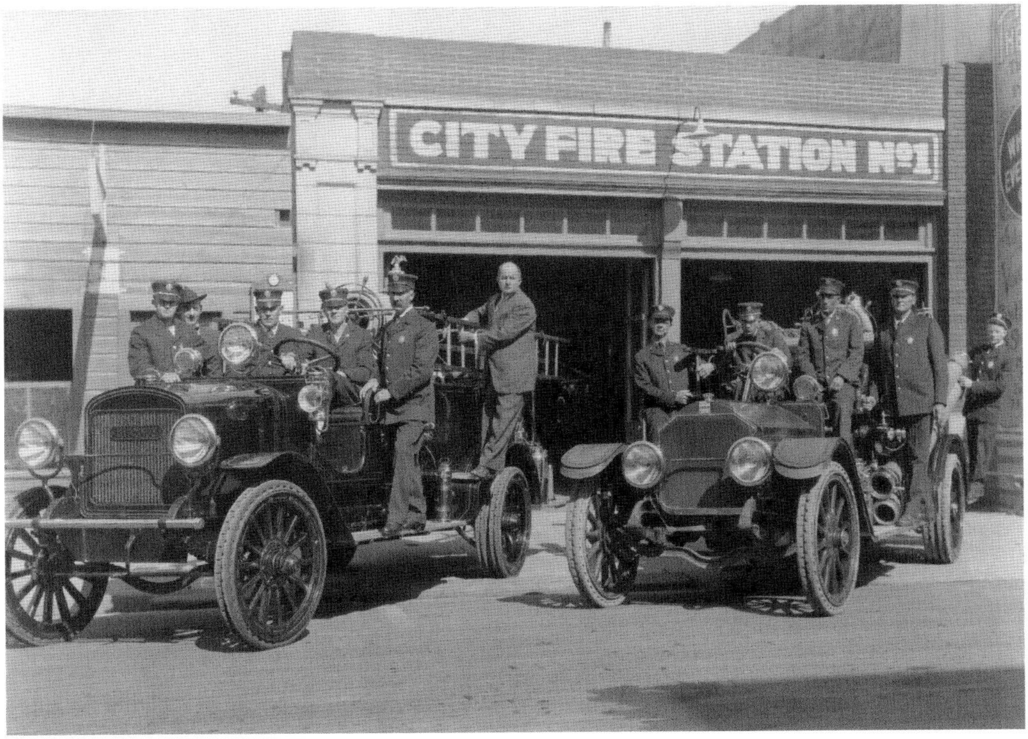

CHAPTER TWO

Main Street USA

Soon after the turn of the 20th century, the motor age came to Idaho Falls, bringing with it roads and car dealerships. In 1911, Idaho Falls became the county seat when Bonneville County was carved out of Bingham County.

There were two disruptions to this otherwise idyllic picture. When the United States entered World War I in 1917, Mayor George Edgington was one of the locals to sign up for military service. All were hailed at a gathering in front of the new Carnegie Library on Eastern Avenue.

Perhaps more terrifying than the war, the Spanish influenza pandemic came in 1918, killing 675,000 people in the United States and more than 22 million worldwide. The *Idaho Register* reported in November of that year that 150 cases had been diagnosed in Idaho Falls. Funerals, as many as 16 in one day, were held on porches or in front yards. Churches, schools, and movie theaters were closed, and no more than six people could be in a bank at one time.

The pandemic subsided in 1919, and Idaho Falls once again returned to its Main Street vision. The Colonial Theatre opened, Idaho's largest vaudeville and motion picture house. A new courthouse and city hall were built, a radio station went on the air, new hospitals were erected, and businesses boomed. In 1927, the Bonneville Hotel, funded by a consortium, became the city's first skyscraper, hosting conventions for decades to come.

In the years following the stock market crash of 1929, Idaho Falls was not spared. Nevertheless, the city managed to build its Lower Power Plant without raising taxes or incurring long-term debt, and continued to grow as a regional commerce center and a place where a person could find entertainment. After the Japanese attack on Pearl Harbor, Idaho Falls stepped forward like all other American towns. A delegation from the city traveled to Portland in March 1944 for the launching of the USS *Idaho Falls*. Castings for the big tanker came from Theo Ballard's Idaho Falls foundry, which also cast a plaque with the inscription "Good voyages from the people of Idaho Falls" and 100 ashtrays as souvenir gifts for the crewmen. The Kiwanis, Lions, and 20–30 clubs contributed subscriptions to *Reader's Digest*, *Saturday Evening Post*, and *Collier's*.

When the war ended, it was time to get back to business. Action on a dam on the South Fork of the Snake River, on hold since 1942, was back on the agenda. Most importantly, city leaders were getting wind of an opportunity of atomic proportions.

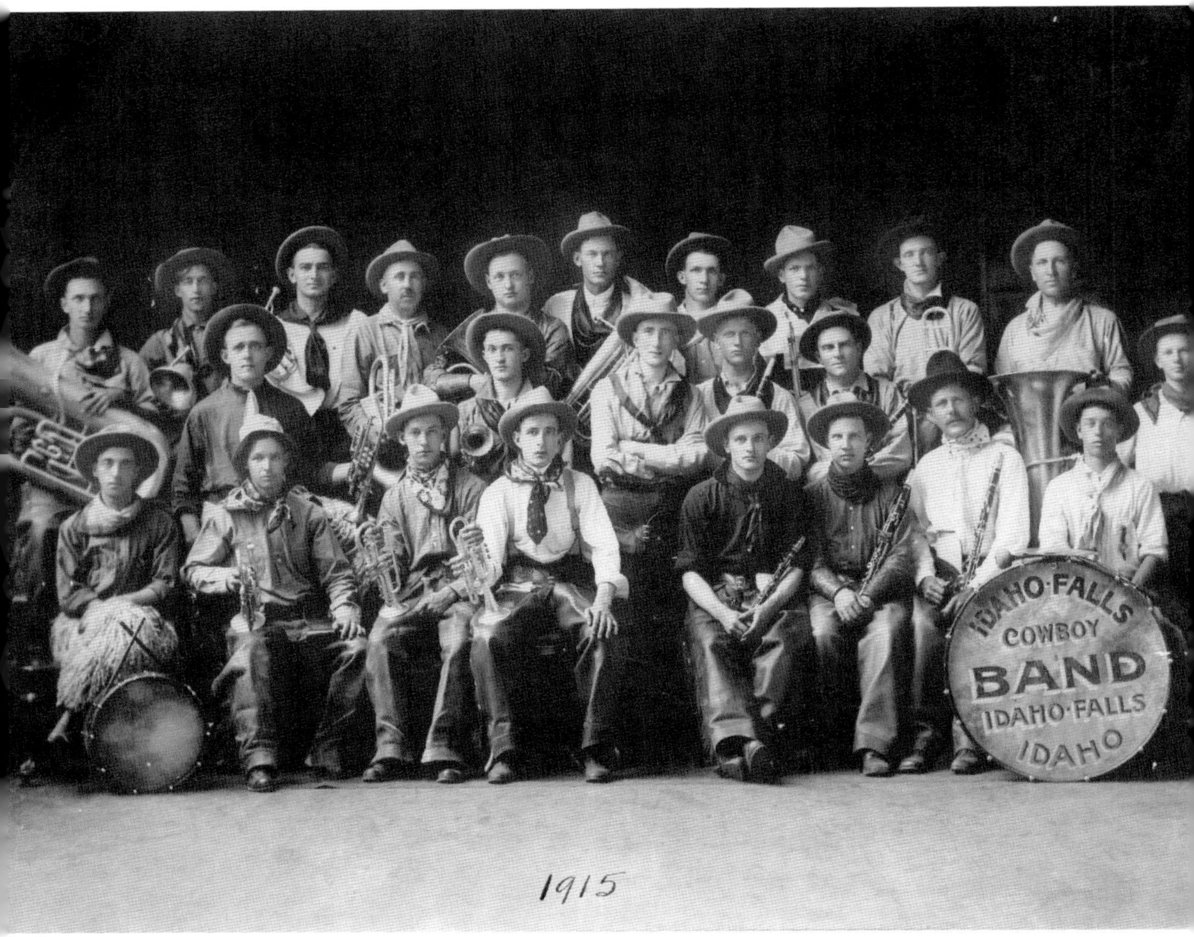

Idaho Falls Cowboy Band

After leaving the Philippines, where he conducted the US Marine Band, Prof. John Von Prosky came to Idaho Falls and assumed leadership of the O.P. Thayer Military Band, which he renamed the Idaho Falls Cowboy Band. When it played at the 1914 Wizard of the Wasatch celebration in Salt Lake City, the band rode their horses into the saloon. In 1917, the city set aside a small salary for the conductor, and in the 1920s passed a special tax levy. The band continued performing until 1942. (Courtesy of the Museum of Idaho.)

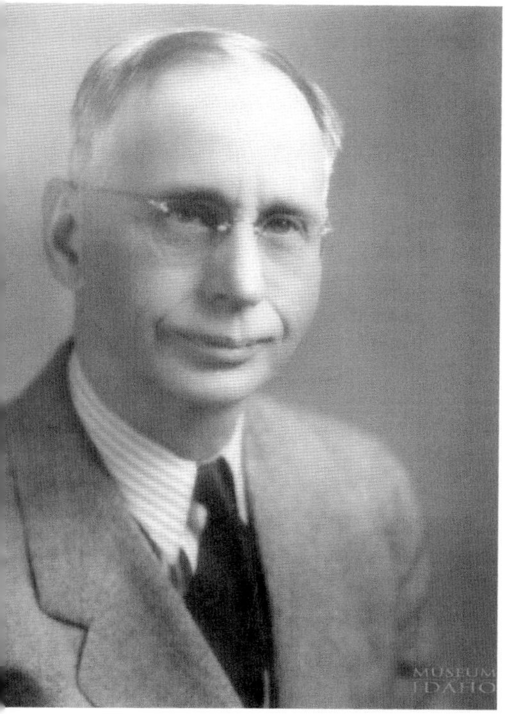

Music Man

Horace Chesbro, a violinist from Seattle, came to St. Anthony in 1911 with his wife, Ella, and their family. After more than a decade there, they moved to Idaho Falls and set up shop on Broadway, where Chesbro Music Co. is today. To create demand for instruments, the Chesbros started school band programs. During the Great Depression, they turned their attention to wholesaling and sheet music, and in future years the company would become the largest distributor of sheet music in the West. (Courtesy of the Museum of Idaho.)

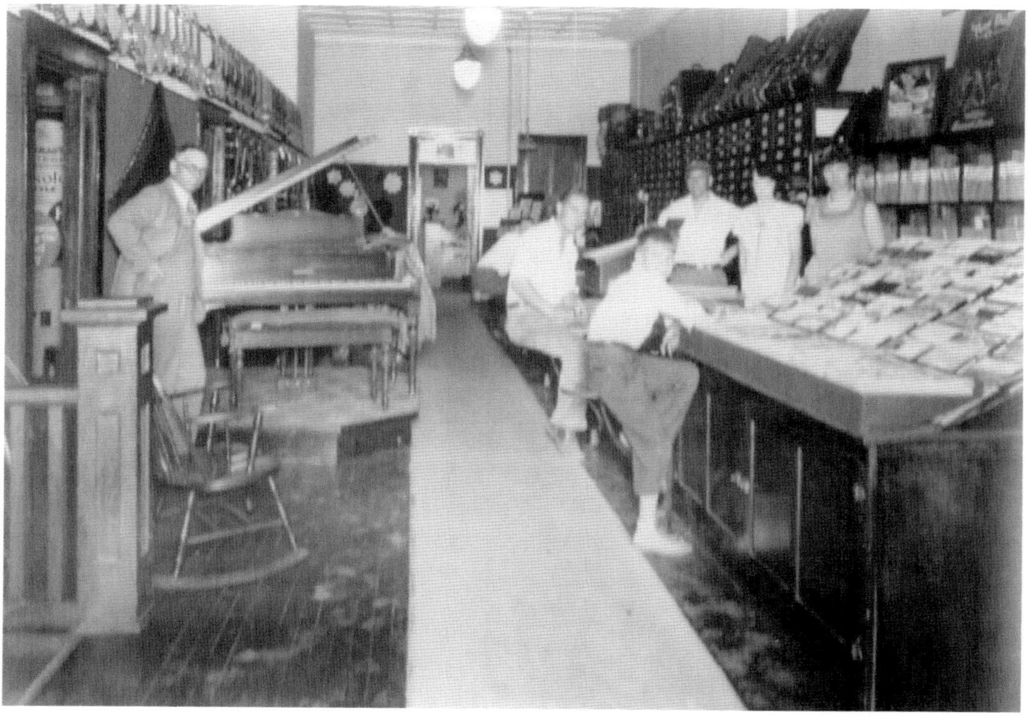

Inside Chesbro Music

Horace Chesbro (left) and his staff pose at their Broadway store. The pneumatic tube system between floors remained in operation until late in the 20th century. (Courtesy of Chesbro Music.)

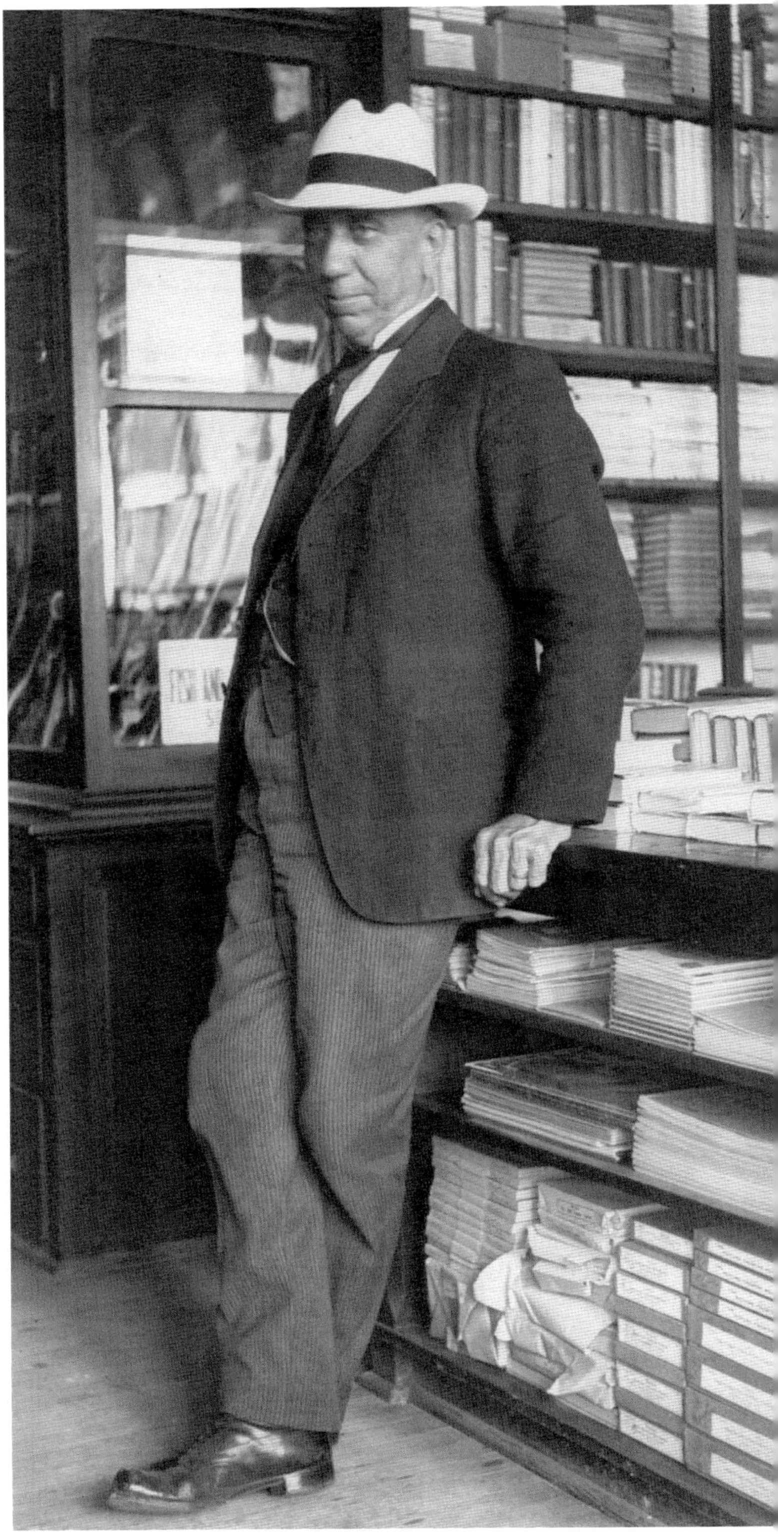

Longtime Store Owner
Alma Marker was a downtown retailer of sheet music, stationery, and other merchandise. He came to Idaho Falls in 1882 and sold goods out of trucks before opening his first store on Capital Avenue. He moved to a new location on Shoup Avenue near Broadway 10 years later, where he was in business until his retirement in 1938. He was a member of the Sportsmen's Association and an avid fisherman. He died in 1956 at the age of 97. (Courtesy of the Museum of Idaho.)

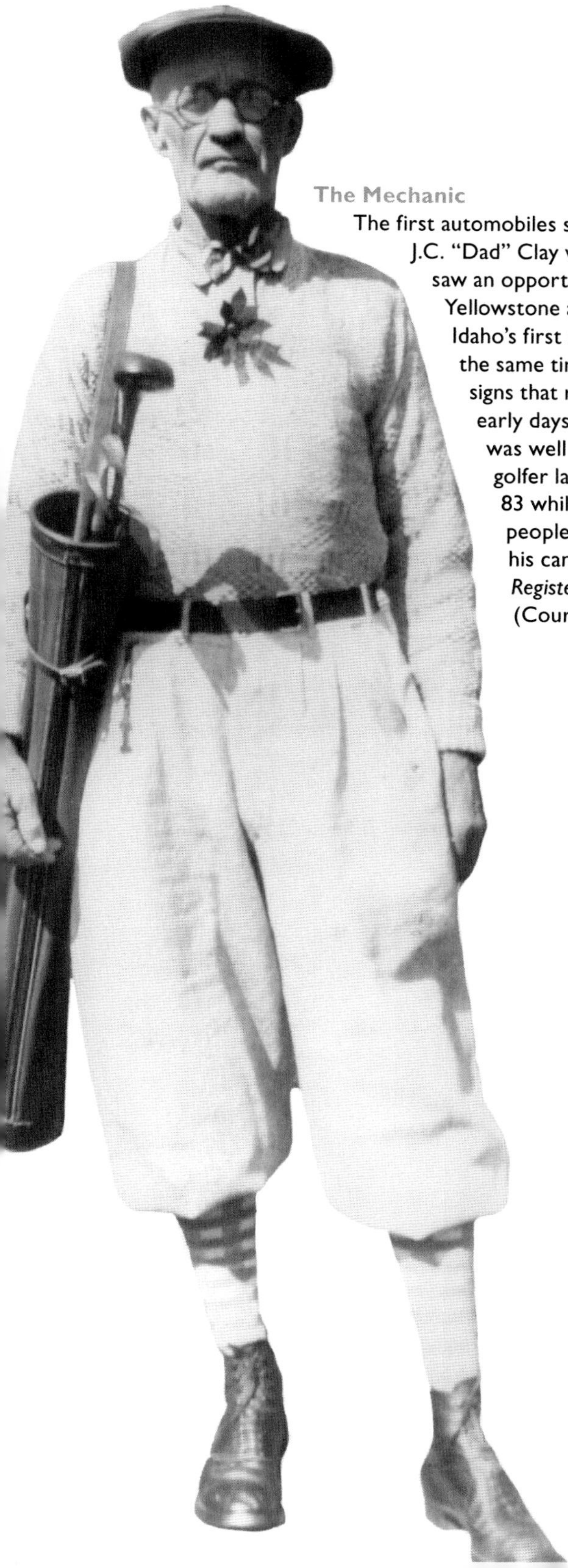

The Mechanic

The first automobiles started appearing in Idaho Falls around 1903. J.C. "Dad" Clay was a mechanic who came to Idaho Falls and saw an opportunity, opening his garage at the corner of Yellowstone and A Streets in 1910. In 1914, he published Idaho's first road log, describing 5,500 miles of roads; about the same time, he began a system of orange and black road signs that read ". . . miles to Dad Clay's Garage." In his early days, he was a cowpuncher and mail stage rider. He was well known as a truthful fisherman and an ardent golfer late in life. He died of pneumonia in 1937 at age 83 while visiting his niece in Los Angeles. "Idaho Falls people will miss the familiar sight of Dad Clay, with his cane and dog, on the downtown streets," the *Post-Register* wrote in a front-page story about his passing. (Courtesy of Idaho Falls Parks and Recreation.)

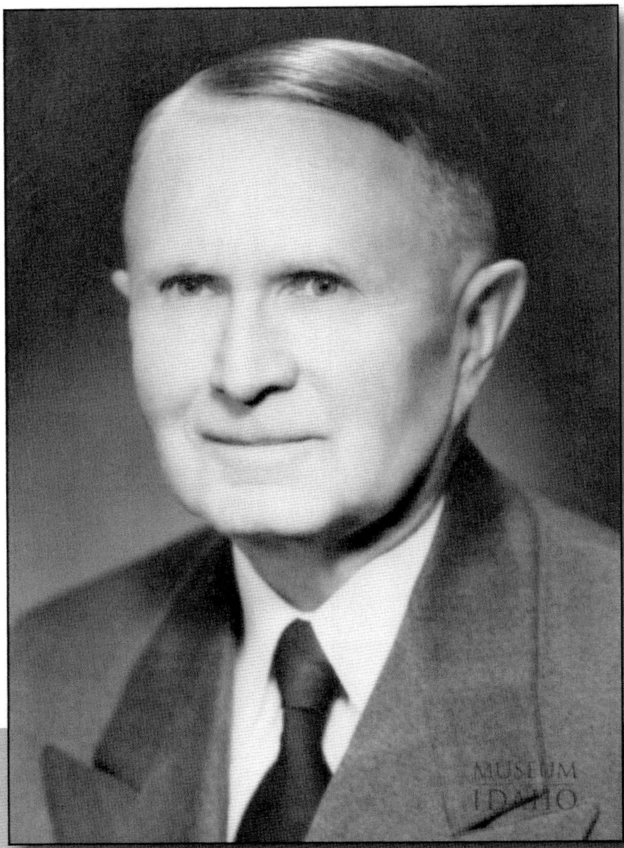

LDS Hospital Pioneer
The son of Utah pioneers, Dr. H. Ray Hatch of Heber City, Utah, was called by LDS church president Heber J. Grant in 1919 to help build what became Idaho Falls LDS Hospital. The hospital opened near the Snake River in September 1923. Hatch and his wife, Mary Leona, remained in Idaho Falls, and the family built a mansion in the country east of town on First Street that is a holistic health center today. (Both, courtesy of the Museum of Idaho.)

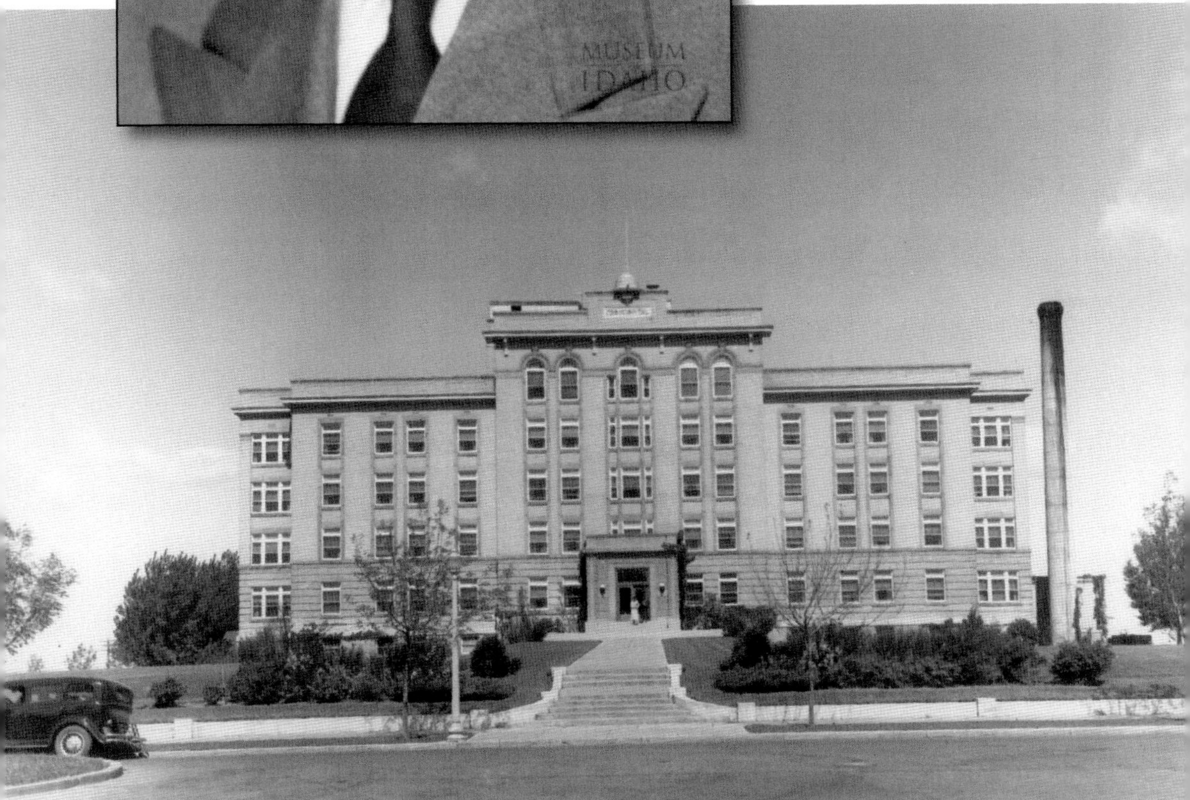

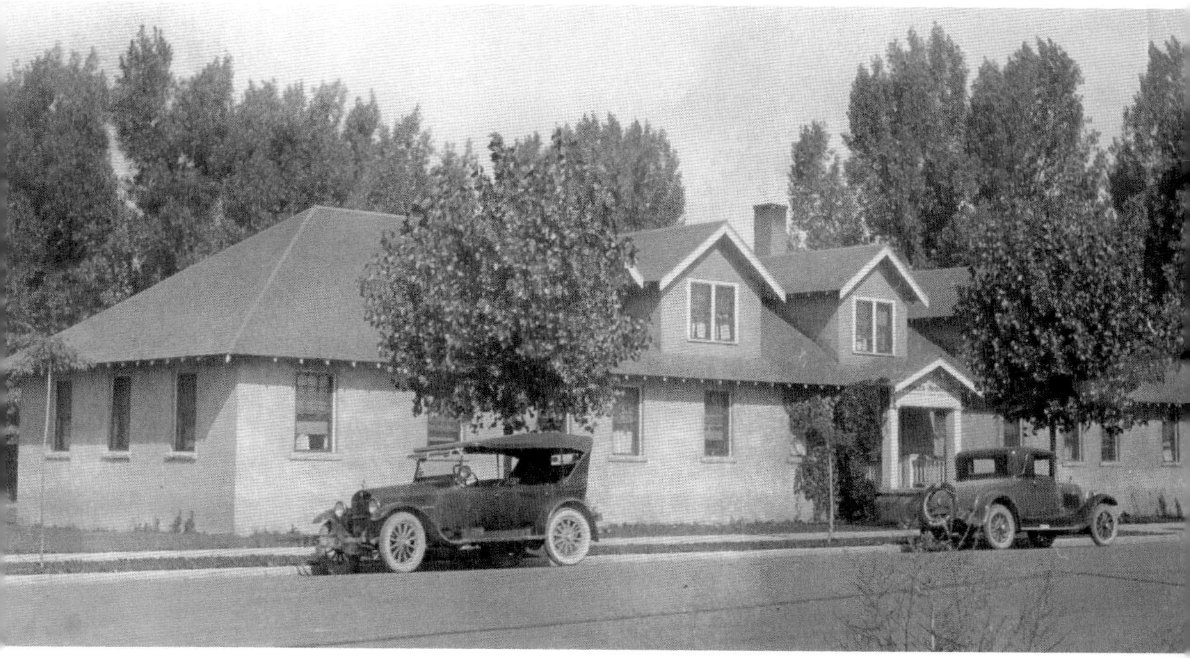

Spencer Hospital
Nurses who trained at Spencer Hospital on South Boulevard lived upstairs. It is now a day care center. (Courtesy of the Museum of Idaho.)

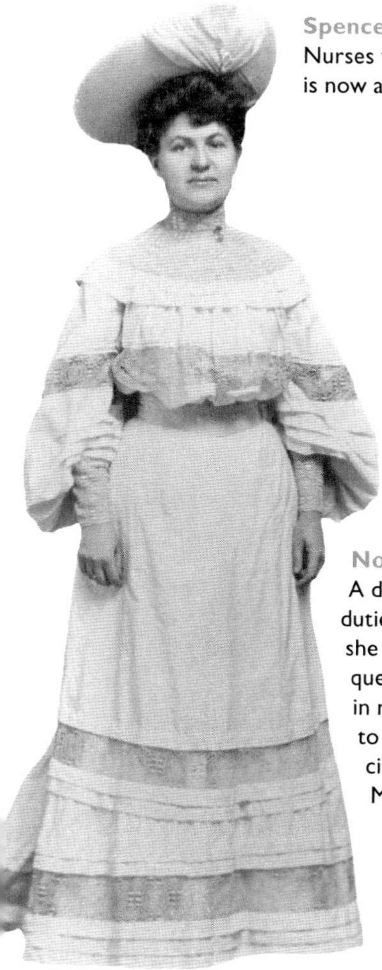

No Nonsense Nurse
A doctor's daughter, Anna Lee Bridges was first called upon for nursing duties during the Spanish influenza pandemic. After the flu subsided, she trained as a nurse at Dr. H.D. Spencer's hospital. When friends questioned the care she provided for the prostitutes who lived upstairs in many buildings downtown, she replied that they might be surprised to hear the stories she heard about some of the town's more reputable citizens. Those were secrets she never divulged. (Courtesy of the Museum of Idaho.)

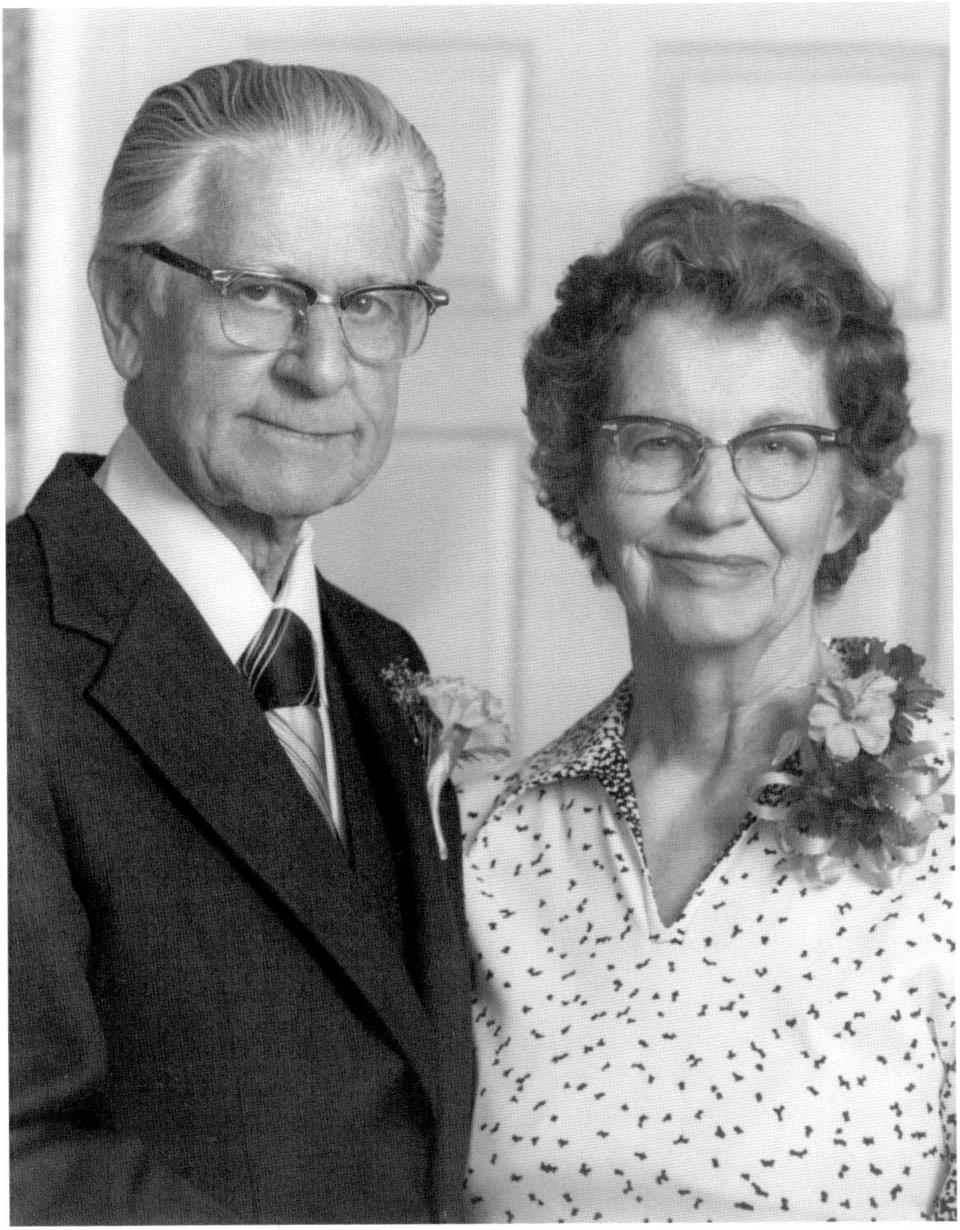

Devout Developer

Born in 1906, few residents exemplified Idaho Falls's 20th century business spirit better than Delbert Valentine Groberg, who founded the D.V. Groberg Co. in 1929. When real estate sales faltered in the early 1930s, Groberg researched the titles of lots on the east bank of the Snake River, ground that later became the site of the Idaho Falls LDS Temple. Groberg's interests expanded into property appraisal and other fields. With partners, he helped found the KID Broadcasting Corp., Idaho Falls's first radio station, the Land Title Co., and the Bank of Commerce. He was also a key player in the effort to bring the Atomic Energy Commission headquarters to Idaho Falls. He and his wife of 74 years, Jennie, represented Bonneville County as grand marshals at the Idaho Centennial Celebration in Boise in 1990. He died in 2004. (Courtesy of Mary Jane Fritzen.)

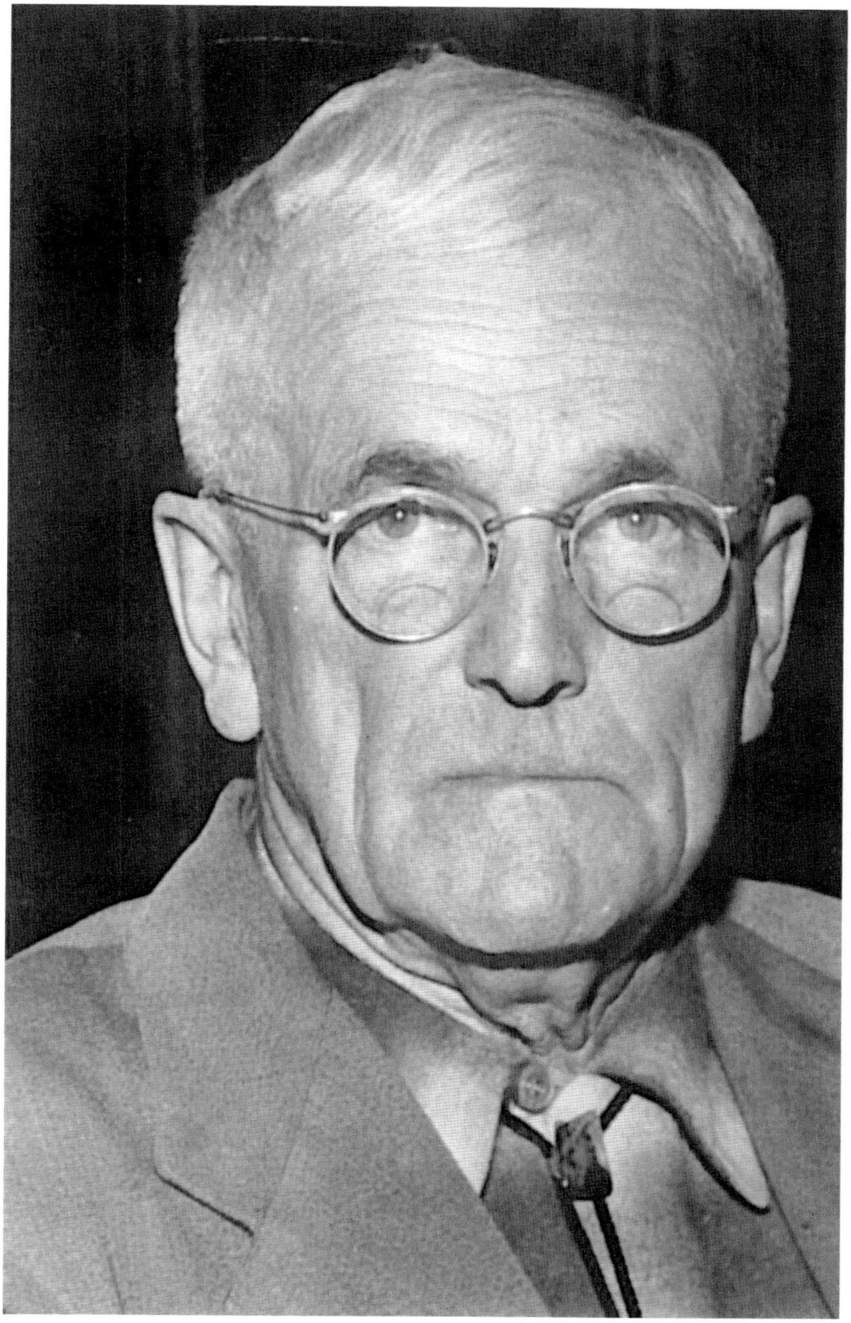

The Water Master

Lynn Crandall managed water distribution of the Snake River and Salmon River for more than 29 years. Born in 1888, he came to Idaho in 1916 to be chief hydrographer for the Twin Falls North Side Land and Water Co. In 1920, he was appointed commissioner in charge of water distribution in the Big Lost River Valley. He was elected water master of the Snake River Water District 10 years later. In 1958, he was the recipient of the Distinguished Service Gold Medal of the US Department of Interior. (Courtesy of the Idaho Department of Water Resources.)

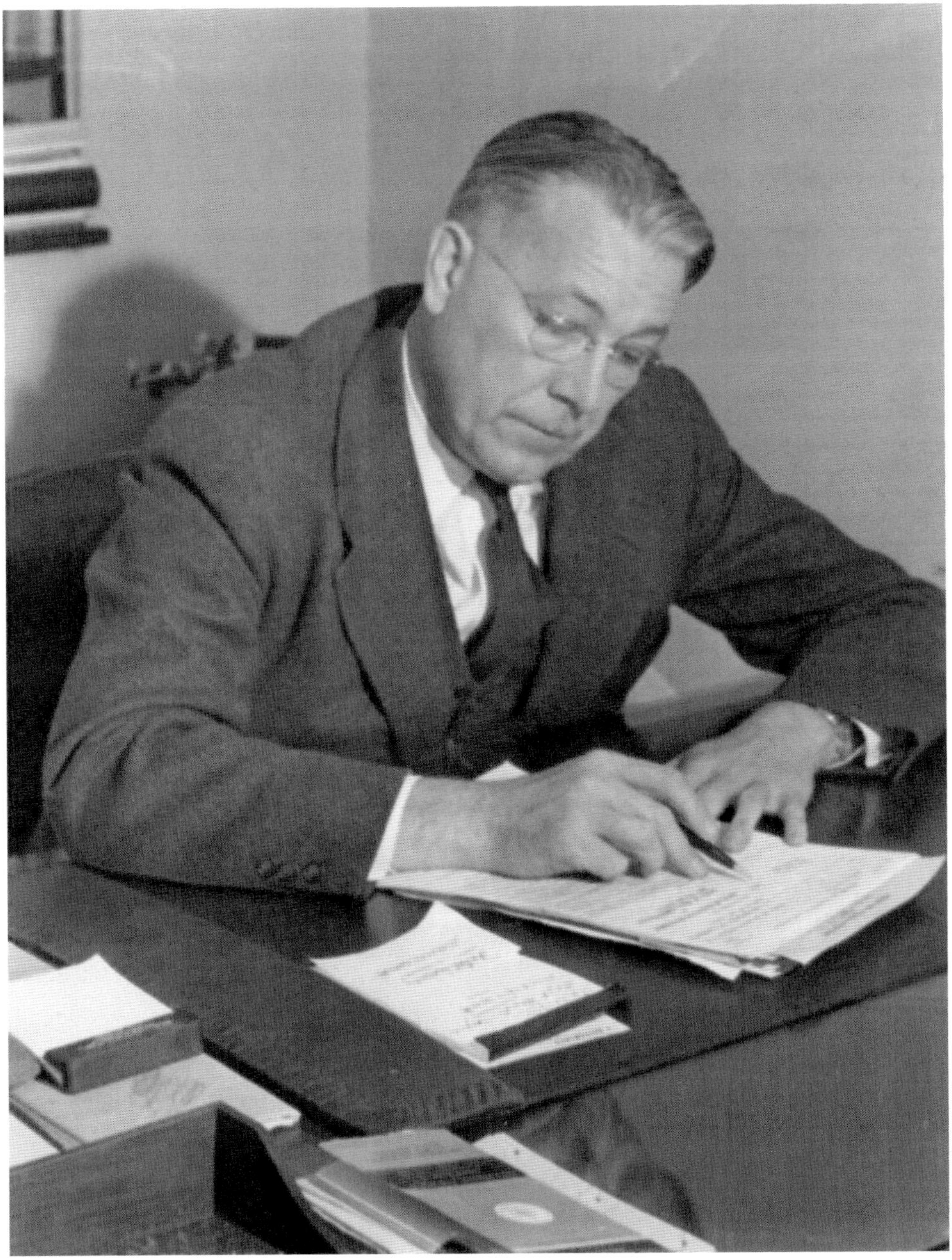

The Publisher

When *Daily Post* publisher J. Robb Brady Sr. died unexpectedly in 1926, it was E.F. McDermott, his general manager, who ended up guiding the newspaper for the next 50 years. In 1931, with the Depression in full swing, he oversaw the merger of the *Times-Register* and *Daily Post* into the *Post-Register*. He was a founder of the Community Chest (later the United Way) and an organizer of the Catholic Church's construction of Sacred Heart Hospital. Most dear to his heart was professional baseball. McDermott was president of the Idaho Falls Baseball Club and later president of the Pioneer League. His legacy at the newspaper is the Goodfellow Fund, an annual Christmas charity drive the paper still manages. (Courtesy of the Idaho Falls *Post Register*.)

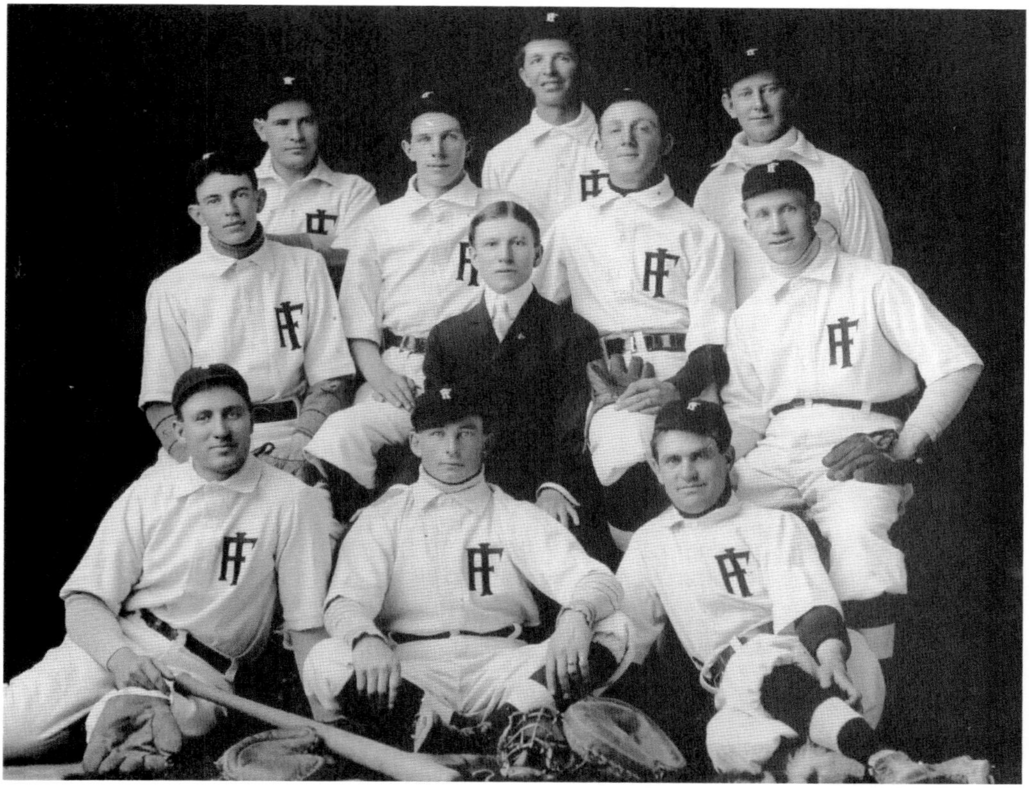

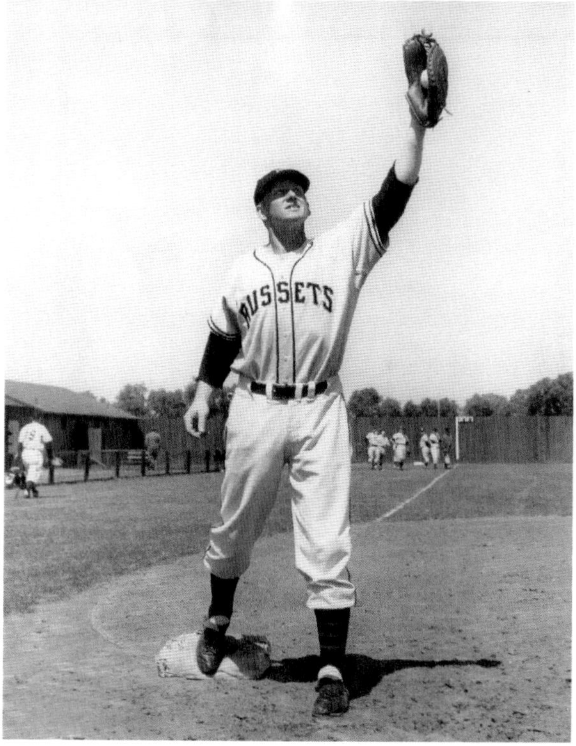

Diamond Stars

Professional baseball in Idaho Falls dates back to the early 20th century. Pictured above is the team of 1906. After World War II, the Russets of the Pioneer League were a rookie farm team for the New York Yankees. Legendary manager Bill Martin played for the Idaho Falls squad in 1946. (Both, courtesy of the Museum of Idaho.)

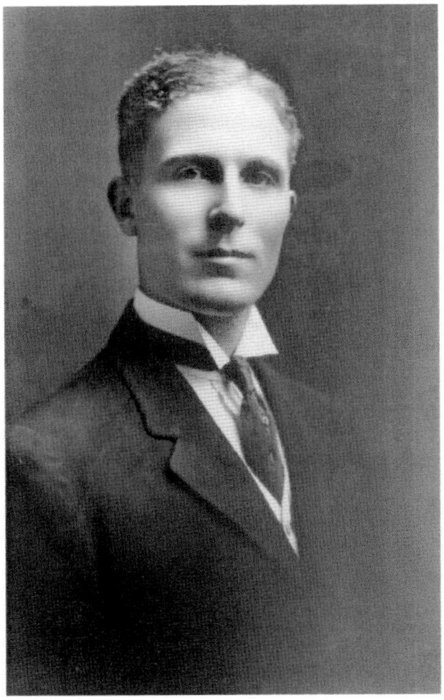

The Young Missionary

David Smith, seen here as a young missionary, became the first president of the Idaho Falls LDS temple. In business, he started a Chevrolet dealership in the lobby of the Idaho Hotel in 1919 with two cars and built it into one of eastern Idaho's largest car retailers. (Courtesy of David John Stosich.)

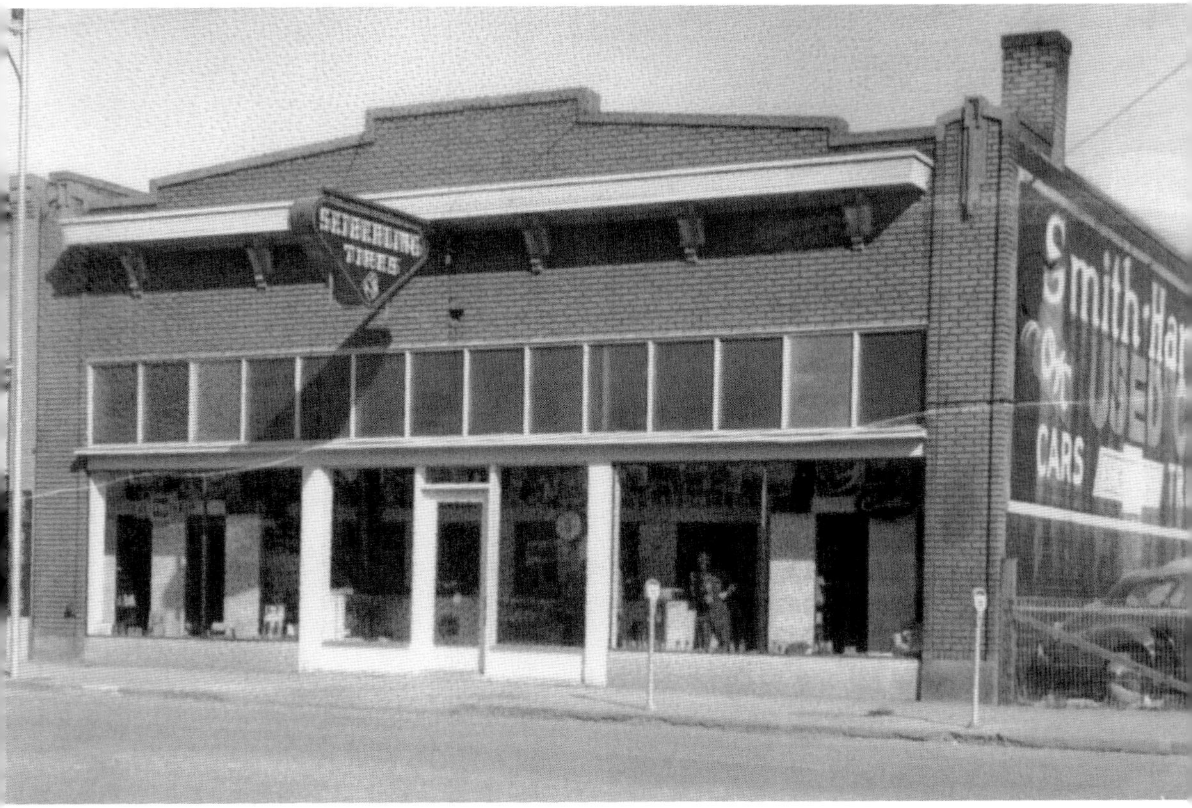

Smith-Hart Chevrolet

The Smith-Hart dealership is shown in 1948, at its downtown location. (Courtesy of the Museum of Idaho.)

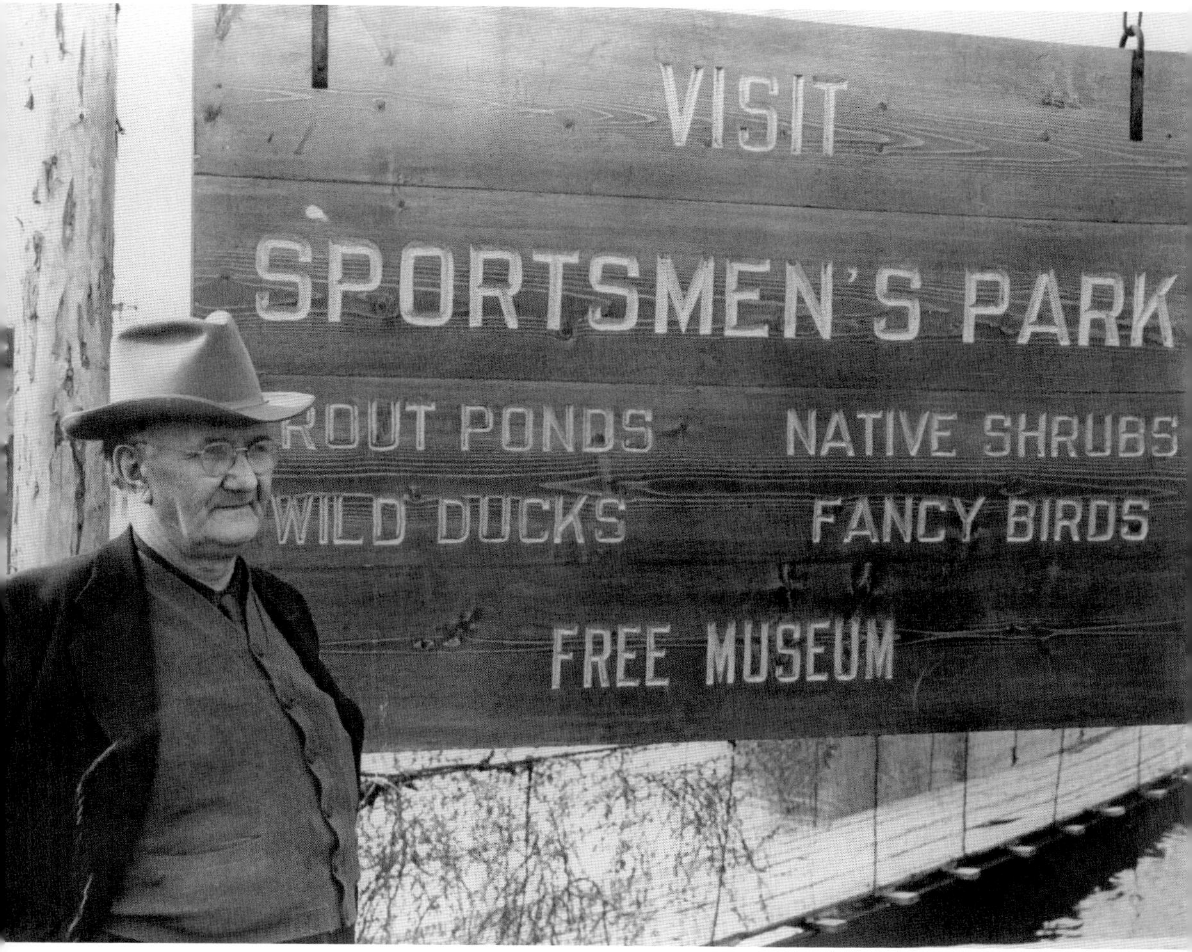

Pedersen Sportsman Park

Born in Denmark in 1875, Peder Pedersen was baptized into the Church of Jesus Christ of Latter-day Saints in 1900 and came to Idaho Falls the next year. A tailor by trade, he was an avid hunter and fisherman who had limited opportunities in his homeland, where such activities were reserved for the nobility and the wealthy. In Idaho Falls, Pedersen became one of the community's strongest advocates for fish and wildlife preservation and management. In the 1930s, under his direction, concrete fish runs were built on an island in the Snake River south of the Broadway Bridge, where millions of fingerlings were spawned and hatched to stock local lakes and streams. Today it is called Pedersen Sportsman Park. The Idaho Falls Sportsman's Association became noted throughout Idaho and the West with an annual jamboree and sportsman's conference drawing hundreds of individuals from all over the West. At his shop, Pedersen ordered suits from a company in Denver and performed alterations himself. He taught the trade to his sons, including the youngest, Soren "Eddie" Pedersen, who was elected mayor of Idaho Falls in 1963 and served three terms. Pedersen's shop was renowned as a place for discussing politics, and whenever Sen. William Borah or Sen. Henry Dworshak came to Idaho Falls, they stopped in to get a feel for public opinion in the Upper Snake River Valley. (Courtesy of the Idaho Falls *Post Register.*)

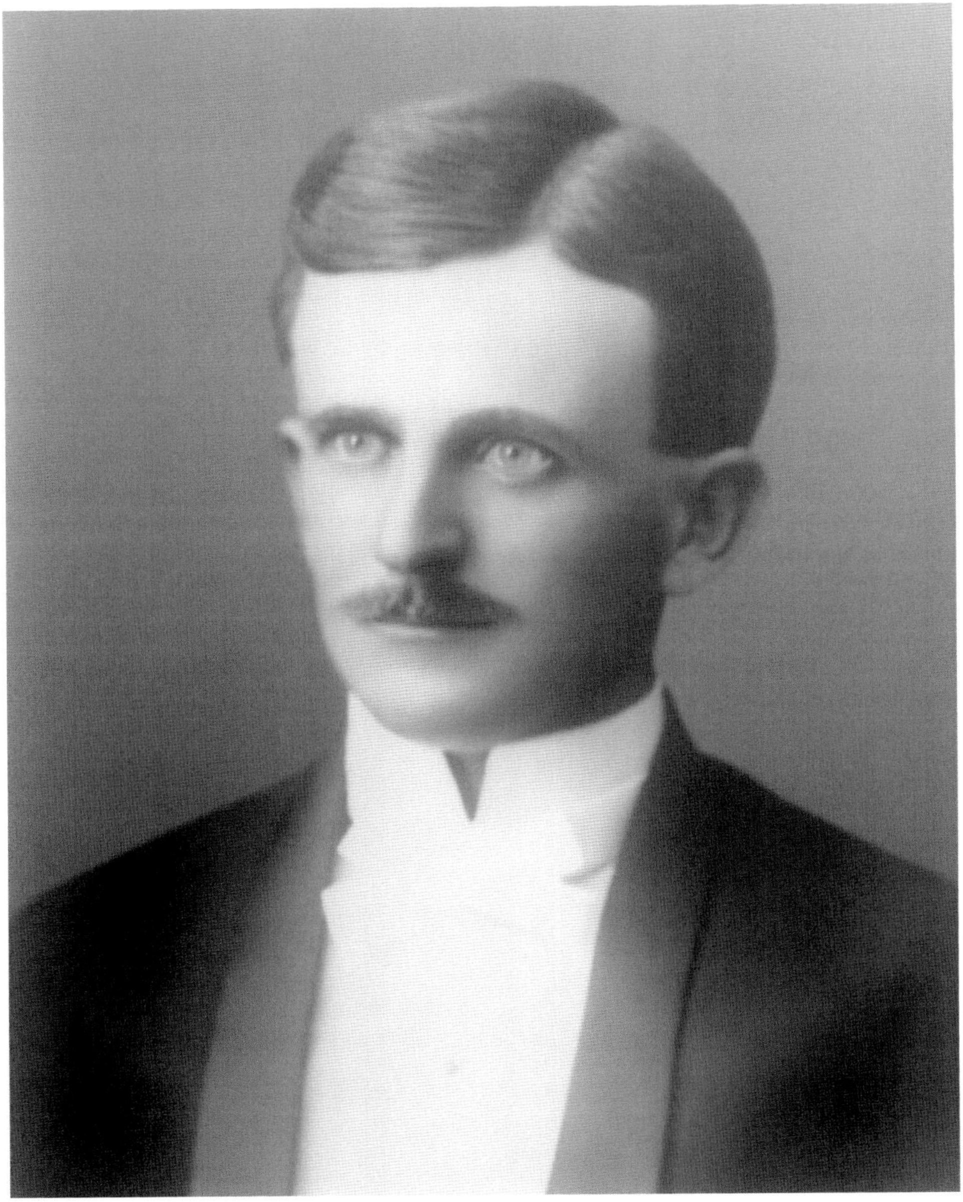

Depression Era Leader

The son of Idaho Falls's first mayor, Barzilla W. Clark attended Rose Polytechnic Institute in Terre Haute, Indiana, and became a licensed engineer in 1905 before returning to Idaho. After two terms on the city council, he served as mayor of Idaho Falls from 1913 to 1915. He left office to pursue mining and development before being reelected in 1926. His administration saw major developments to the city's services, including Municipal Hydroelectric Plant No. 1, the new city hall and fire station, airmail service, enlarged municipal parks, and new wells. In 1936, he was elected governor of Idaho. During his tenure, a state tuberculosis hospital was authorized, a new pardon and parole system was installed, and junior college districts were established. Clark left office in January 1939 and returned to Idaho Falls, where his younger brother Chase became mayor the same year. He succumbed to lung cancer in 1943 and is buried in Rose Hill Cemetery. (Courtesy of the City of Idaho Falls.)

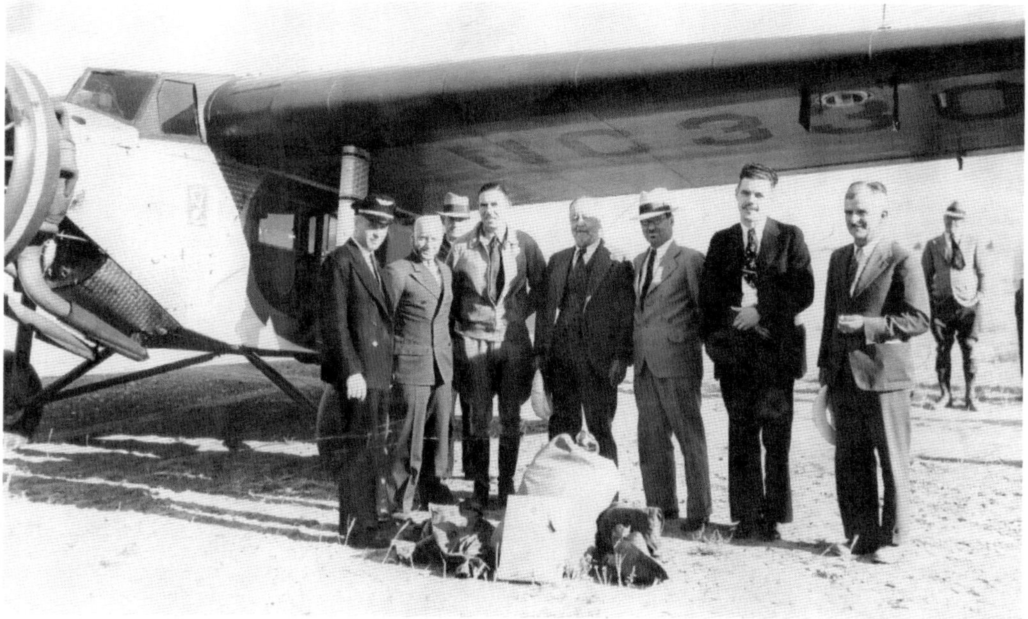

Energetic Executive

The above photograph shows Idaho Falls mayor Barzilla W. Clark (right) on the day airmail service came to Idaho Falls in 1934. Below, Clark signs a bill into law as governor of Idaho, an office he held for two years. (Both, courtesy of the Museum of Idaho.)

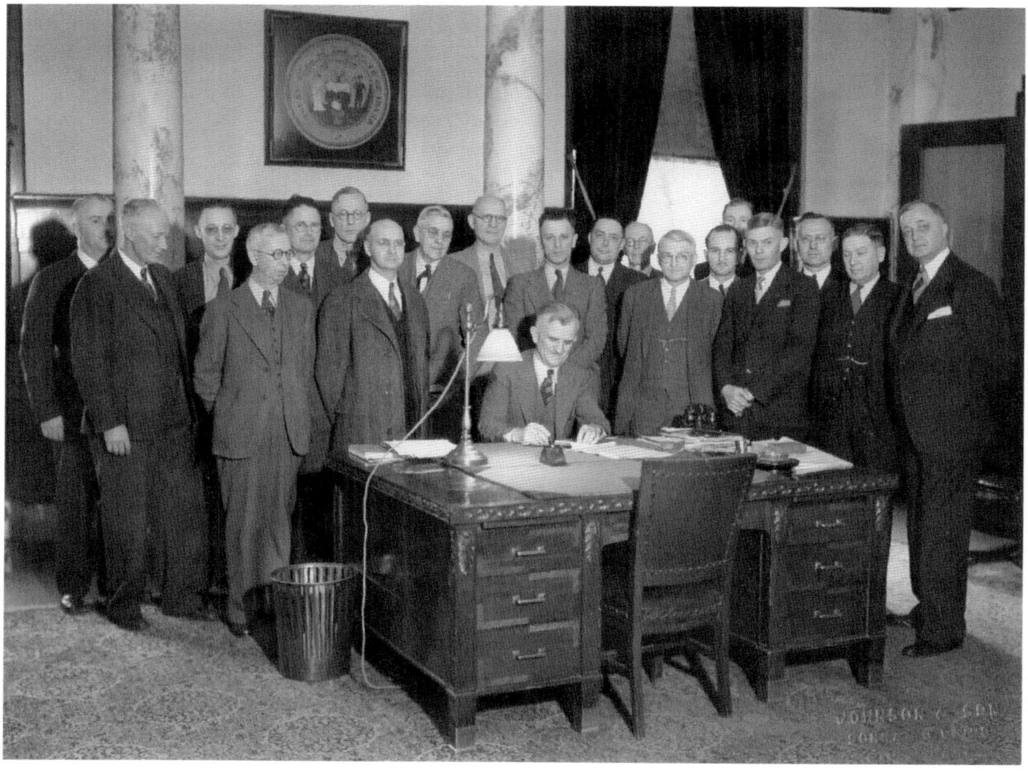

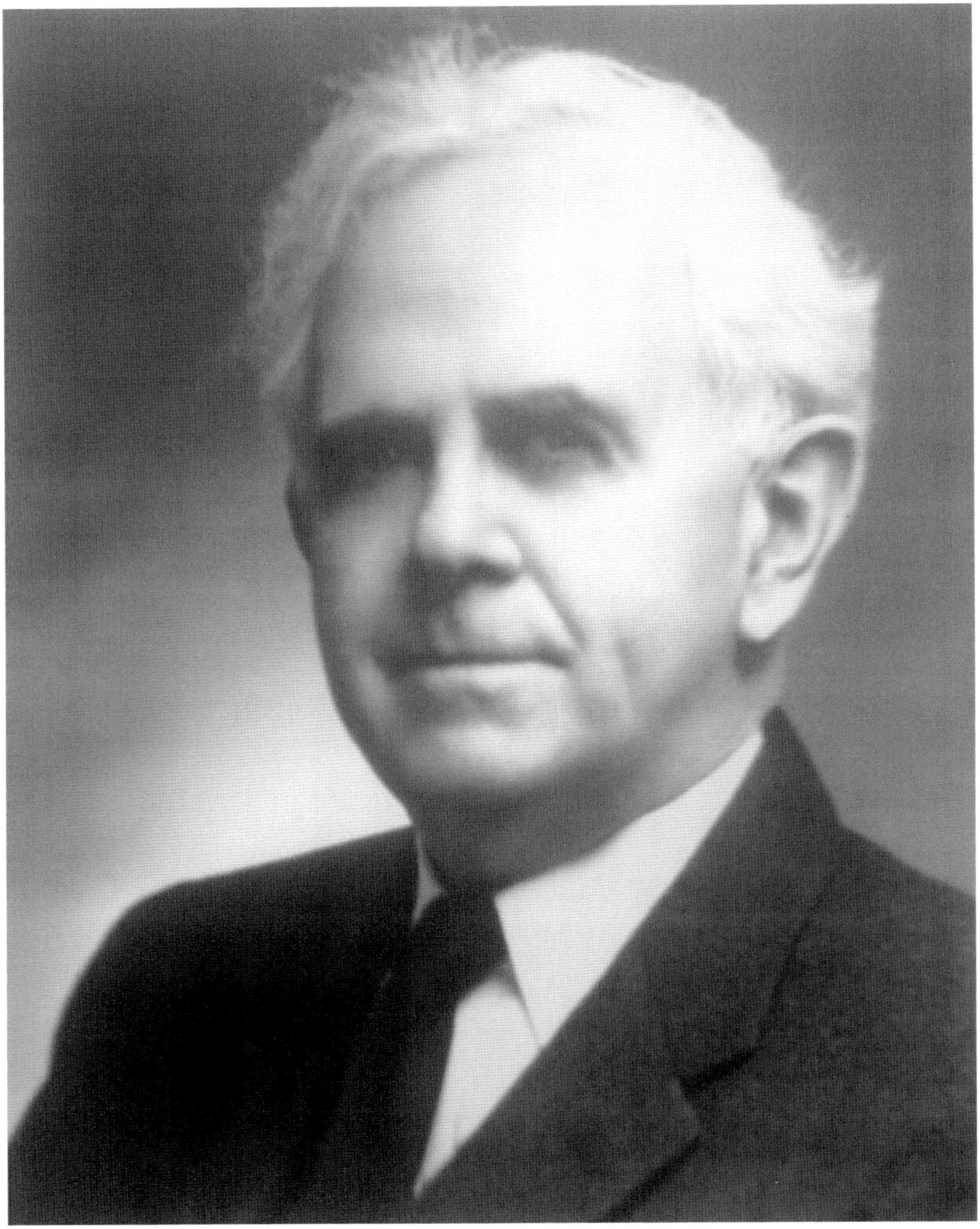

The Younger Brother

The youngest son of Joseph Clark, Chase A. Clark, was active in real estate and land development. He was elected to the Idaho legislature from Custer County in 1911 and 1913, but left to serve with the US Army in 1916 in Mexico. He eventually returned to Idaho Falls and was elected mayor in 1939, succeeding his older brother Barzilla. He was elected governor in 1940 and held office until 1943, when Pres. Franklin Roosevelt appointed him a United States district judge. He retired from the bench in 1964 and died in 1966. He was the father-in-law of US senator Frank Church. (Courtesy of the City of Idaho Falls.)

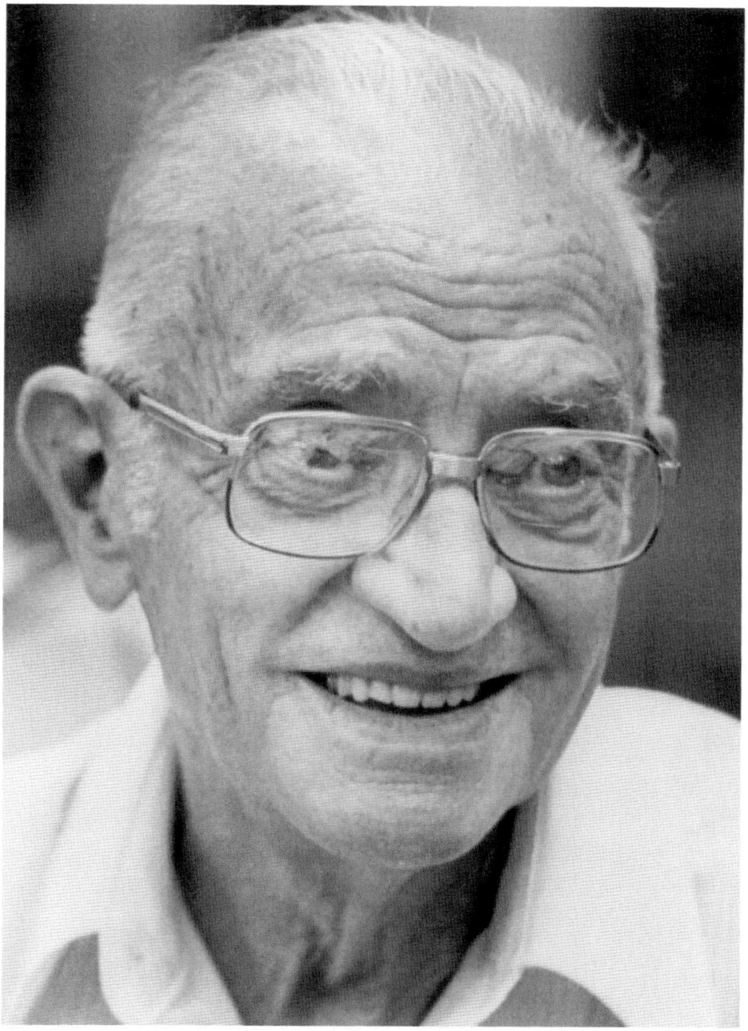

A Place for Tourists

The son of Barzilla and Ethel Clark, Ferris Clark built two cabins in 1928 along the Snake River to provide lodging for a growing number of tourists. Over 50 years, these dwellings expanded into the Westbank. Below is a postcard from the Westbank as it appeared in the 1960s (an eight-story tower would be built in the 1970s). Clark left the hospitality business at age 72 and died in 1987. After changing owners several times, the Westbank is now the Hotel on the Falls. (Both, courtesy of the Idaho Falls *Post Register.*)

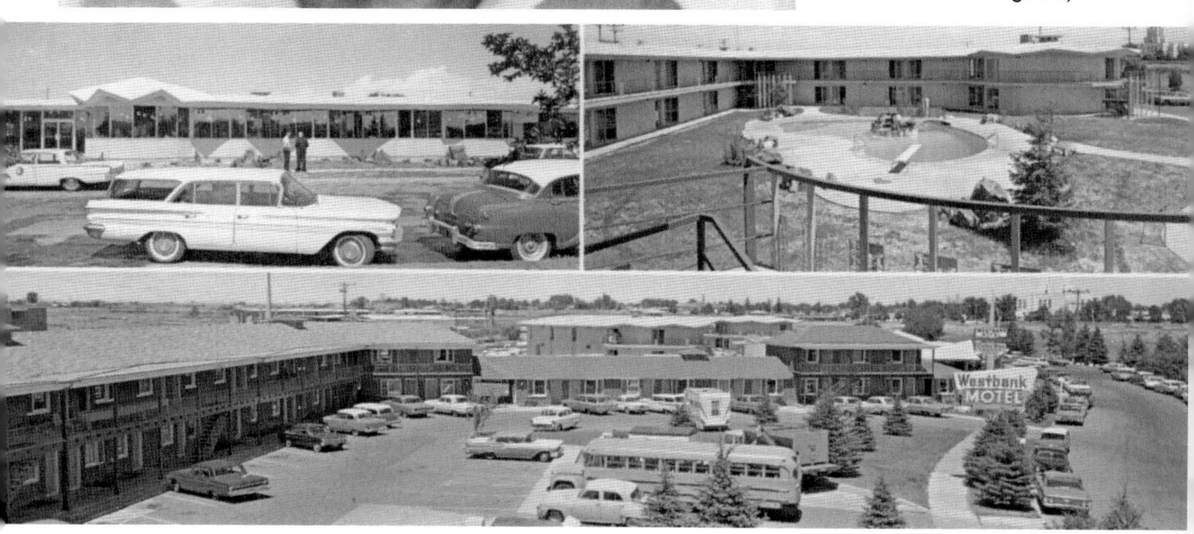

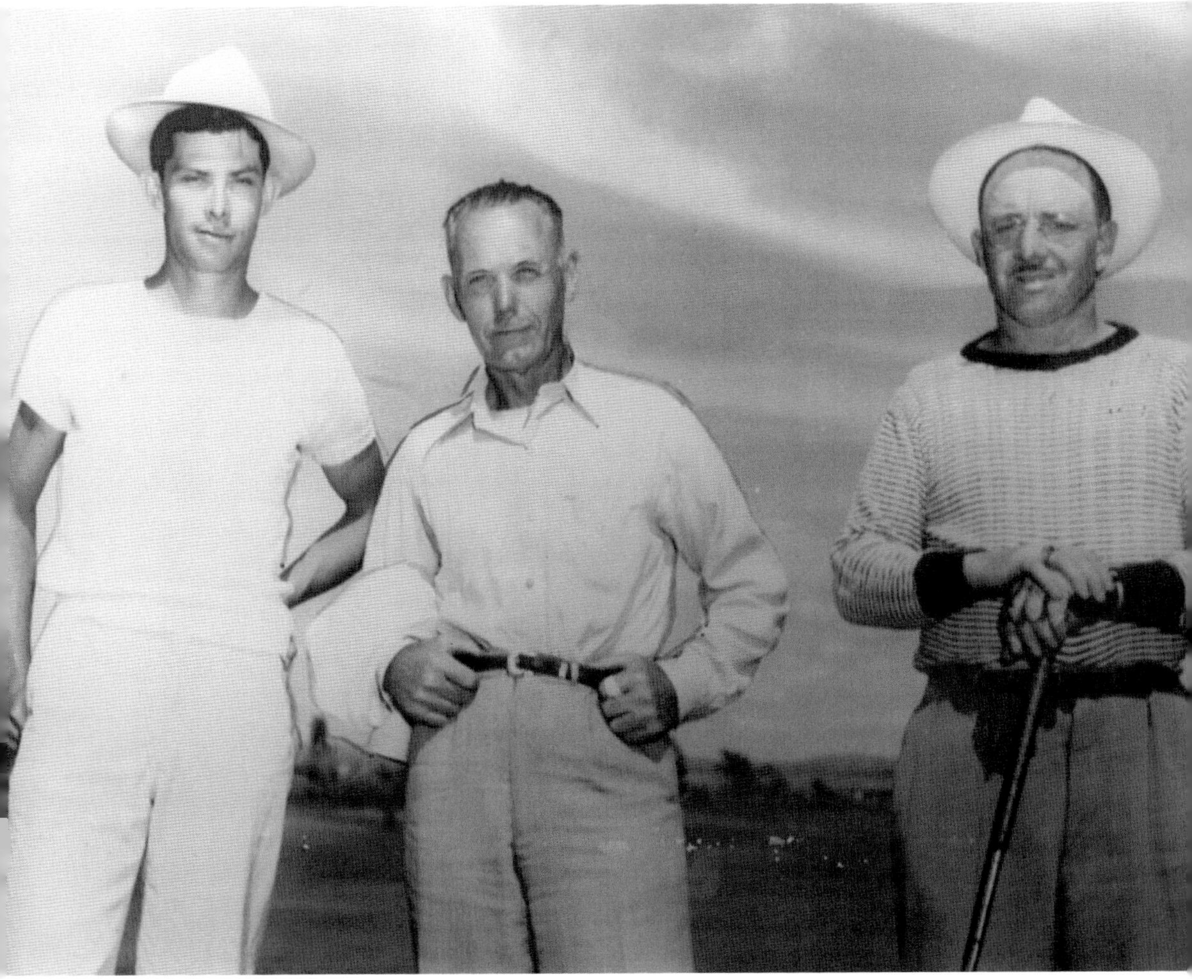

Planner and Planter

A city councilman for 18 years, Russell A. Freeman (center) is hailed by many as the father of the Idaho Falls park system. In charge of buying land and developing parks, planting, and landscaping, he also chaired the committees for the Idaho Falls Civic Auditorium and Ravsten Stadium. With George Orullian, he took the lead in developing the municipal golf course. Freeman Park, at the north end of the Snake River Greenbelt, is named after him. In this image he is flanked by his son Jim (left), later an Idaho Falls city councilman, and a friend, Otto Rast. (Courtesy of Pinecrest Municipal Golf Course.)

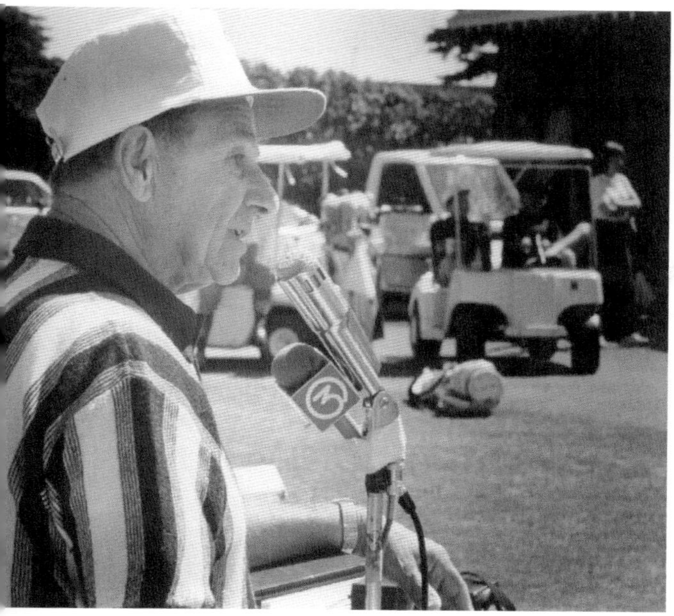

"Godfather of Golf"

George Henry Orullian was the city's first golf pro. Born in Armenia in 1909, he came to the United States as an infant with his parents, who settled in Salt Lake City. He and his wife, Gertrude, moved to Idaho Falls in 1936, and he became the supervisor of the city's first municipal course, Pinecrest. He held the position until 1974. He was a lifetime member of the Professional Golfers Association of America and a leader of Elks Lodge No. 1087. Here, he is pictured speaking at Pinecrest's 50th birthday celebration in 1986. (Courtesy of the Idaho Falls *Post Register.*)

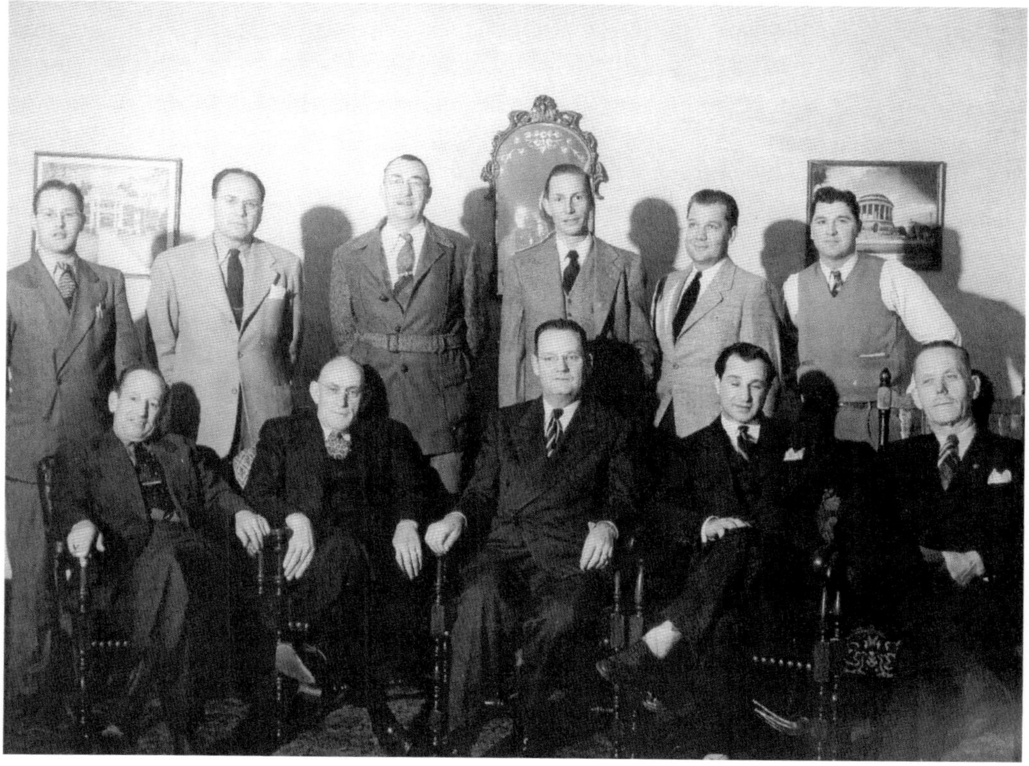

In the Clubhouse

Idaho Falls Golf Association members posing in the Pinecrest Clubhouse in 1948 are, from left to right, (first row) Spike Ballard, Bill Gourley, B.L. Harris, George Orullian, and Russ Freeman; (second row) Jack Couch, A.M. Smith, Ross Corbett, N.O. Anderson, S. Eddie Pedersen, and J. Robb Brady. (Courtesy of Idaho Falls Parks and Recreation.)

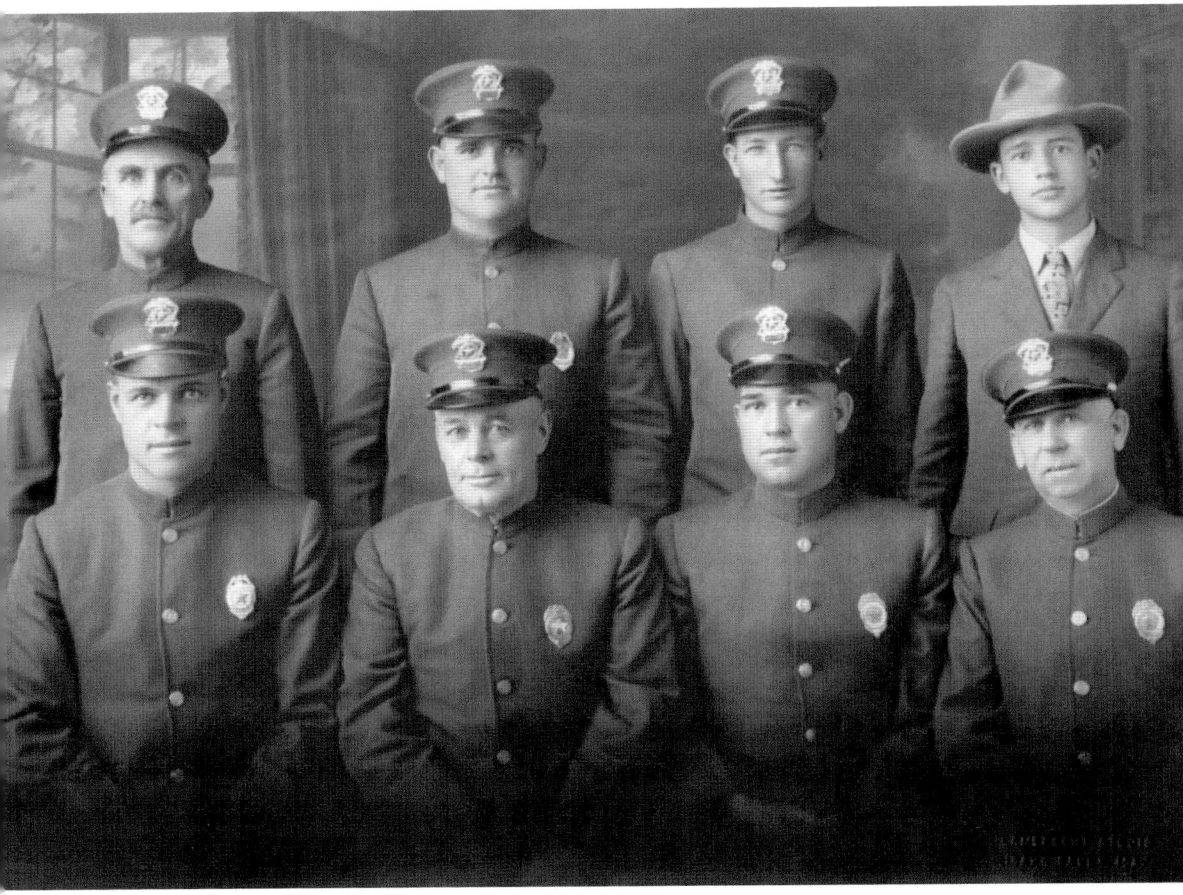

Idaho Falls's Finest

Idaho Falls had a small police force when this photograph was taken in 1927. From left to right are (first row) Harry Neppin, Chief Larry Hanson, R.E. Gillespie, and Sidney Whitehead; (second row) William Hayward, R.V. Hogue, Harold Arva, and William S. Holden. Holden, who would become one of the city's most prominent attorneys and civic leaders, was home from George Washington University Law School for the summer. (Courtesy of the Holden family.)

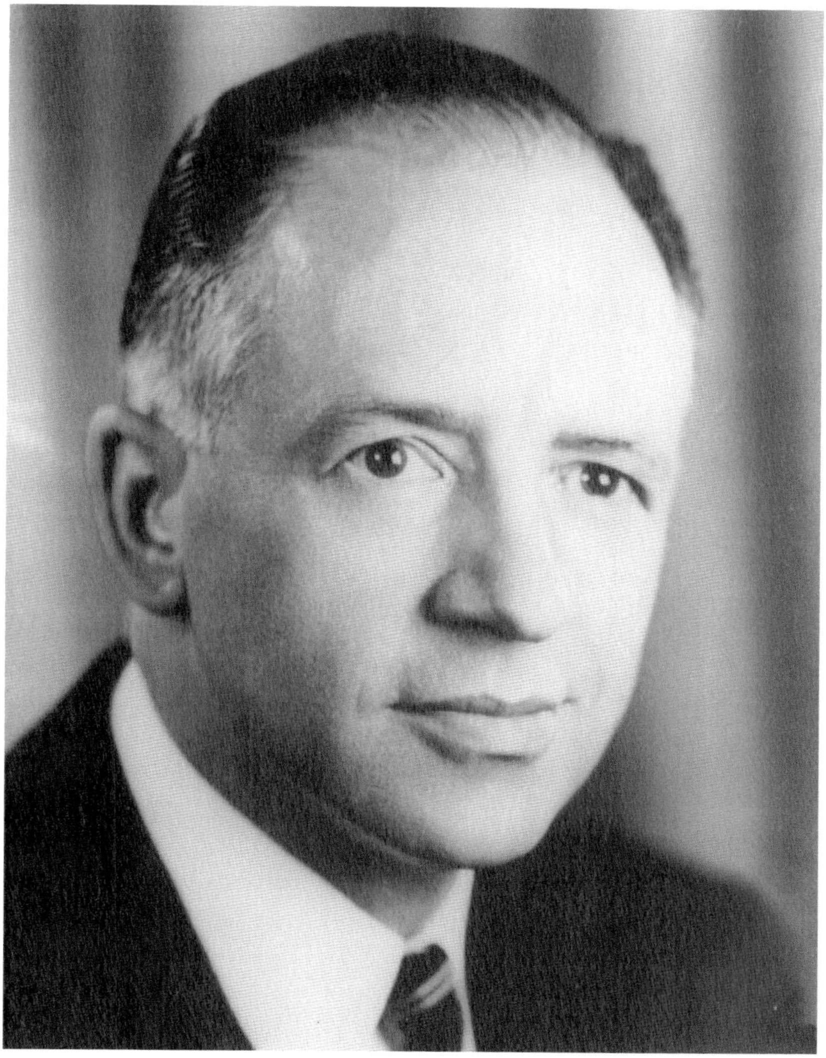

Community Leader

The son of an attorney and the nephew of three others, William S. Holden led the team of community leaders responsible for bringing the Atomic Energy Commission (AEC) headquarters to Idaho Falls in 1949. When it was announced that the AEC would be locating its nuclear reactors on the Snake River Plain, Holden and Mayor Tom Sutton led a delegation to Washington, DC, to lobby for Idaho Falls. The choice came down to Pocatello and Idaho Falls, and while Pocatello offered a staid all-male delegation to tout its advantages, Idaho Falls, following Holden's directions, rustled up every "winsome young wife" it could find to host dinners and receptions. This was called "the Party Plan." To cover for Idaho Falls's lack of a paved road to the desert where the reactors were to be built, Holden persuaded Sutton to put crews to work on the west side of town, to give the appearance that road construction was already underway. The AEC picked Idaho Falls, population 19,000, and the city entered a new phase of explosive growth. As one of the West's preeminent water lawyers, Holden was also a key player in the construction of the Palisades Dam in the mid-1950s. He was a stalwart of the Idaho Republican Party and challenged incumbent GOP senator Herman Welker in 1956. Due to another moderate candidate on the ballot, Welker, a McCarthyite, held the nomination but lost that fall to Democrat Frank Church. Holden died in 1988 at age 81. (Courtesy of Greater Idaho Falls Chamber of Commerce.)

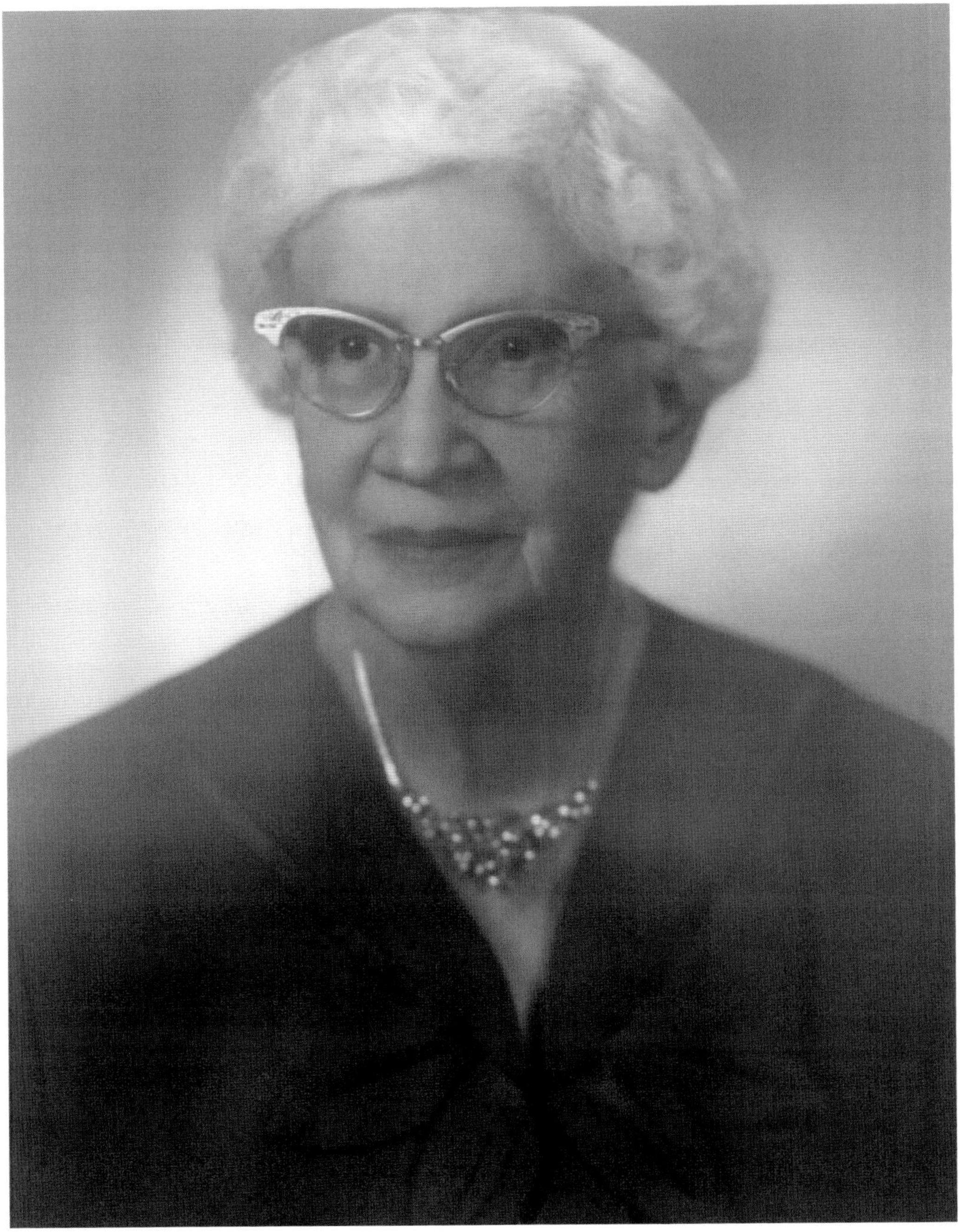

Elementary Presence
In a career that spanned 45 years, Ethel Boyes was one of Idaho Falls's earliest educators. Born in 1886, she was 18 when she took the state-required test to become a teacher. Attending Albion Normal School, she received her degree in 1912. She taught at Central Junior High School and became the principal at Emerson Elementary. She received the Kiwanis International Distinguished Service Award in 1963 and was honored by the Bonneville Historical Society in 1978, the same year an Idaho Falls elementary school was named after her. She died in 1985. (Courtesy of the Idaho Falls *Post Register.*)

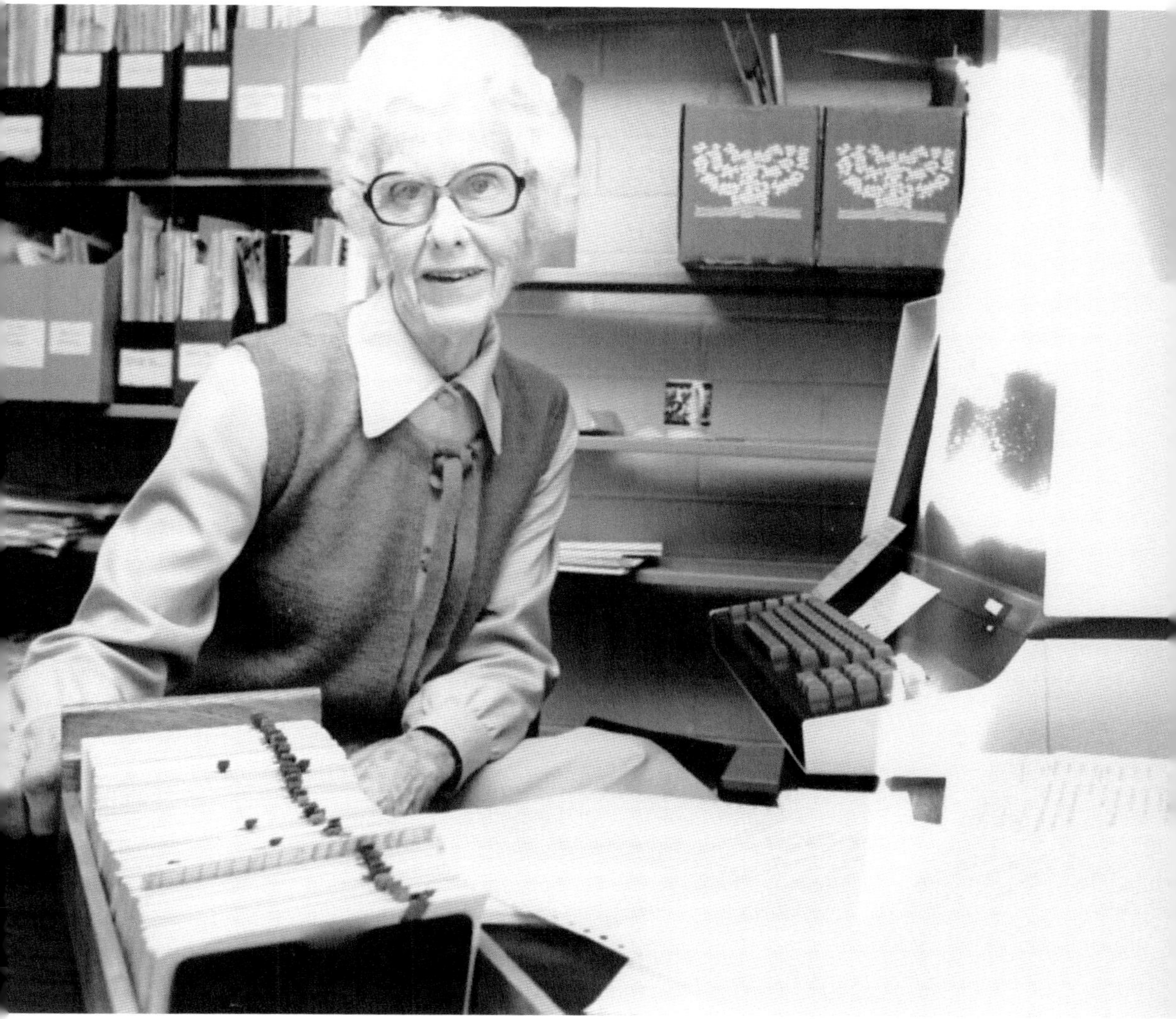

College Prep
Few teachers in Idaho Falls had more impact than Mae Neuber, who taught from 1927 to 1968. In 1951, she started a world history class at Idaho Falls High School restricted to college-bound seniors. Students brave enough to enroll in "Senior World" drew maps to scale with crow quill pens and India ink and applied themselves to essays that had to be completed in an hour. Most of the course was lecture-based, and many students took their notebooks with them to college. One of her pupils, Rodney Merrill, graduated from Harvard in 1962 and nominated her as one of the best college prep teachers in the country. She and three others were chosen from 350 candidates to fly to Boston for a commendation and a check for $1,200. It was her first trip to the East Coast and gave her a chance to visit New York City and Washington, DC. After retiring, Neuber became active in community programs and the Idaho Falls Public Library, where she volunteered three days a week, rebinding more than 1,000 books and saving the library an estimated $35,000. In 1987, five years before her death at age 91, she was honored by friends and former students when the foundation they had set up in her name made a gift of two dictionaries and seven atlases to the library. Today, a plaque with her picture hangs in the entryway. (Courtesy of the Idaho Falls *Post Register.*)

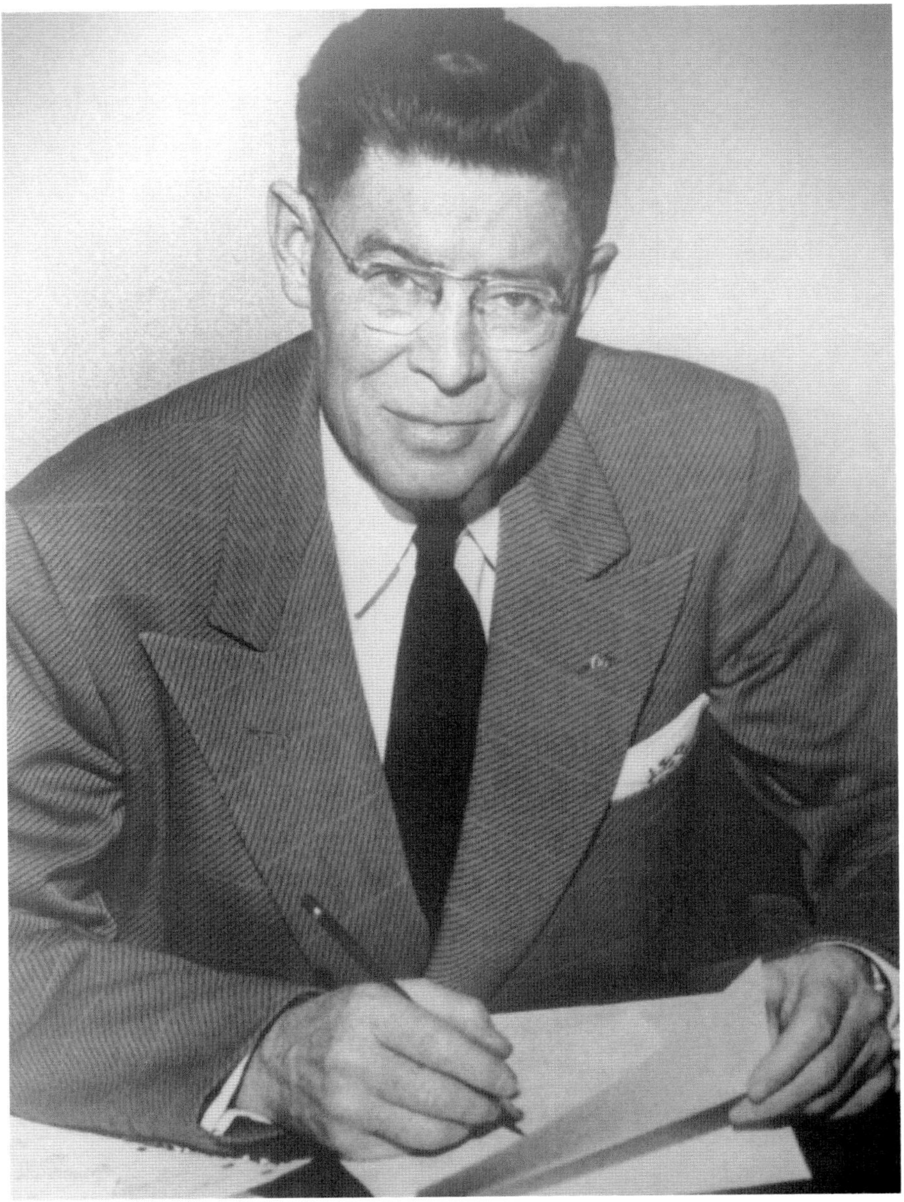

The Principal

Arthur Harold Bush was an Idaho Falls educator for 45 years, serving 42 of them as an elementary school principal. Born in 1901, he came to Idaho Falls to teach general science and geography. He was the city's first male teacher below the senior high level. He was named principal at Riverside School, where he served for 28 years. He moved to Whittier Elementary in 1954, and after he retired in 1968, it was renamed for him. He served on virtually every level of teacher and education associations from local to district to state, including several Idaho Education Association committees. His philosophy was simple: "If we can make our students happy little individuals through the first three or four years, who get along with their school mates and like to play in organized sports, then we have done our job." He died in 1973. One of his sons, Eugene L. Bush, was a prominent Idaho Falls attorney and state legislator. (Courtesy of A.H. Bush Elementary School.)

Longtime City Attorney

The Idaho Falls city attorney for nearly 50 years, Ralph Albaugh gave the mayor and council legal advice on many important developments. When the city received $29,572 from S.H. Kress in 1928 for its downtown fire station, it was Albaugh who handled the sale and the purchase of the land where city hall stands. A reserved man who preferred to function behind the scenes, he was granted an honorary lifetime membership by the Greater Idaho Falls Chamber of Commerce in 1953. He died in 1974 at 80 years old. (Courtesy of Tom Albaugh.)

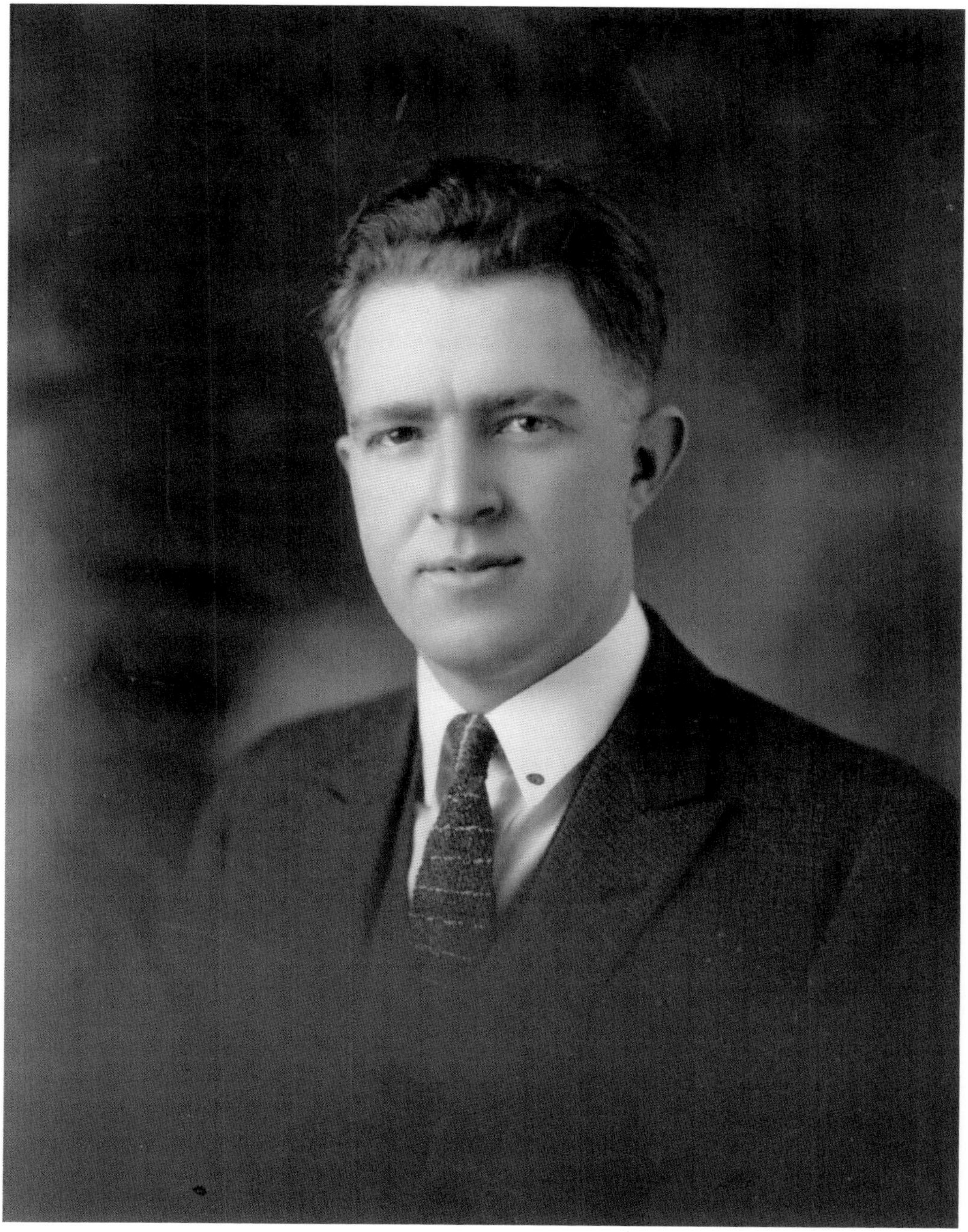

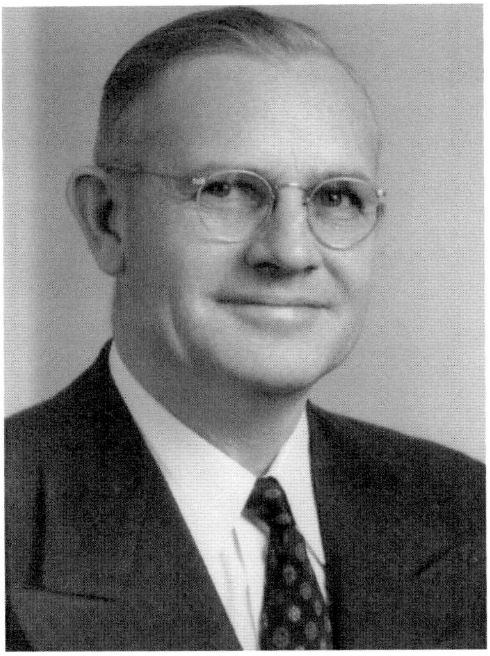

City Engineer

Everything built in Idaho Falls in the mid-20th century was under the eye of Claud R. Black, city engineer from 1930 to 1959. From the Lower Power Plant to the grandstands at Highland Park, from Pinecrest Golf Course to Fanning Field, it was Black who signed off on the plans. Born in 1890, he served on the city council before becoming a city employee. Black was a lifelong member of First Baptist Church, a deacon, a choir member, and a teacher of youth and adult classes. (Courtesy of Terri Fohrenck.)

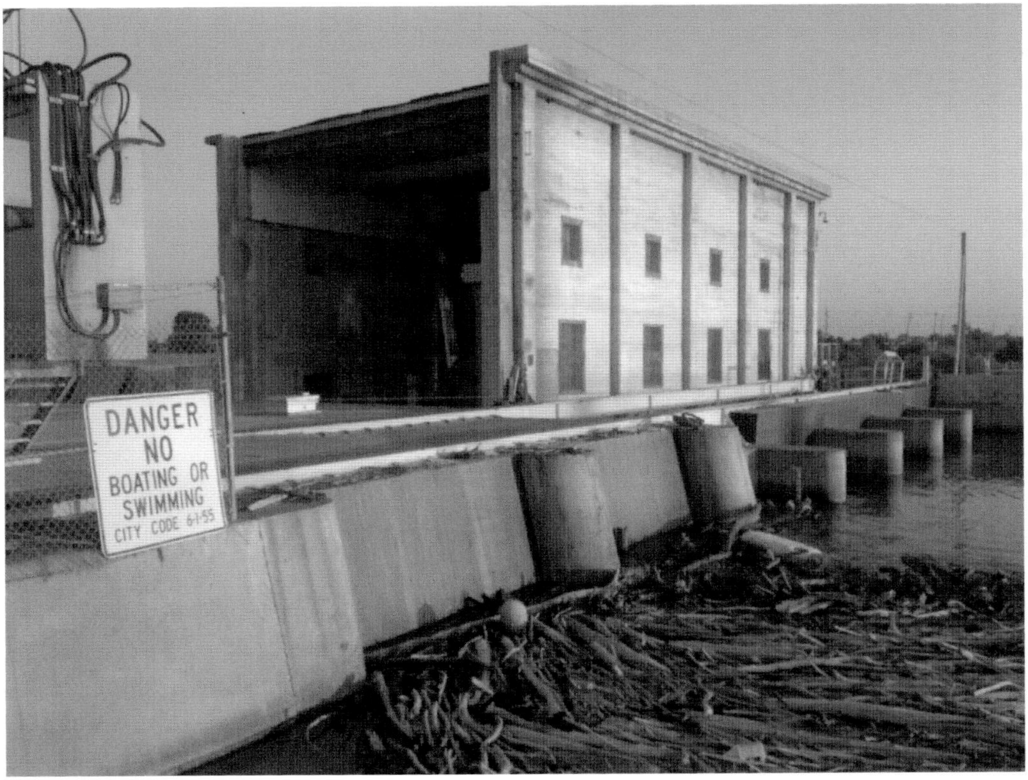

Public Utility

Pictured here is the city of Idaho Falls's Lower Power Plant as it looks in 2013. The plant was originally built in 1937 while Claud Black was city engineer. (Author photograph.)

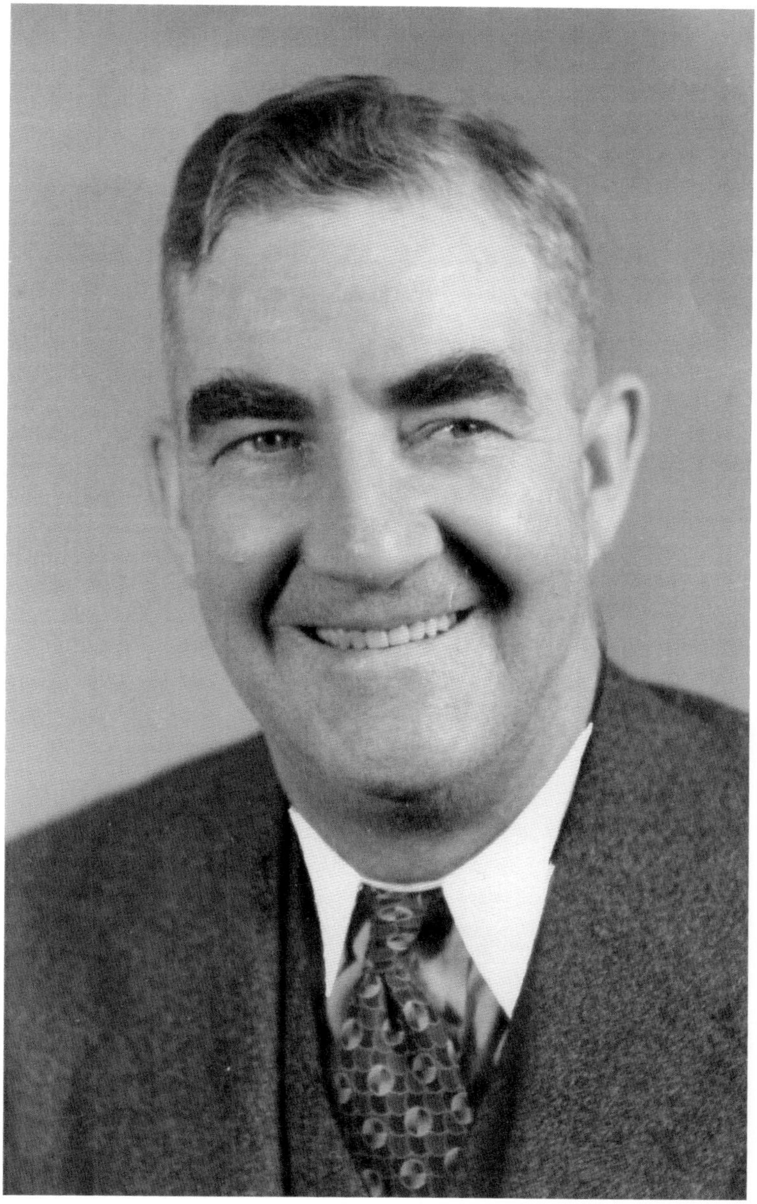

From Altar Boy to Mayor
Born in Eagle Rock in 1889, Ed Fanning was elected to the Idaho Falls city council in 1922 and served four years under Mayor Ralph Lewis. He left to pursue business interests, but in 1937, he was appointed to fill a council vacancy and named mayor when Chase A. Clark went to Boise. Fanning held office until 1949, when he lost to Thomas Sutton, then returned in 1951 and served until 1956, when he died in office. He was mayor when the Atomic Energy Commission built the National Reactor Testing Station. During his terms in office, Idaho Falls's population increased by nearly 10,000 people. A Catholic, he was the city's first altar boy and was among the laymen who helped finance and build Holy Rosary School, church, and Sacred Heart Hospital. The year before he died, he became the first Catholic layman in Idaho to be knighted by the Order of St. Gregory the Great, an honor granted to him by Pope Pius XII. (Courtesy of the Museum of Idaho.)

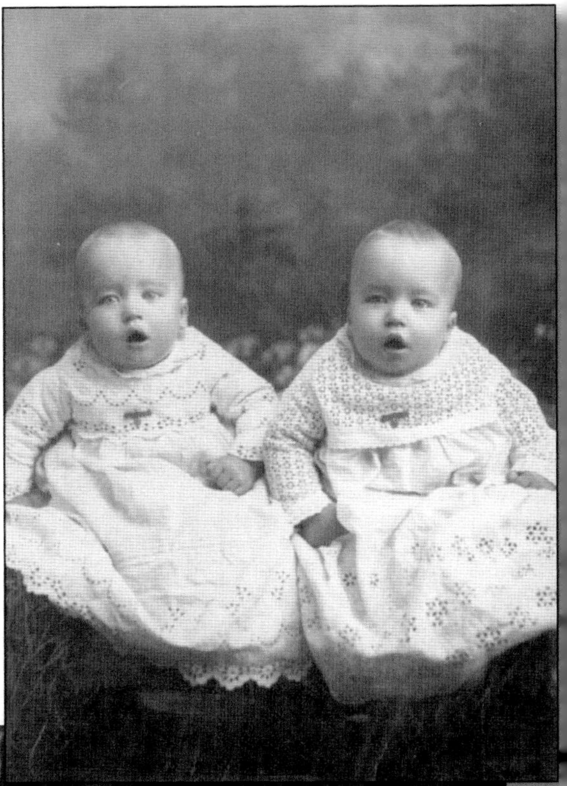

The Keefer Twins

Fred and Frank Keefer were twin sons born to William Keefer in 1891. Both would grow up to become cowboys, builders, and notorious raconteurs. Fred Keefer, pictured below in later years at home among his artifacts, built the log cabin on the island below John's Hole now known as Keefer's Island. (Both, courtesy of the Museum of Idaho.)

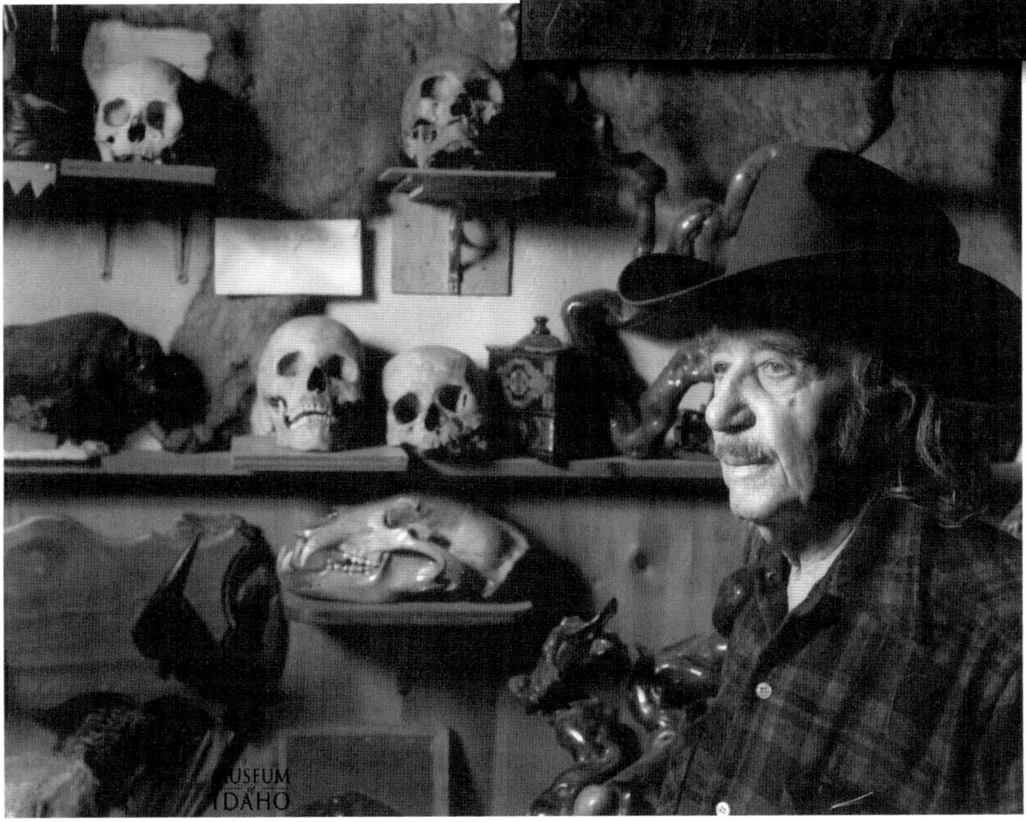

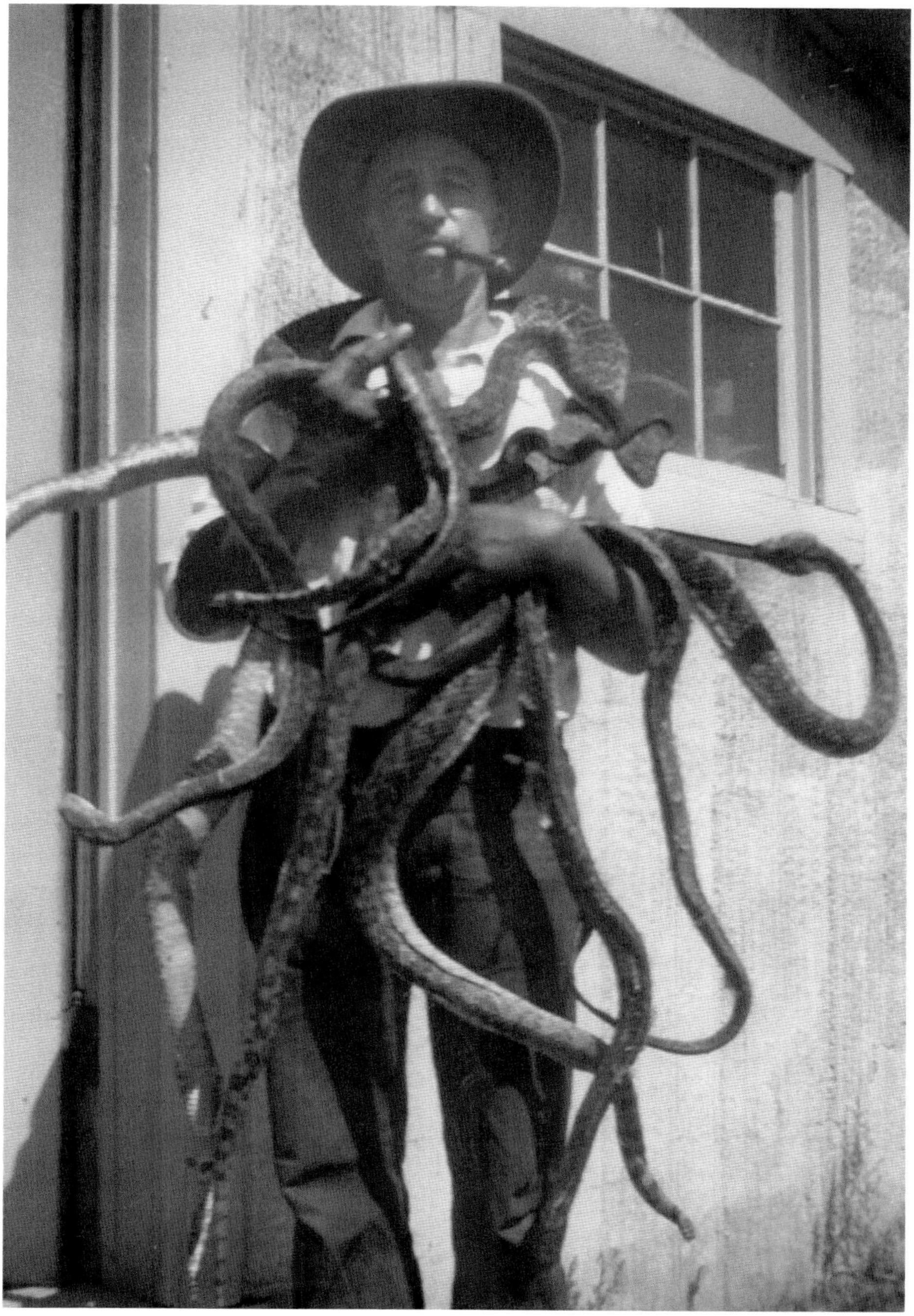

On the Midway

Frank Keefer's most novel claim to fame may have been his time as a snake handler with Siebrand Brothers Carnival, but he also served in the US Army during World War I. He and his brother Fred left a unique wealth of artifacts and writings with the Bonneville Museum, now at the Museum of Idaho. Colorful tales abound; some of them are even true. Frank died in 1976, and Fred followed a little over a decade later in 1987. (Courtesy of the Museum of Idaho.)

Closing the AEC Deal

Mayor from 1949 to 1951, Tom Sutton played a key role in the Atomic Energy Commission's decision to locate its National Reactor Testing Station headquarters in Idaho Falls. He came to Idaho Falls in 1917 to work for Anderson Lumber Company. After serving in the US Marine Corps during World War I, he returned to marry his sweetheart, Idaho Falls native Jennie Seedall. He went into the grocery business and served 16 years on the city council before being elected mayor. He died in 1979. (Courtesy of the City of Idaho Falls.)

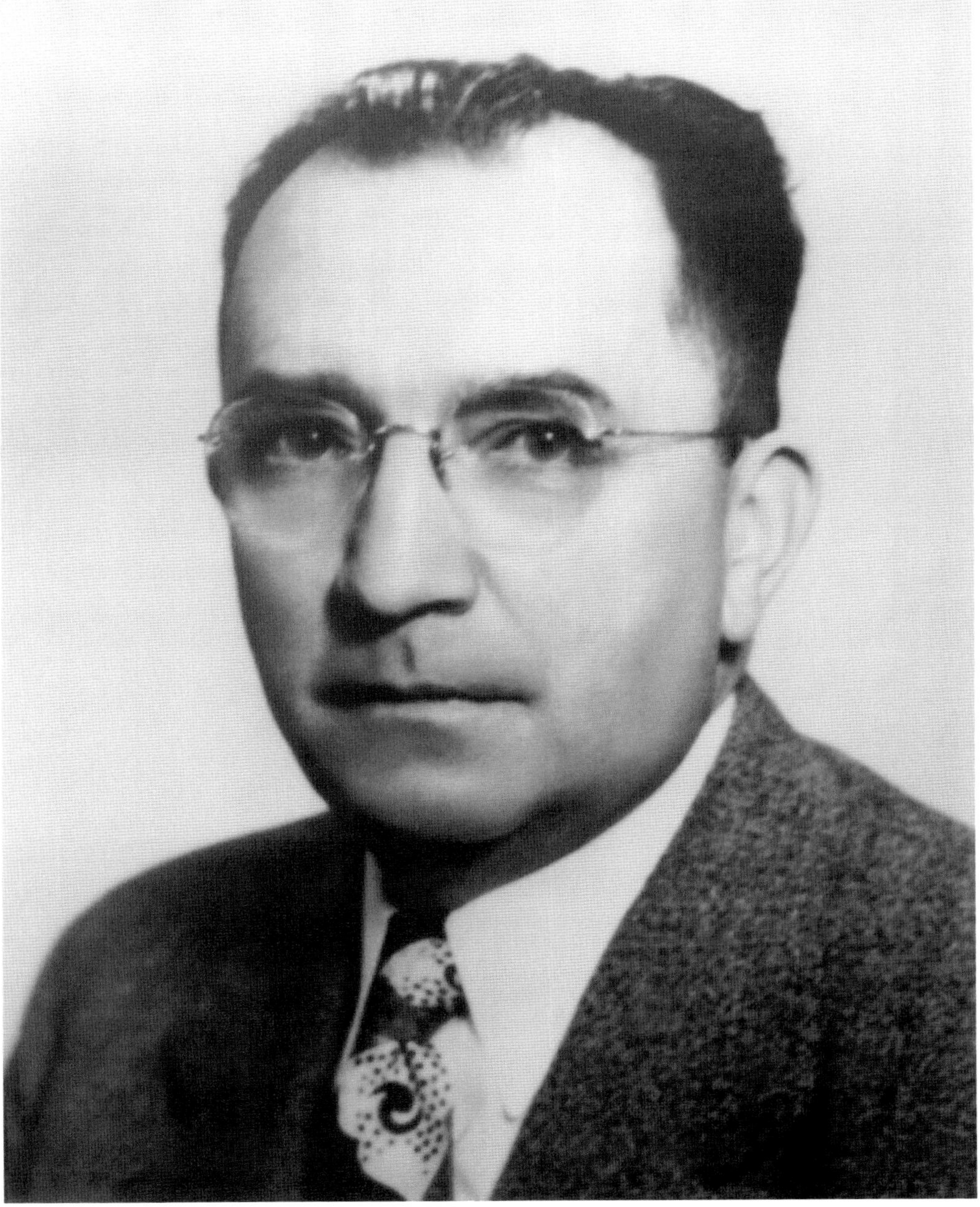

CHAPTER THREE

The AEC Years

At the beginning of August 1946, with Hiroshima and Nagasaki barely a year past, Pres. Harry Truman signed the McMahon Act, transferring control of atomic energy from military to civilian hands and creating the Atomic Energy Commission.

The new agency would inherit the work of the Manhattan Project—all the plants, laboratories, equipment, and people assembled during World War II to produce the atomic bomb. The AEC's mission was to develop peacetime atomic science and technology, and one of the first decisions that had to be made was where to build new reactors.

The first sustained chain reaction had been achieved in 1943 at the University of Chicago, under the squash court stands. To build a full-scale, working reactor, a remote location was preferable. While the commission's eyes were first on Montana, the focus quickly shifted to the Naval Proving Grounds on the Snake River Plain, where the US Navy test fired big, re-lined guns before sending them into action. Once the decision was made that the National Reactor Testing Station would be in eastern Idaho, the next question was where to put the AEC Idaho Operations headquarters.

Four communities made a bid for the opportunity: Blackfoot, Arco, Pocatello, and Idaho Falls. Blackfoot and Arco were quickly ruled out because of their size, and while Pocatello's civic leaders were willing to tout their city's advantages, their effort was half-hearted compared to the ardent wooing of Idaho Falls. Mayor Tom Sutton and attorney William S. Holden flew to Washington, DC, to meet with AEC officials, and parties and receptions were held.

After the AEC opted for Idaho Falls, the community was never the same. Changes were due anyway as the Baby Boom was beginning, but the in-migration of scientists and engineers, as well as the new construction jobs, meant new neighborhoods and schools, streets, and public facilities. Between 1950 and 1960, Idaho Falls's population grew 72.5 percent, from 19,218 to 33,161.

A new high school was built along with a civic auditorium, new roads were paved, and new wells were dug. A symphony orchestra and an opera company were established. Professional baseball returned and thrived.

Today, only two of the 52 reactors built in the Idaho desert remain in operation. The US Navy, which trained its sailors on prototypes at the Naval Reactors Facility, left in 1995. But the Idaho National Laboratory's focus has diversified, and it continues to have a huge effect on the local economy and the community's collective outlook.

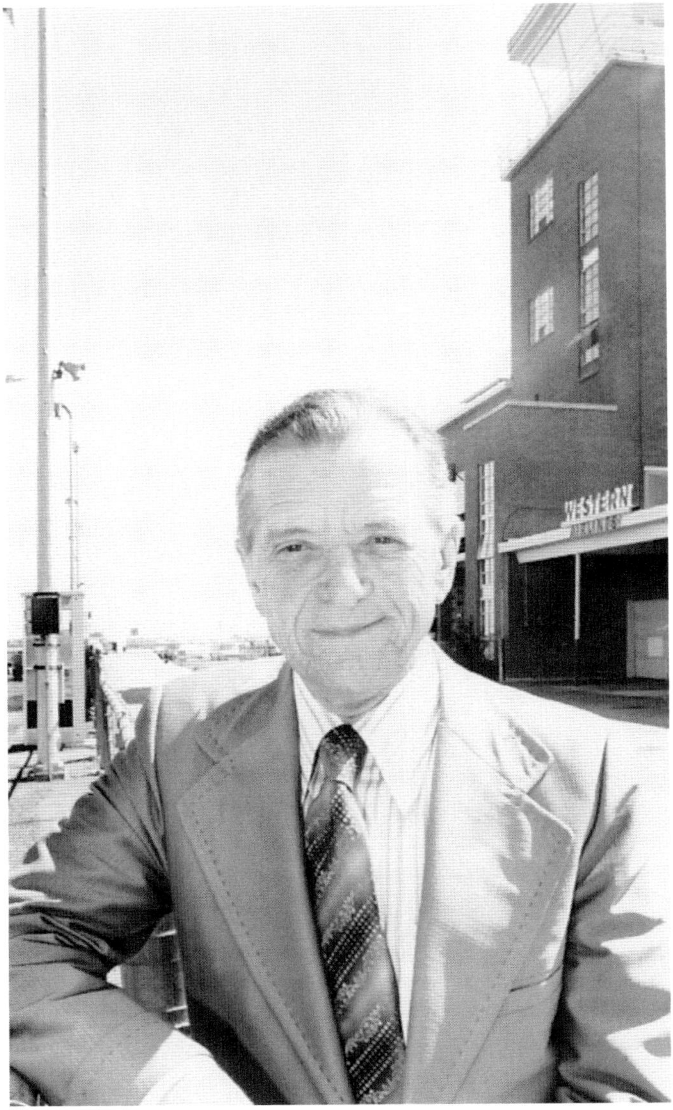

The Aviator

If anyone put Idaho Falls on the aviation map, it was Harold Prester "Pete" Hill. The son of a Kansas aviation pioneer, Hill's pilot's license was signed by Orville Wright. "Pete was probably the last of the old breed, from the helmet-and-goggles days," said city councilman Wes Deist. Leaving a job in Seattle with the Civil Aeronautics Administration, Hill took over the Idaho Falls airport in 1953. At that time, there was nothing but the log hangar and hut built by the Works Projects Administration. Hill's plan was to make the airport self-sufficient in 20 years. His company, Idaho Aviation Center, was one of two civilian flight companies in the nation to contract with the Atomic Energy Commission. Hill would fly his Cessna 195 to Denver to pick up Adm. Hyman Rickover, who would sleep on Hill's couch when he stayed in Idaho Falls. For inspection of the Navy's reactors, Hill would fly the admiral out to a desert road where the officers and sailors would be lined up to salute. As a teacher, Hill taught a person not only how to fly but how to think. "Pete could be pretty demanding and intimidating," said Bob Hoff, CEO of Aeromark, the Idaho Falls Regional Airport's fixed base operator since 1983. "He demanded that you do well and never settled for less." Hill died in 1999, at age 86. (Courtesy of the Museum of Idaho.)

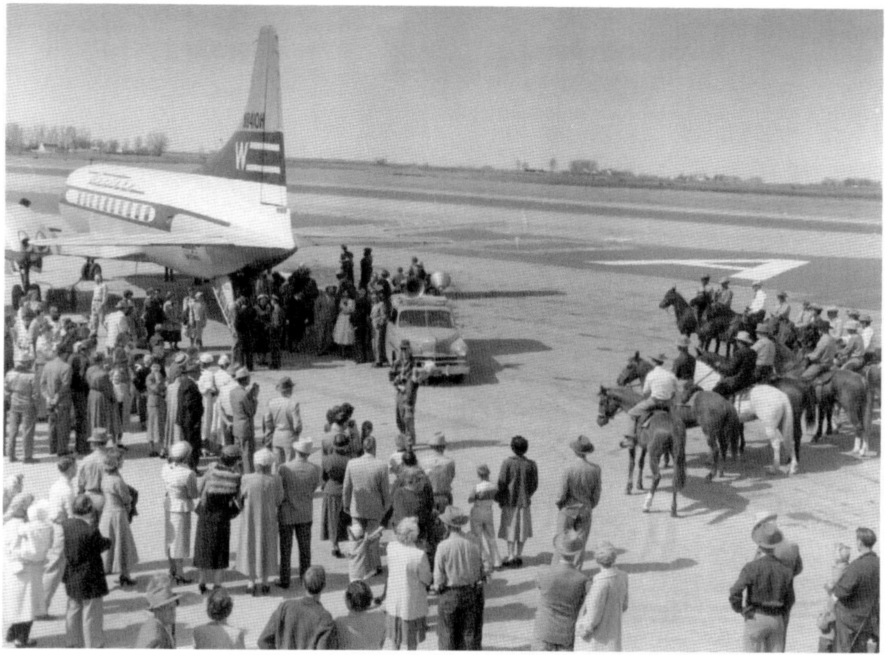

Commercial Service

Above, the Bonneville County sheriff's posse showed up at Fanning Field in 1953 to see the first Western Airlines flight leave. Below, businessmen load Idaho potatoes, normally shipped by rail, onto a small plane. (Both, courtesy of the Museum of Idaho.)

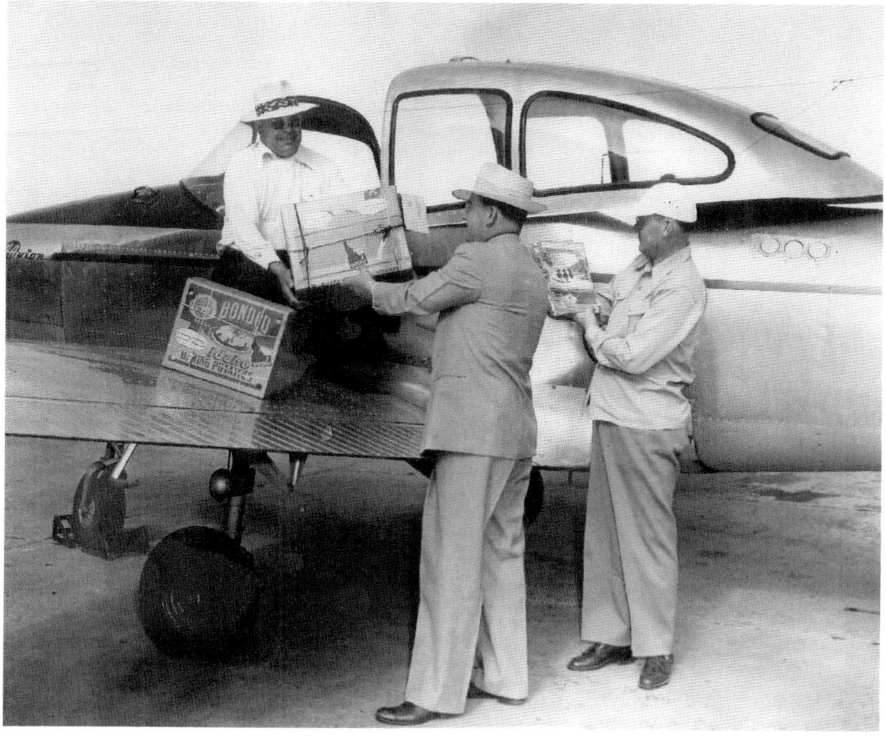

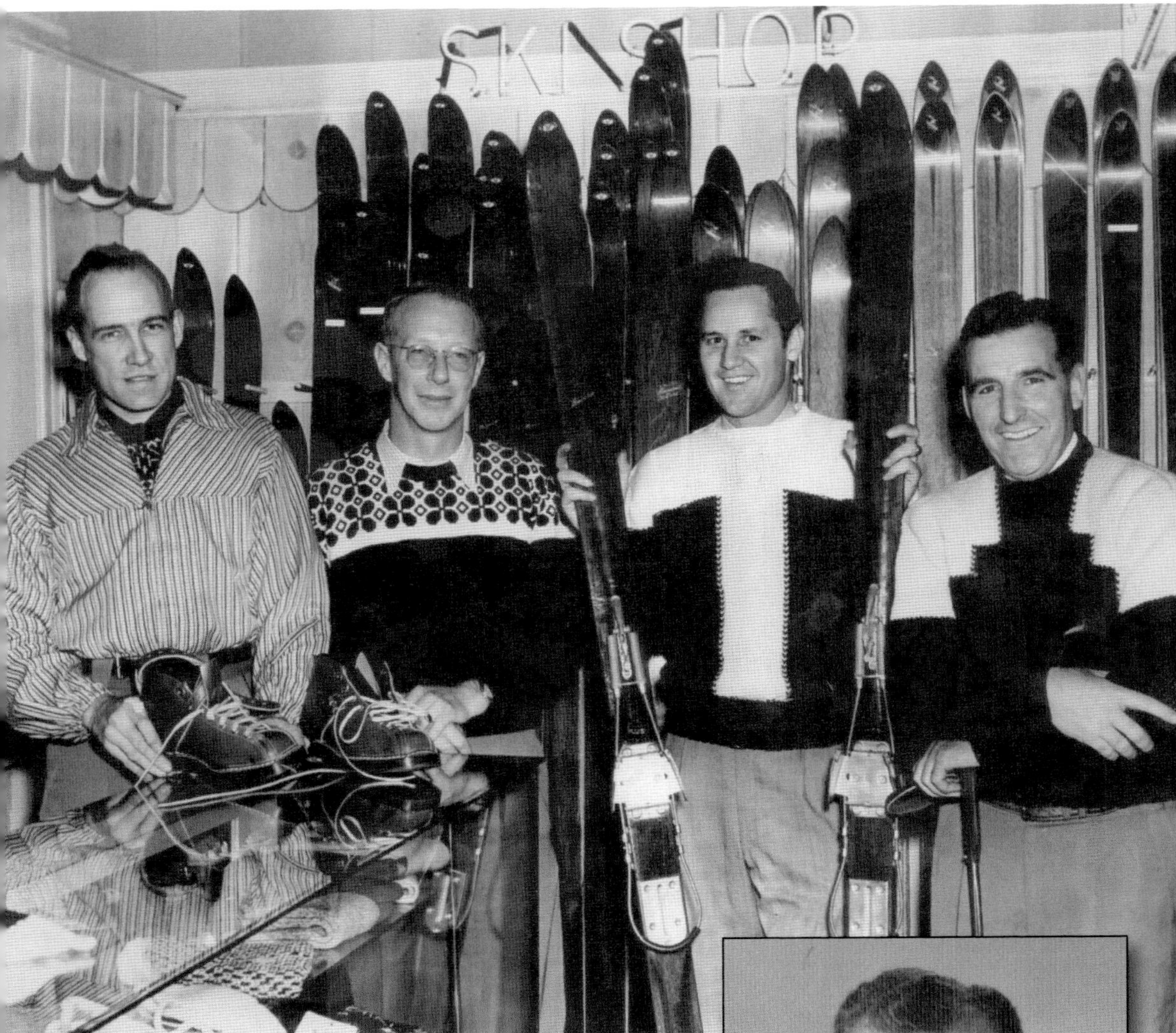

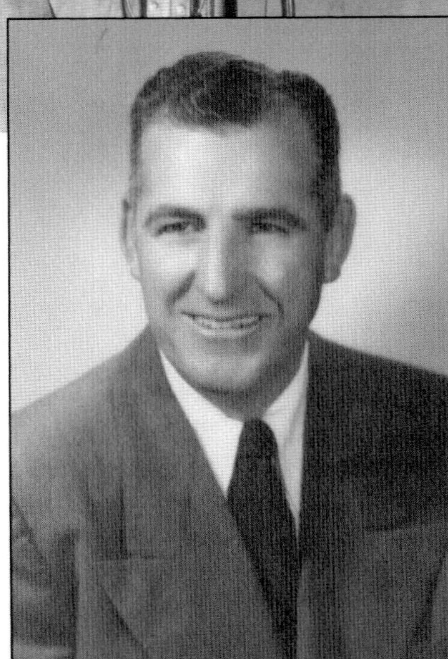

School for Skiers

James M. Brady was the quarterback of the Notre Dame football team made famous in *Knute Rockne, All American*. In his hometown, his greatest accomplishment may have been to make skiing a lifetime sport for an entire generation. In 1947, he founded the KIFI Ski School, named after the Idaho Falls radio station he started the same year. In its heyday, as many as 17 buses were going from Idaho Falls High School to Pine Basin, often in treacherous conditions. Pictured above from left to right are Joe Poitevin, Dan Kelly, Bob Bybee, and Brady at the Outdoorsman, a ski shop in downtown Idaho Falls. The school's success created what is today one of the largest skiing communities in the country. (Both, courtesy of Jill Groth.)

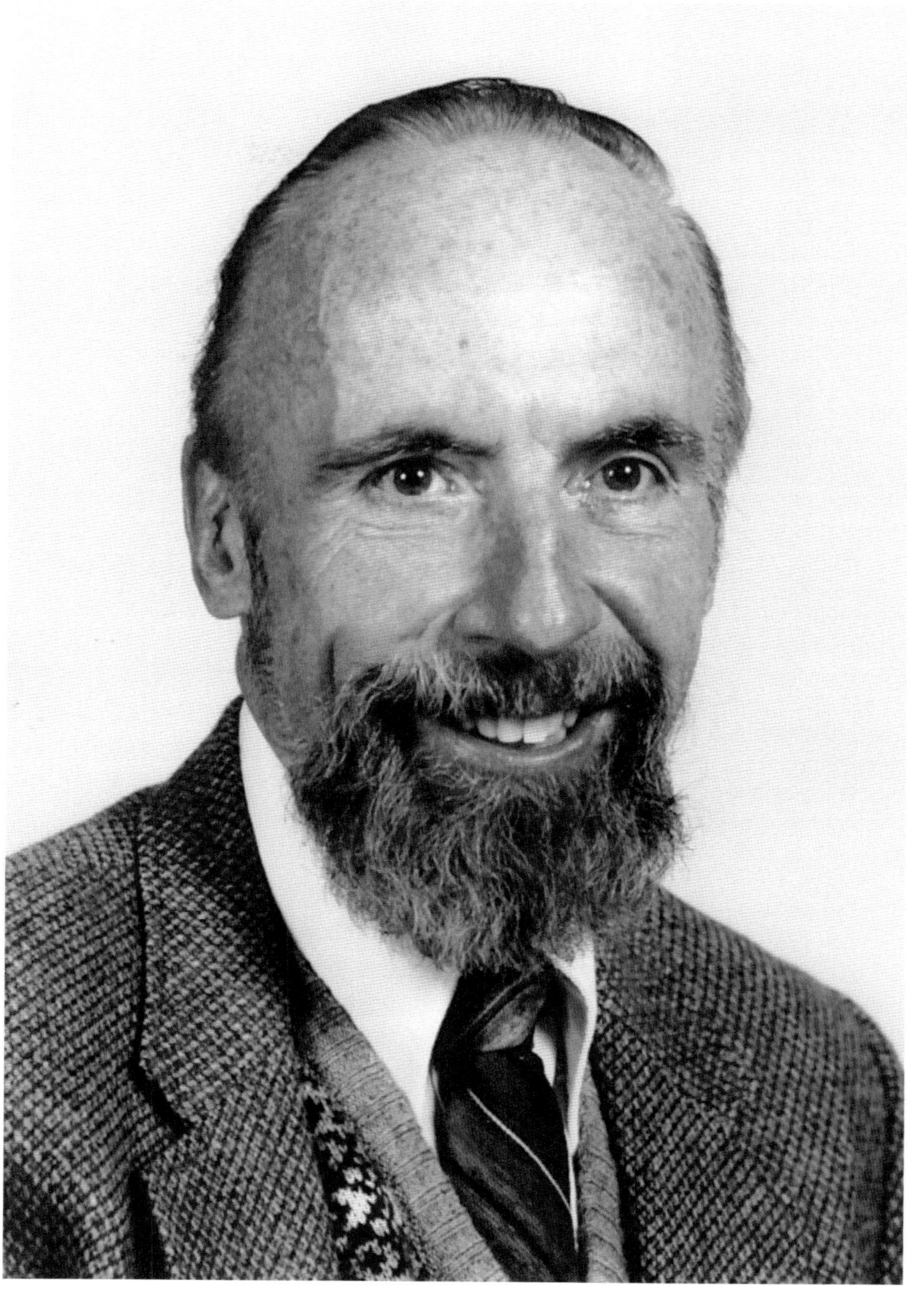

Under the Sea

When the USS *Nautilus* dove under the polar ice cap in 1957, Frank Fogarty, an assistant engineer, knew the 100-man crew was going where no one had gone before. An Annapolis graduate, Fogarty had volunteered for Adm. Hyman Rickover's nuclear navy, and learned the basics of nuclear physics alongside future president Jimmy Carter. Fogarty served on other subs before the Navy gave him command of the *Nautilus*, which he held until 1967. He later came to work at the Naval Reactors Facility where the prototype reactor for the *Nautilus* had been built. He retired in 1993. (Courtesy of the Idaho Falls *Post Register*.)

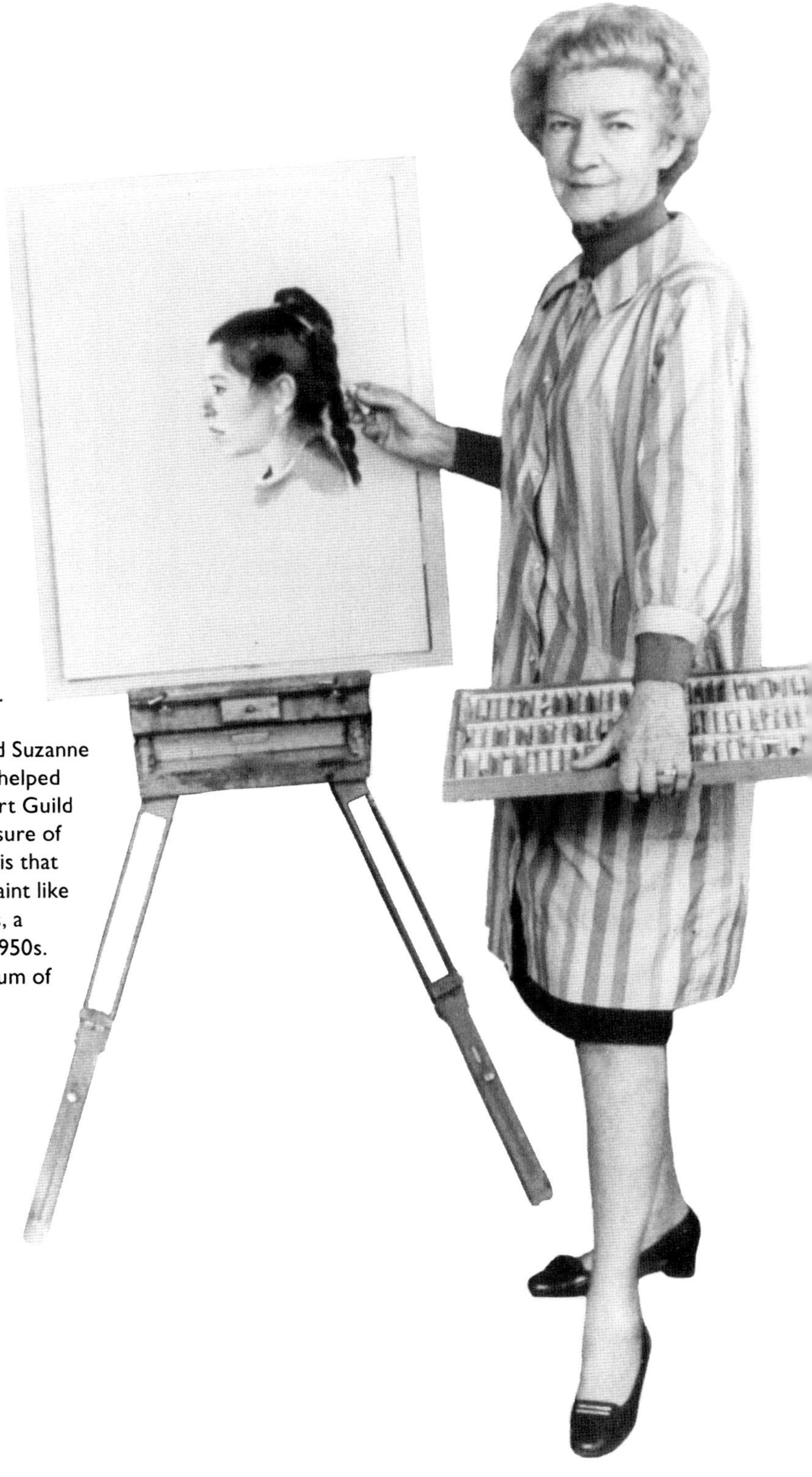

Artistic License
If there were an "Idaho Falls School" of painting, Helen Hoff Aupperle would be its founder. An Idaho Falls native, Aupperle was the youngest student accepted to the Chouinard Art Institute. She returned to Idaho Falls in 1940 and taught art for nearly 30 years at Idaho Falls High School. Along with Fred Ochi, Ina Schwartz Oyler, and Suzanne Fonnesbeck, Aupperle helped found the Idaho Falls Art Guild in 1948. "The real measure of her ability as a teacher is that none of her students paint like her," said Roy Reynolds, a student from the late 1950s. (Courtesy of the Museum of Idaho.)

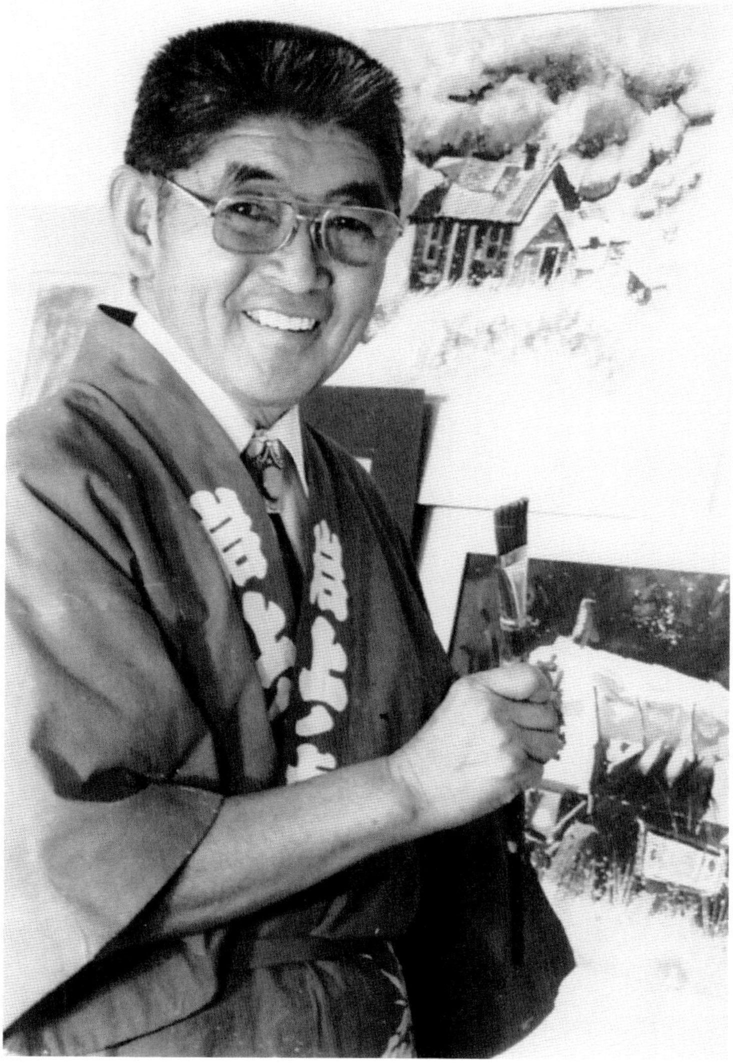

"Fastest Brush in the West"
Fred Ochi's paintings hang in homes, churches, schools, and businesses all over eastern Idaho. As 20th century American journeys go, Ochi's was unique. He was president of the Japanese American Citizens League in San Mateo, California, when Pearl Harbor was attacked in 1941. As the West Coast became hostile to individuals of Asian descent, he left his job as chief display artist for Fox West Coast Theatres and headed inland, settling in Idaho Falls in 1942. He picked up the thread at the Paramount Theater (now the Colonial), married, and started his sign-painting business, Fred's Signs. In 1948, he helped start the Idaho Falls Art Guild. He could do two or three paintings on a Tuesday night at the guild's log hut in Highland Park. "I called him 'the fastest brush in the West,' but, you know, he knew what he was doing," said Marilyn Hoff-Hansen, a longtime friend. Ochi received the Idaho Governor's Award in the Arts in 1998. At that point, his brush had begun to slow down, due to what the family later discovered had been a series of strokes. While his memory began to fail, the one thing that never changed was his personality. "Even when he was having a hard time getting around, he would say, 'Everything's fine, no trouble,' " said his son, Jon Ochi. "It was his way of saying, 'I'm okay; don't worry about me.' " (Courtesy of the Idaho Falls *Post Register.*)

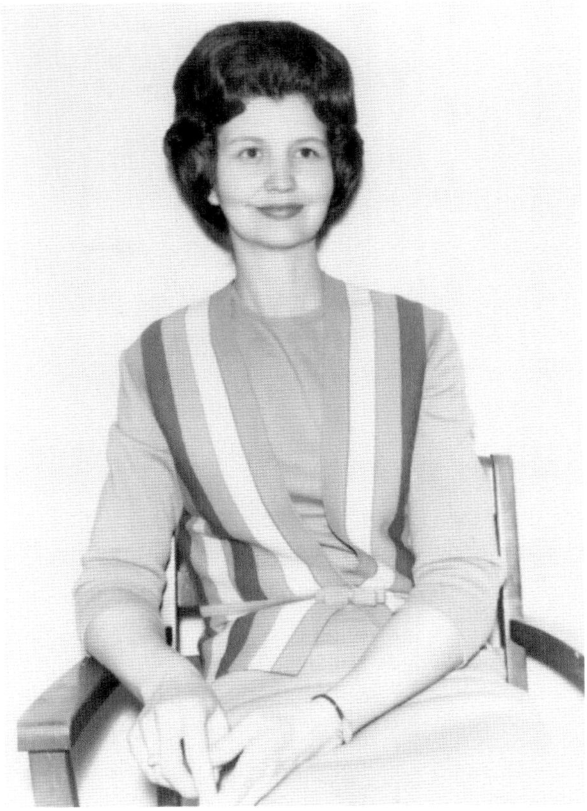

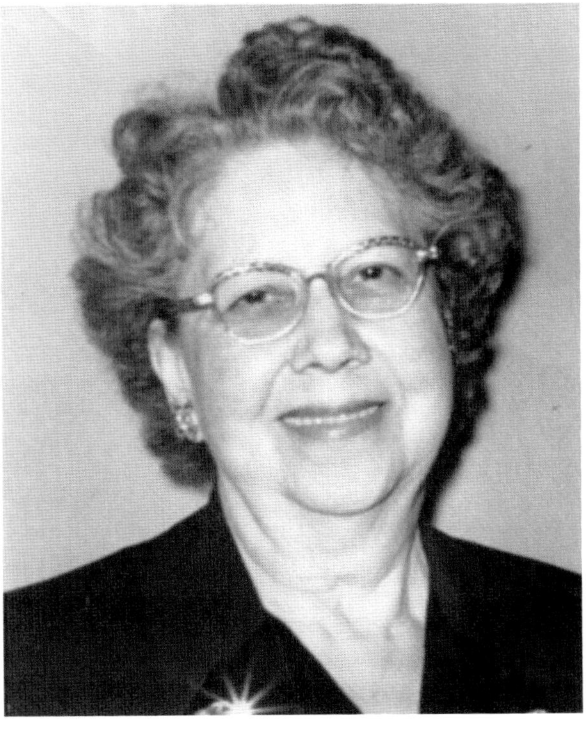

Global Business Vision

With a degree in economics from Stanford, Joan Chesbro was one of two women chosen by Wells Fargo Bank in 1953 for management training. When her parents and brother were killed that year in a plane crash, however, she returned to Idaho Falls to join her grandmother, Ella Chesbro (bottom), in managing the family music business. Over 40 years, she built Chesbro Music Co. into one of the nation's largest wholesalers of sheet music and musical instruments. In the early 1970s, the company became one of the first big distributors in the United States of Japanese brands like Yamaha, Ibanez, and Tama. She was the first woman to be admitted to the Idaho Falls Rotary Club. She served on the CHC Foundation board of directors and Junior Achievement. Her support was critical to the growth of the Idaho Falls Symphony and Idaho Falls Opera Theatre. She died in 1999. (Both, courtesy of Chesbro Music Co.)

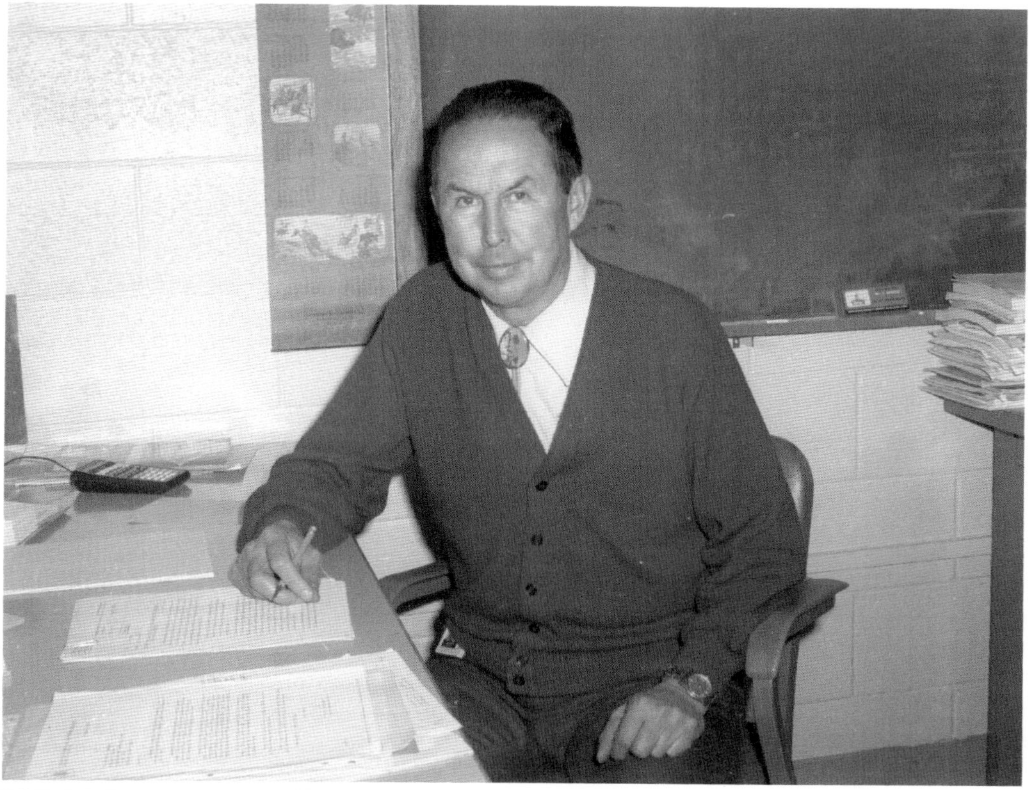

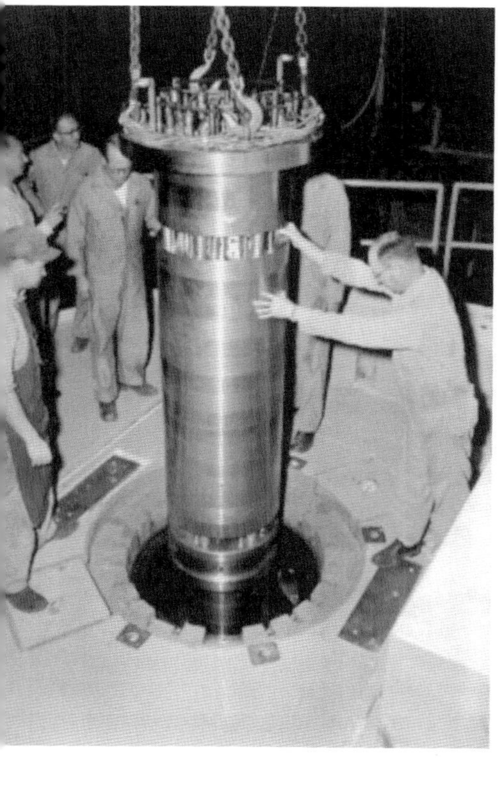

Present at the Creation
Known to everyone as "Kirby," George Kirby Whitham was present when the first civilian nuclear power was generated in Idaho. Whitham had joined the Manhattan Project in the waning days of World War II, then went to work for Argonne National Laboratory, where he and fellow research scientists designed the Experimental Breeder Reactor (left). In 1951, this reactor produced enough electricity to illuminate four 200-watt bulbs. Whitham worked on the BORAX-III reactor before becoming construction and project manager for EBR-II. After retiring in 1985, he remained active in the American Nuclear Society and freelanced as a consultant to Argonne. He died in 2011. (Both, courtesy of Mary Ann Whitham, Idaho National Laboratory.)

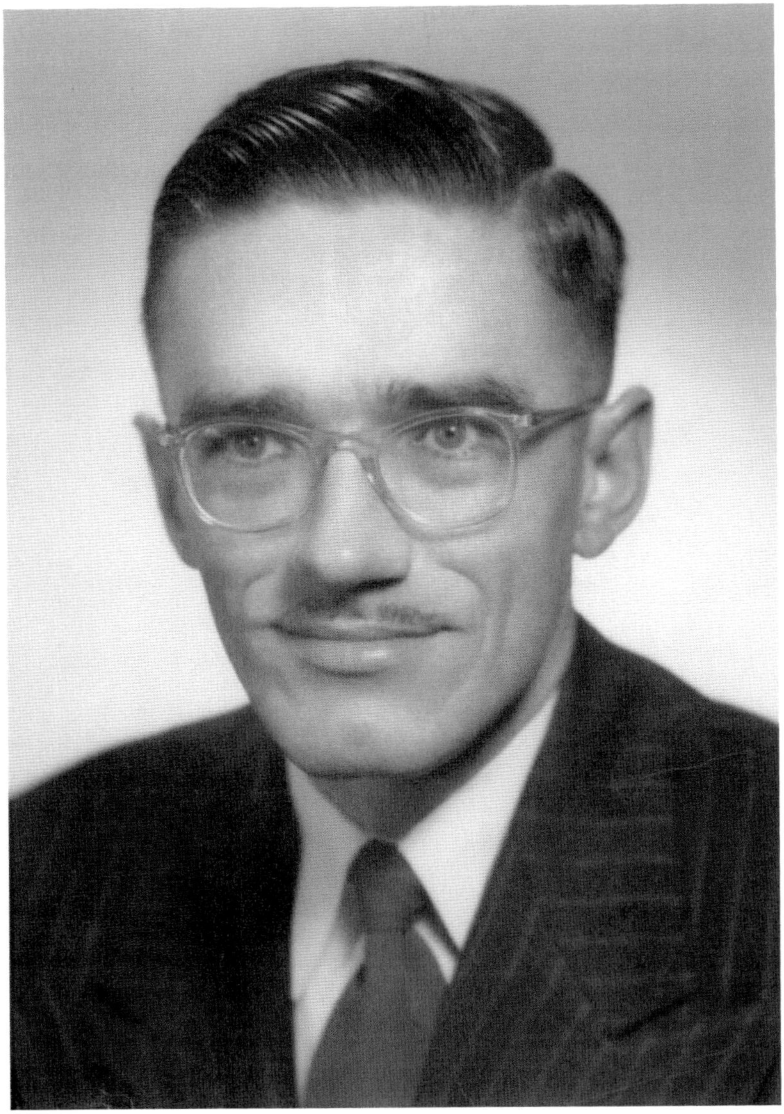

Storyteller

Joe L. Marker became a reporter at 17 when he applied for a job in the *Salt Lake Tribune*'s Idaho Falls office. Bureau chief Carl Hayden asked if he could take pictures, and Marker said he would try. Today, the Museum of Idaho is the repository of his extensive cache of photos. He served in World War II, seeing action in France, Belgium, and Germany. When he returned to Idaho Falls, he resumed his career in journalism as the *Deseret News* bureau chief. On the day the *Post-Register* building on Capital Avenue caught fire, Marker was on the scene with his camera before the paper's own photographer. Soon after that, publisher E.F. McDermott offered him a job. He worked for the *Post Register* from 1959 until his retirement in 1988. Marker made a few unsuccessful bids for political office, and the highest compliment a person could receive from him was, "That's very Democratic of you." Besides traveling with his dogs à la John Steinbeck, one of Marker's greatest sources of pleasure was playing the organ in Virginia City, Montana, and around Idaho Falls. For years, he gave a recital at St. John's Episcopal Church on the Sunday closest to the Fourth of July and an annual Christmas concert at Trinity United Methodist Church on December 22, his birthday. Marker died in 2004 at age 86. (Courtesy of the Museum of Idaho.)

Pride in Publishing

The son of the *Daily Post*'s first publisher, J. Robb Brady Jr. became one of the community's strongest voices for conservation when he took the paper's reins. Orphaned at six, he was raised by an aunt. After graduating from Notre Dame, he began working in 1941 at the *Post Register* as a sports reporter. He became managing editor, then publisher in 1977 after the death of E.F. McDermott. Brady and his wife of 69 years, Rose Poitevin Brady, established the Haven Temporary Shelter for homeless families. His other affiliations included the Idaho Conservation League and the Nature Conservancy. (Courtesy of the Idaho Falls *Post Register*.)

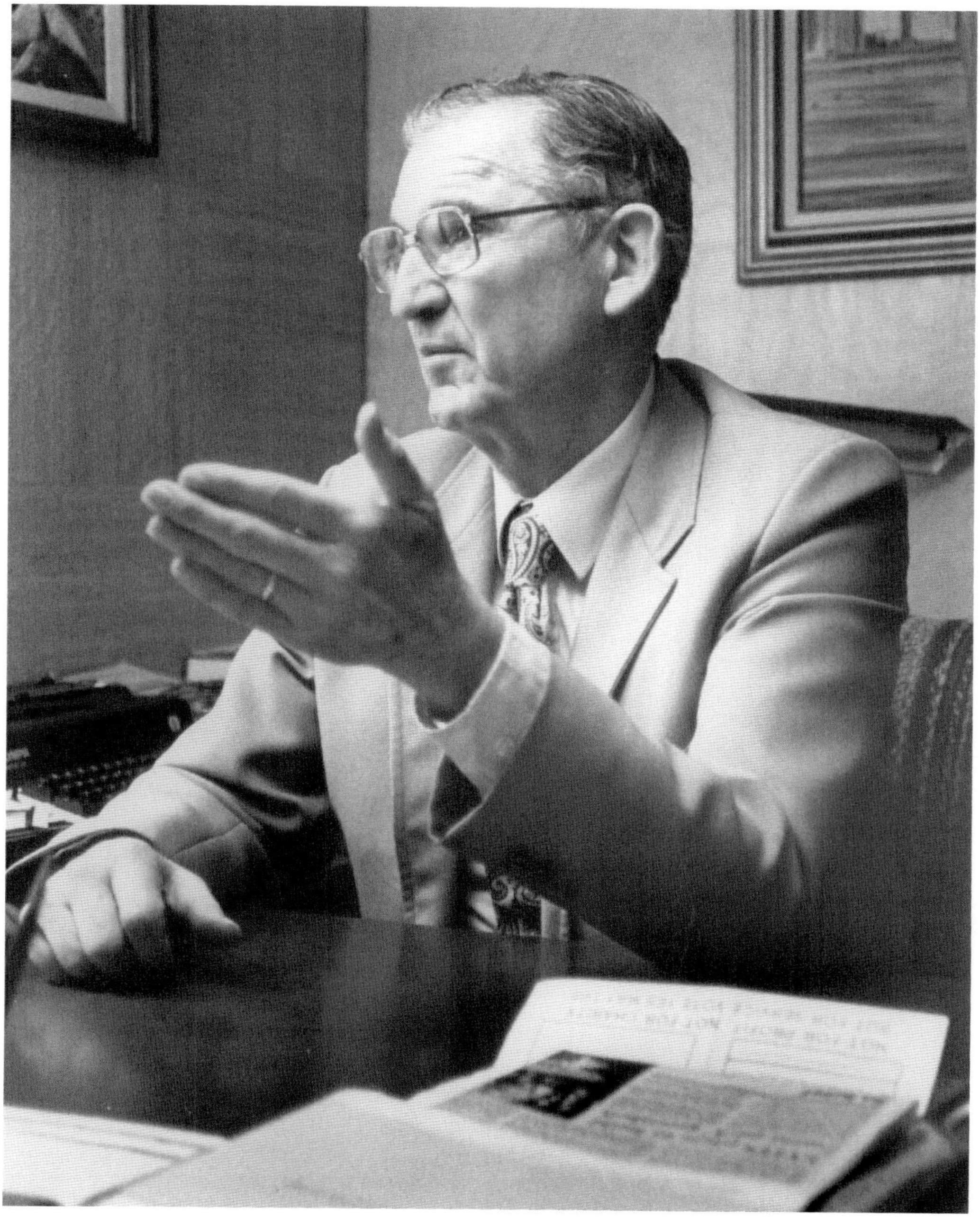

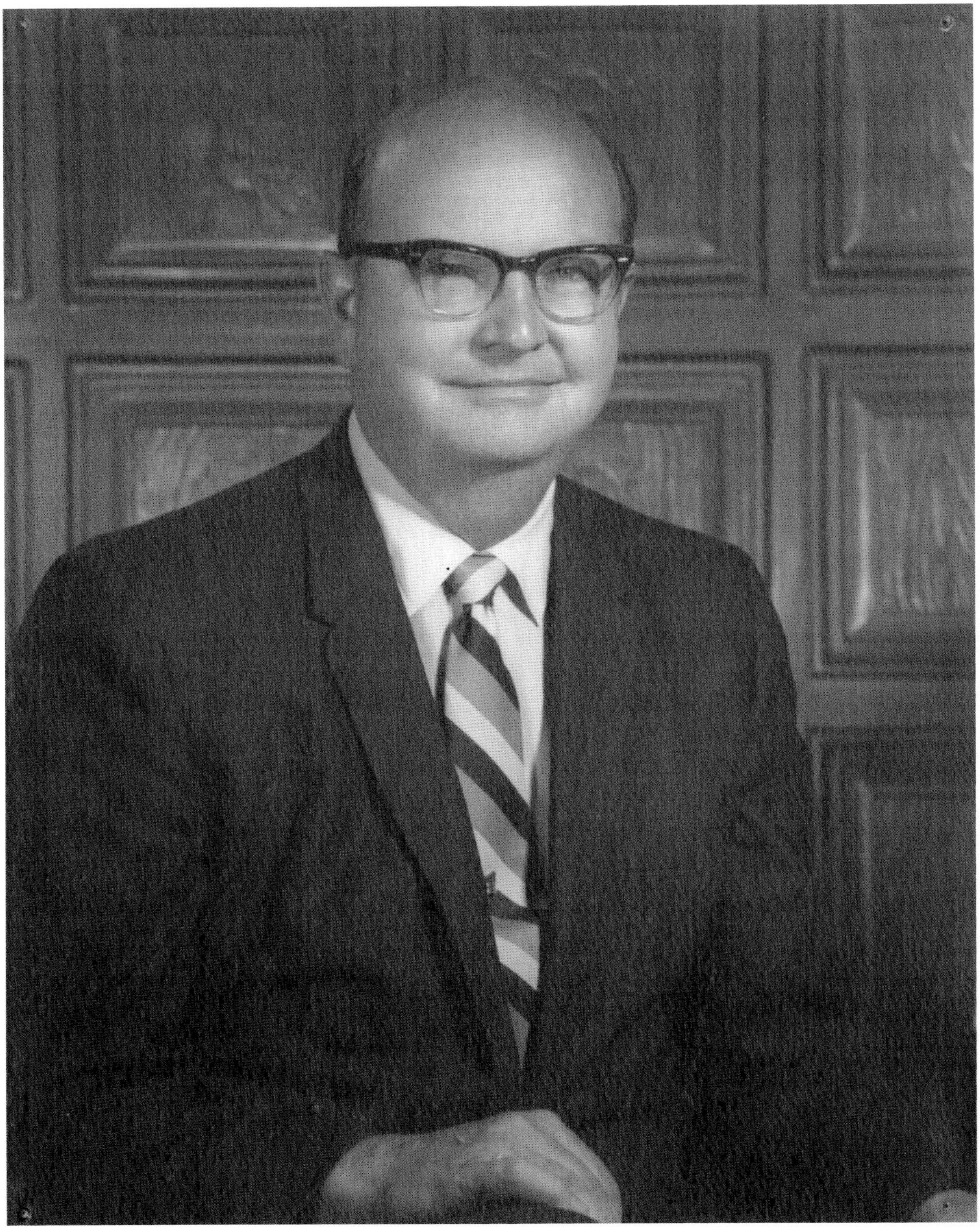

The Spoken Word

J. Allen Jensen was Salt Lake City's first television announcer in 1949, and was a substitute narrator for *Music and the Spoken Word*, the LDS Church's nationwide Sunday morning broadcast. He came to Idaho Falls in 1961 to manage KID Broadcasting Corp. He served on the Radio Code Board of the National Association of Broadcasters and as a member of the All-Industry Radio and Television Music Licensing committees. Locally, he was president of the United Way, Rotary Club, Chamber of Commerce, Idaho Falls Symphony, and Eastern Idaho Nuclear Industrial Council. He died in 1995 at age 87. (Courtesy of Greater Idaho Falls Chamber of Commerce.)

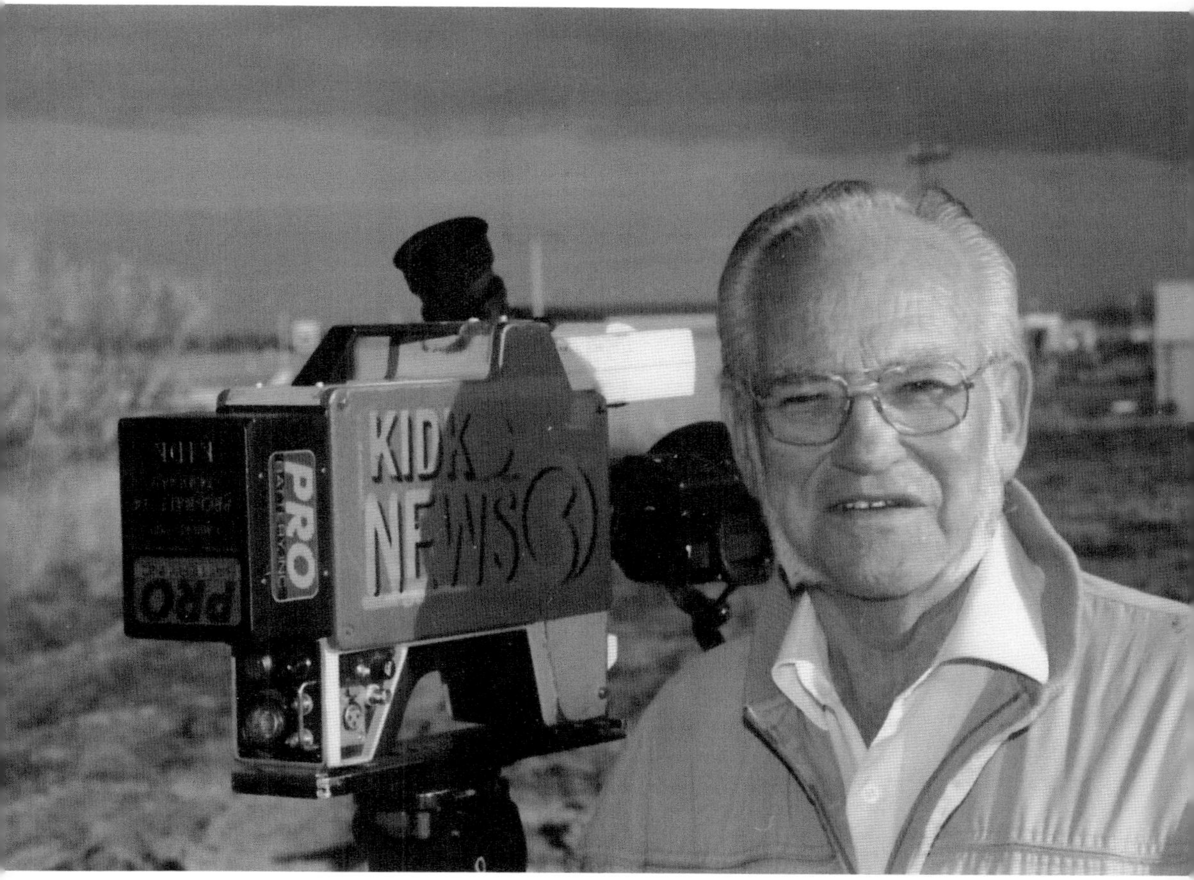

The Camera Eye

Quincy Jensen worked for KID and KIDK television for nearly 40 years. Born in 1922 in the farming community of Burton, he received his first camera as payment for cutting grain. During World War II, he took his camera with him to France, Belgium, and Germany, chronicling the collapse of the Third Reich (he returned home with the last Nazi flag to fly over the Bergen-Belsen concentration camp, which he kept in a box in the KID basement on 17th Street). Jensen was chosen Upper Valley Historian of the Year in 1987 by the Upper Snake River Valley Historical Society. He died in 1993. (Courtesy of Lisa Whipple.)

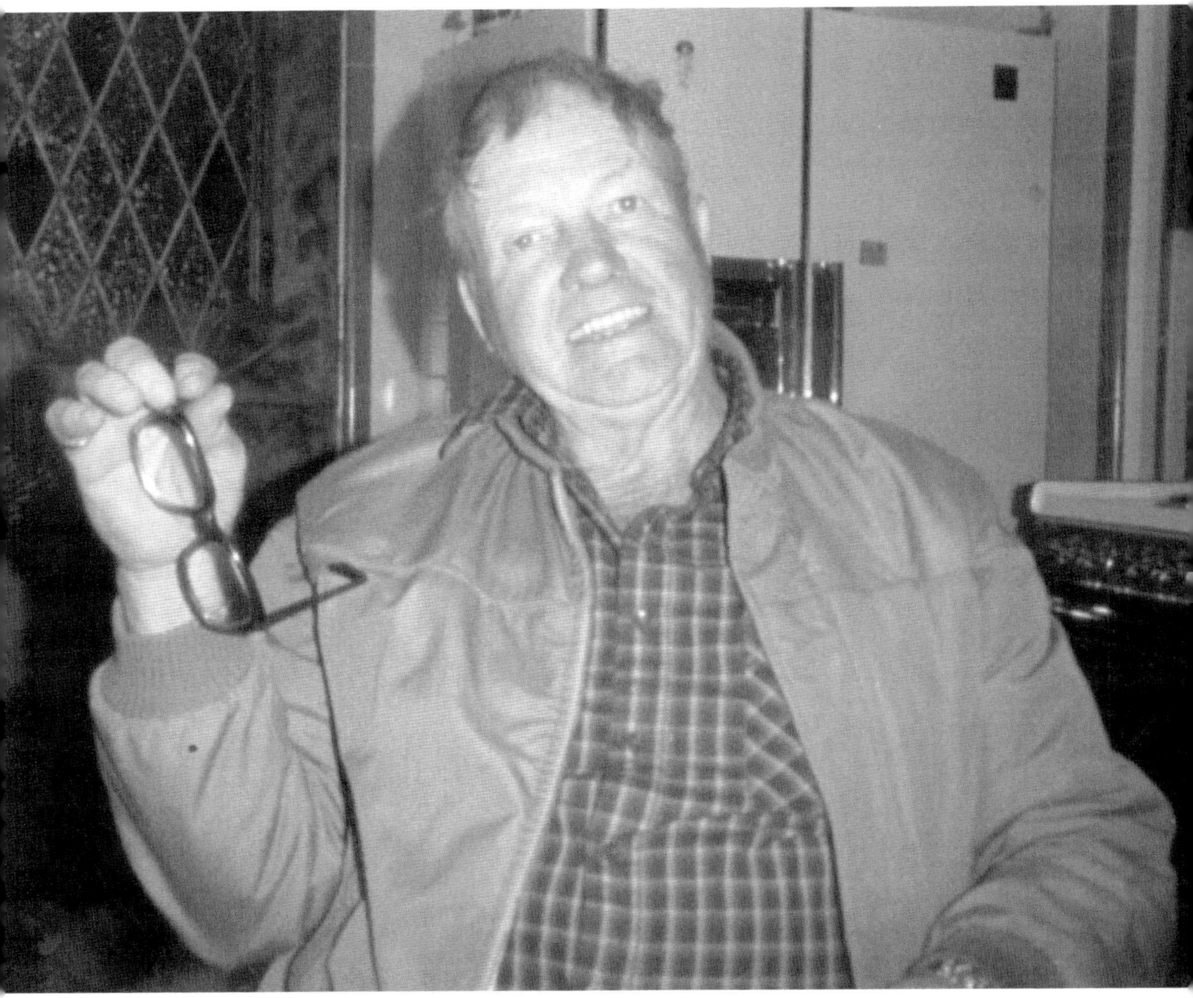

Life on Two Wheels

No one was more responsible for getting Idaho Falls onto two wheels in the years following World War II than Bill Murdock, who opened Bill's Bike Shop with his wife, Alice, in 1947. The first store, on Chamberlain Avenue, sold bicycles and also performed locksmithing and lawnmower blade sharpening. In 1970, they picked up Honda and the businesses split into Bill's Bike Shop and Bill's Cycle Shop. Bill's Bike Shop moved to South Holmes Avenue in the 1980s and remained there until Murdock's son Stan sold the business in 2010 to Gary Wight. Despite new ownership, the store retained the name. (Courtesy of the Murdock family.)

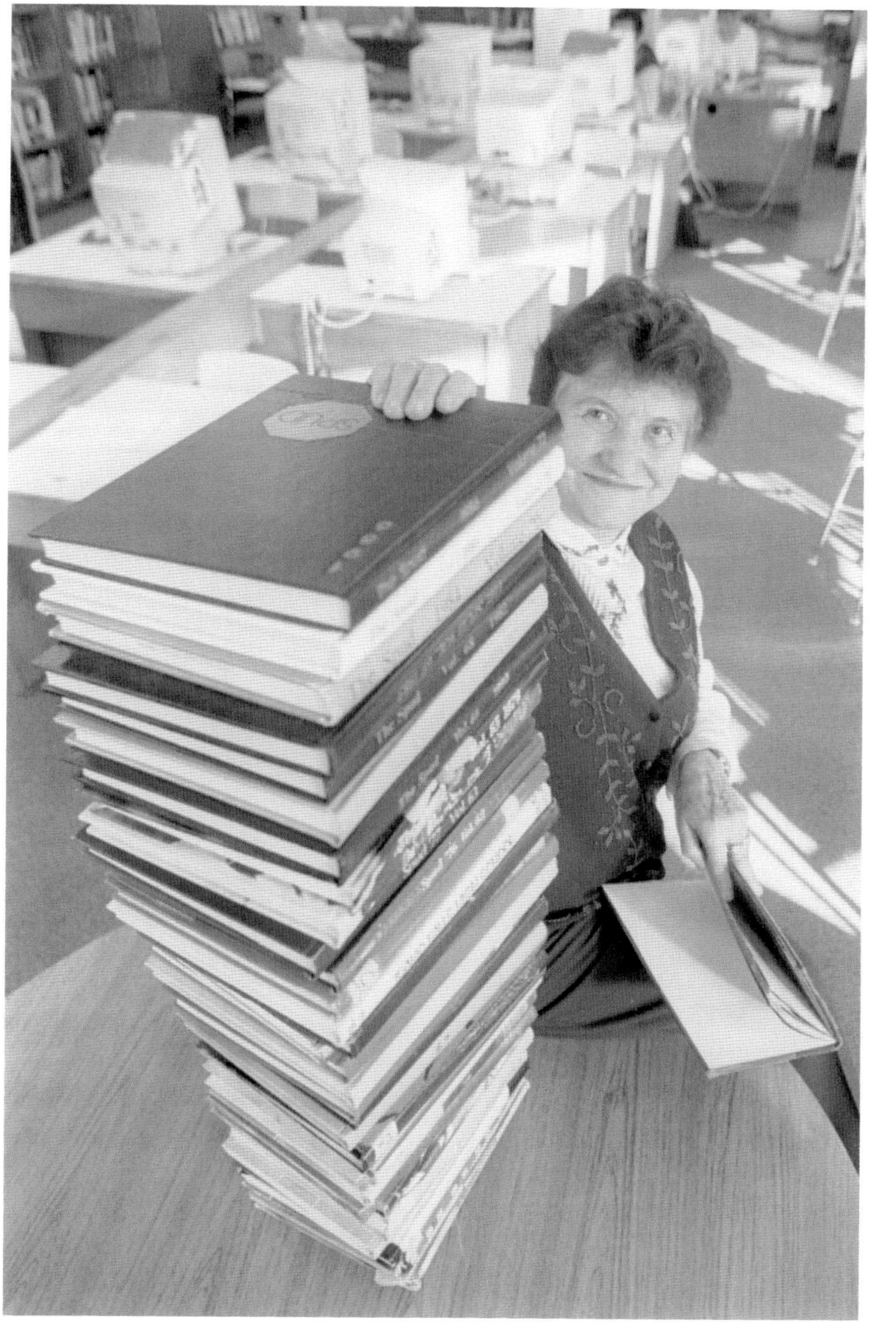

A World of Words

Words have been Afton Bitton's mainstay for more than 80 years. A native of Swan Valley, she was women's page editor of the *Post Register* from 1946 to 1949. But she is better known as "Miss Bitton." For 35 years, she taught English, yearbook, creative writing, journalism, and senior composition at Idaho Falls High School. Since her retirement, she has been involved in local history as a contributor to the Beautiful Bonneville project in 1989 and with her book *Trumpeter's Dell*, published in 2011 in honor of Bonneville County's centennial. (Courtesy of the Idaho Falls *Post Register*.)

Broad Scope in Business

Ray Groth had a hand in a wide variety of Idaho Falls businesses. Born in 1911 in Utah, he came to Idaho Falls for Standard Oil and founded Ray Groth Oil Co. In his 62 years in business, he developed 26 retail gasoline dealerships, some of which included new car agencies. He was one of the first developers at Fanning Field, and he and Frank Brown opened Brown's Menswear on Park Avenue, which later became Brown & Gesas. In 1986, he sold the oil business and bought KUPI Radio. He died in 2002. (Courtesy of Greater Idaho Falls Chamber of Commerce.)

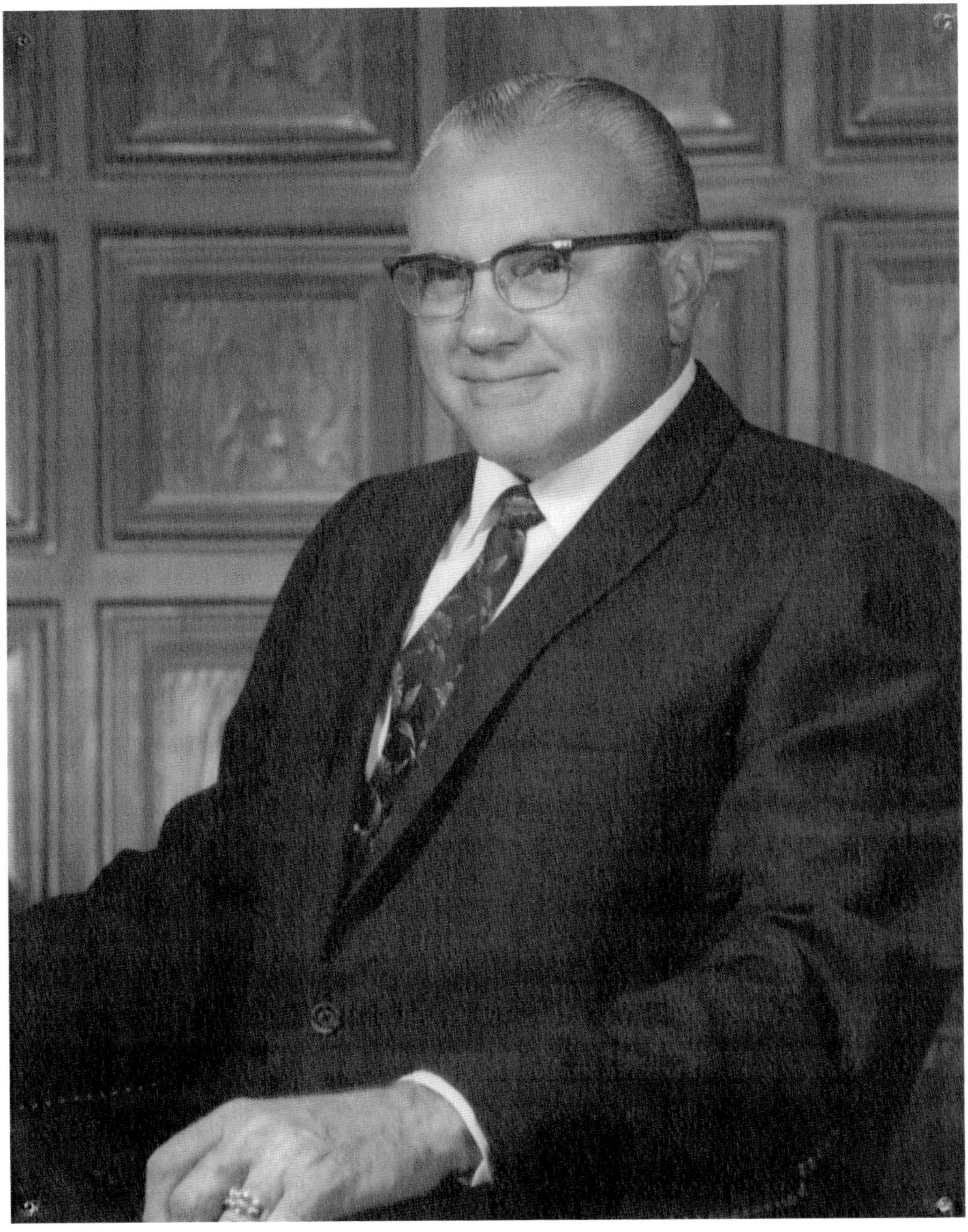

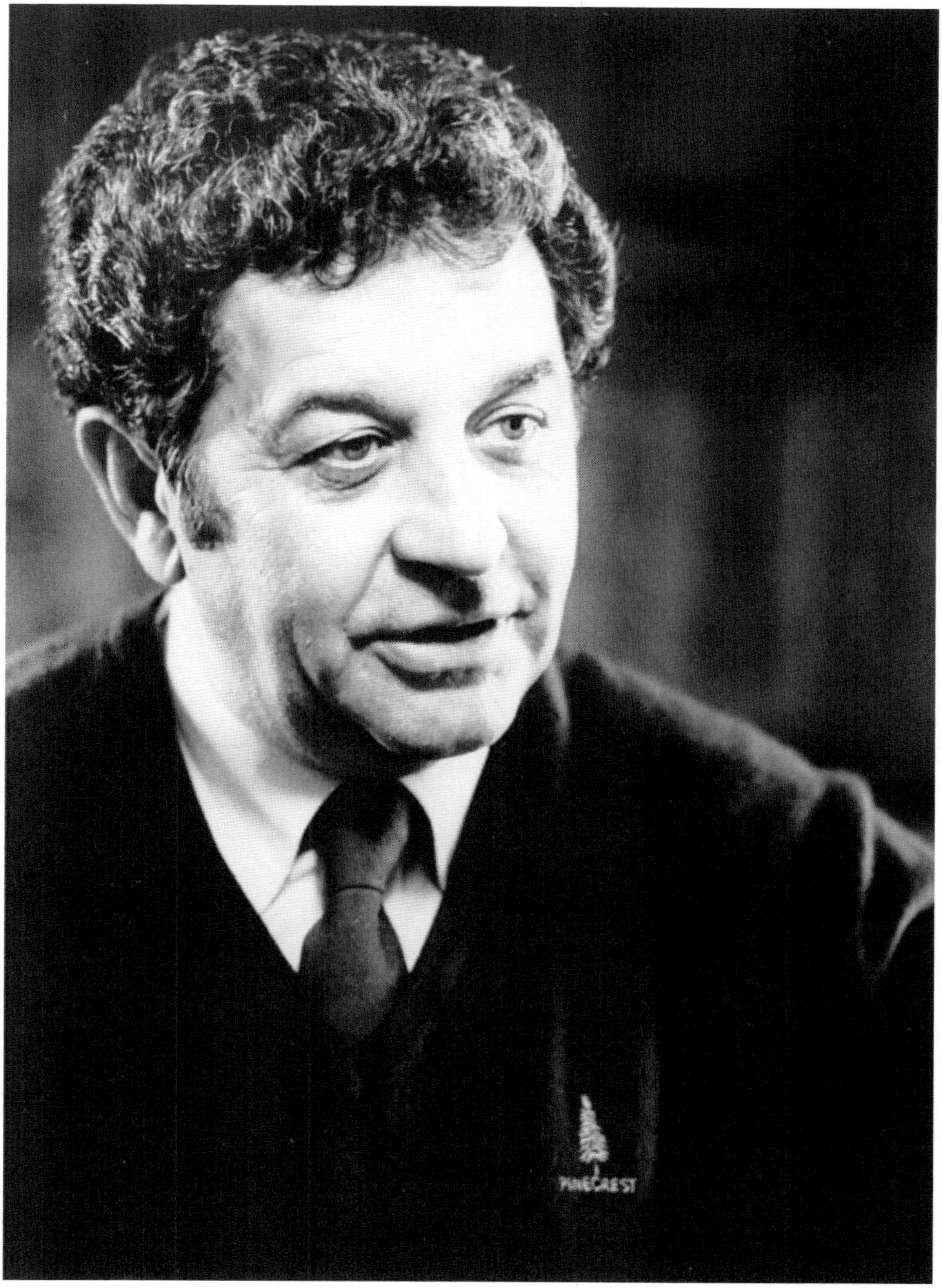

King of the Ice

No person in Idaho Falls may be more responsible for the popularity of hockey than Joe Marmo, a Boston transplant who came in the early 1960s to work for the Atomic Energy Commission. Marmo, who had organized a program in upstate New York, was ready to see the game grow. Because hockey was so new, much of the Idaho Falls program's focus was getting kids onto the ice. Under Marmo, it grew from 20 players to hundreds, and Marmo became president of an 11-state region of the Amateur Hockey Association and one of the national directors. (Courtesy of the Idaho Falls *Post Register.*)

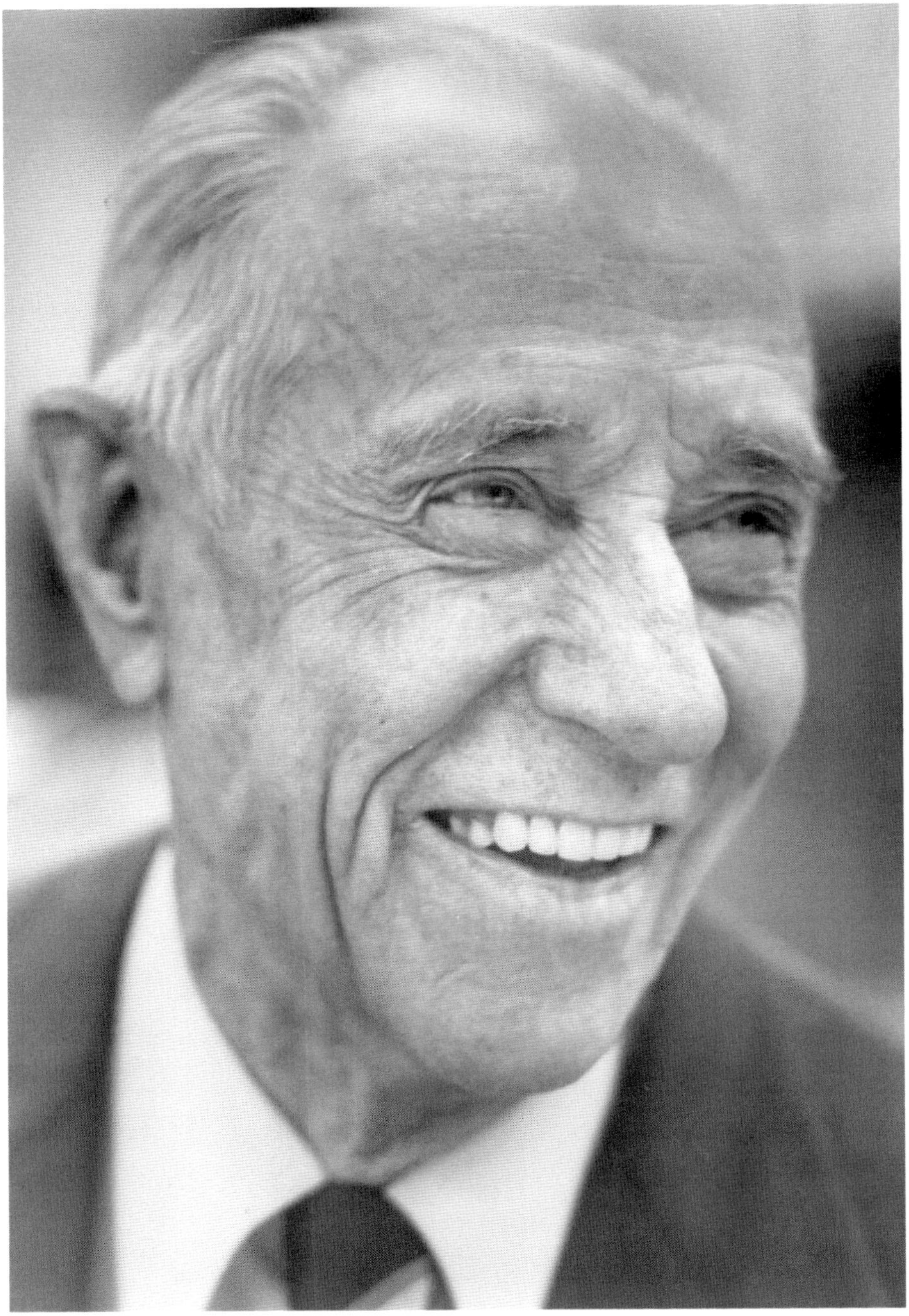

"Mayor of Eleventh Street"
Some have called Ray H. Wood the best public relations man the Bank of Commerce ever had. "The Mayor of Eleventh Street" was hard to miss in his fedora or cowboy hat, cruising the streets of Idaho Falls in his red Cadillac. Born in 1901, Wood came to Idaho Falls in 1939 as a field man for the Ogden-Denver Union Stockyards. Besides managing the bank's farm customers, Wood also created the Eastern Idaho Agricultural Hall of Fame, which recognized successful pioneer farmers for their contributions to their communities and the state. (Courtesy of the Idaho Falls *Post Register.*)

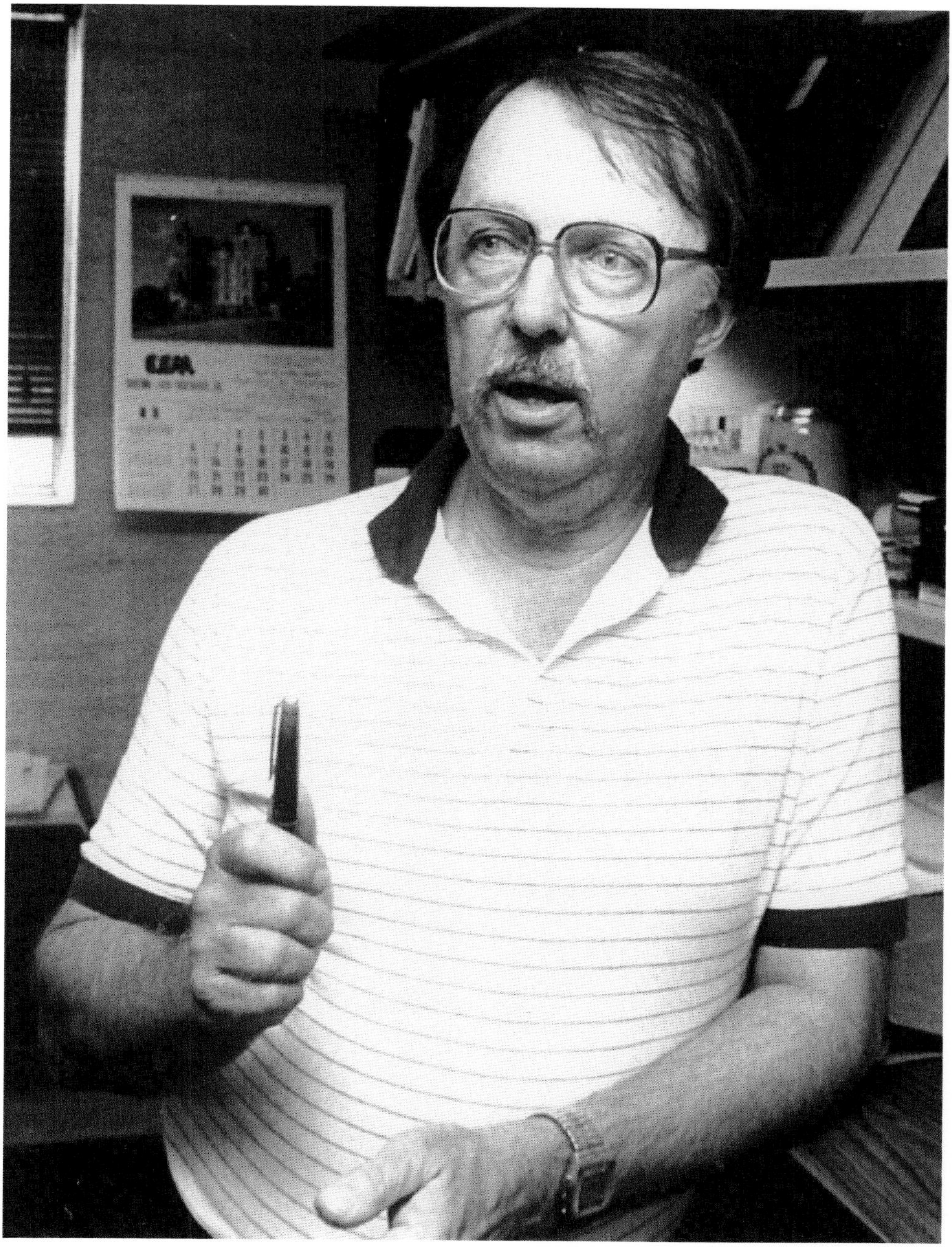

Artist and Inventor

Inventor, businessman, philanthropist, and musician Miles Willard came to Idaho Falls in 1955 after Rogers Bros. Co. became interested in the dehydrated potato flakes he had developed for the US Department of Agriculture. With his own company, Willard went on to develop dozens of patents for snack foods sold worldwide. Willard's other legacy to Idaho Falls was the Miles and Virginia Willard Arts Center. He was an enthusiastic singer with the Idaho Falls Opera Theatre, and at the state level, he served nine years on the Idaho Arts Commission. In 1996, he received the Governor's Award for Support of the Arts. (Courtesy of the Idaho Falls *Post Register.*)

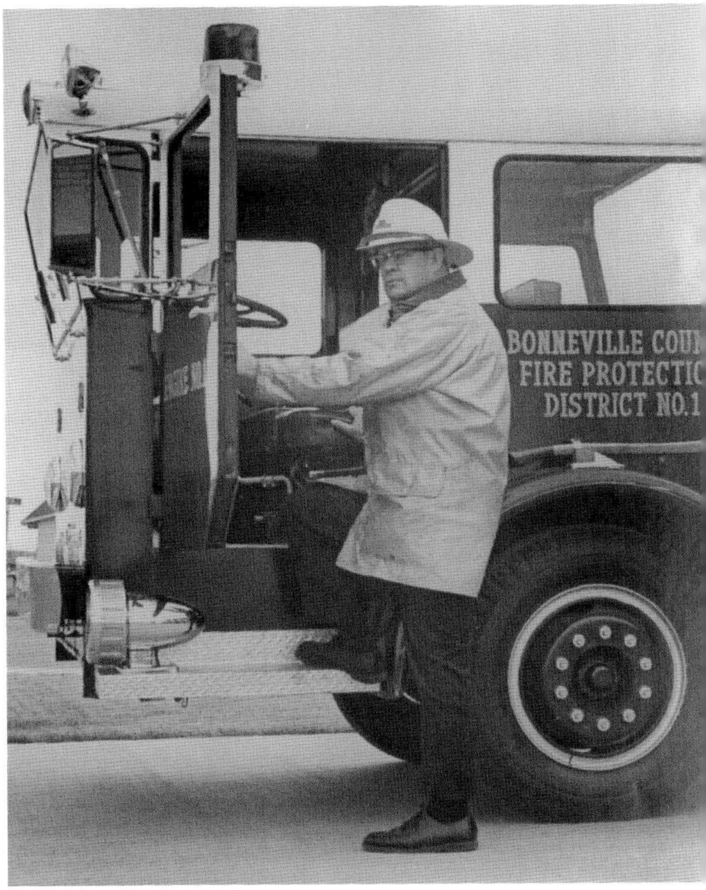

Emergency Service Innovator

In his 27 years as a firefighter and chief, Carl Poulter helped direct major changes in the area's emergency services. He was Idaho Falls's fire chief briefly in the mid-1960s, before going on to head Bonneville County Fire Protection District No. 1, coordinating efforts between city and county. During Poulter's tenure, the fire trucks changed color from red to yellow, for better visibility. In honor of his service, in 2006, Poulter was given the title of Idaho Falls Fire Chief Emeritus. He died in 2010. (Courtesy of Jan Brown.)

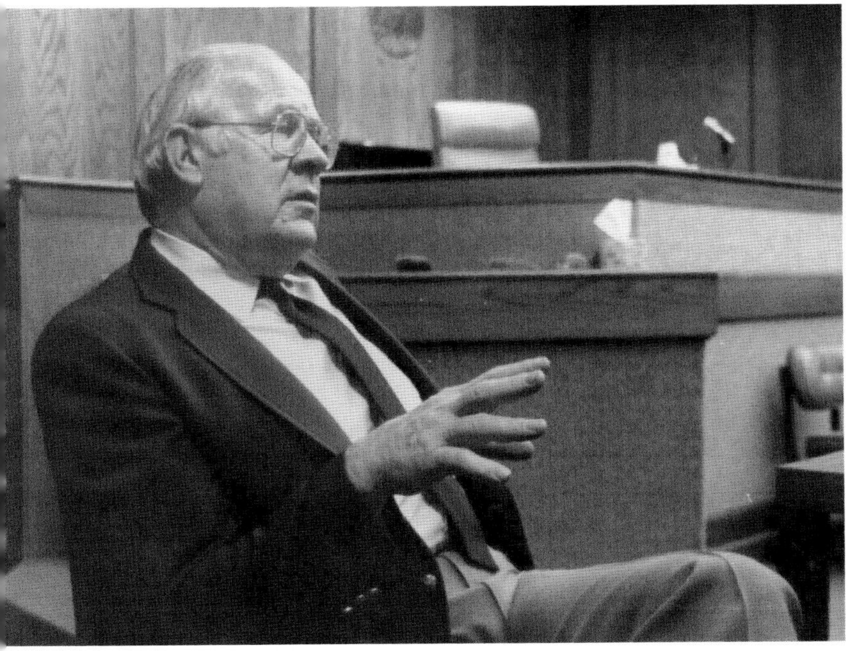

Court Bailiff

After leaving the fire district, Carl Poulter served as a Seventh District Court bailiff for 10 years. (Courtesy of the Idaho Falls *Post Register*.)

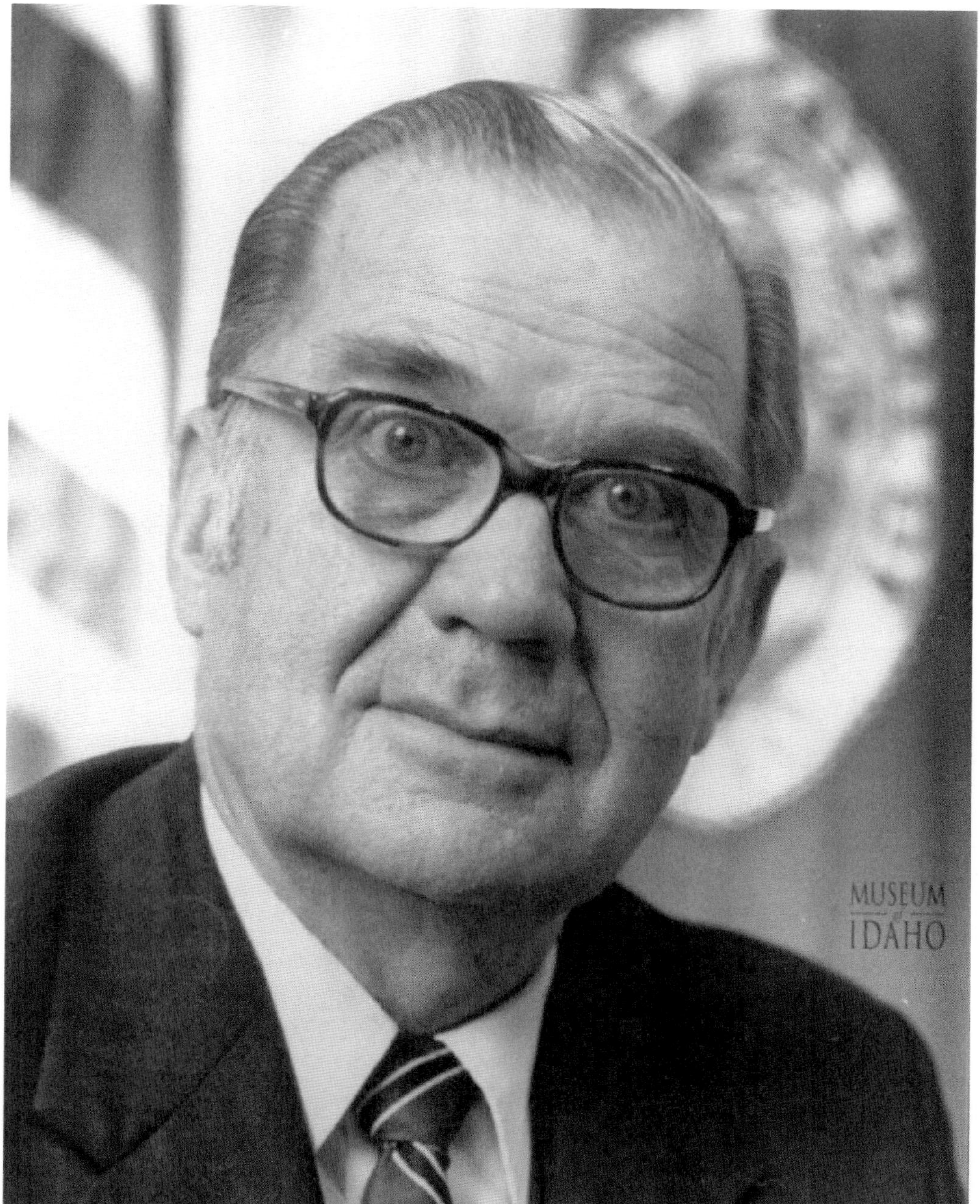

Full-Time Mayor

A tailor by trade, S. "Eddie" Pedersen, mayor of Idaho Falls from 1964 to 1978, grew up steeped in politics. When William Borah and Henry Dworshak came to town, Pedersen's was where they'd get the latest news. Because the shop was heated with a small pot-bellied stove, regulars called themselves the "Hot Stove League." With the city's population nearing 35,000 in the early 1960s, Pedersen's campaign promise was to sell his business and serve as a full-time mayor. He was known for his uncanny ability to remember people's names, and his favorite saying was, "I just never have a bad day." He died in December 1986. (Courtesy of the Museum of Idaho.)

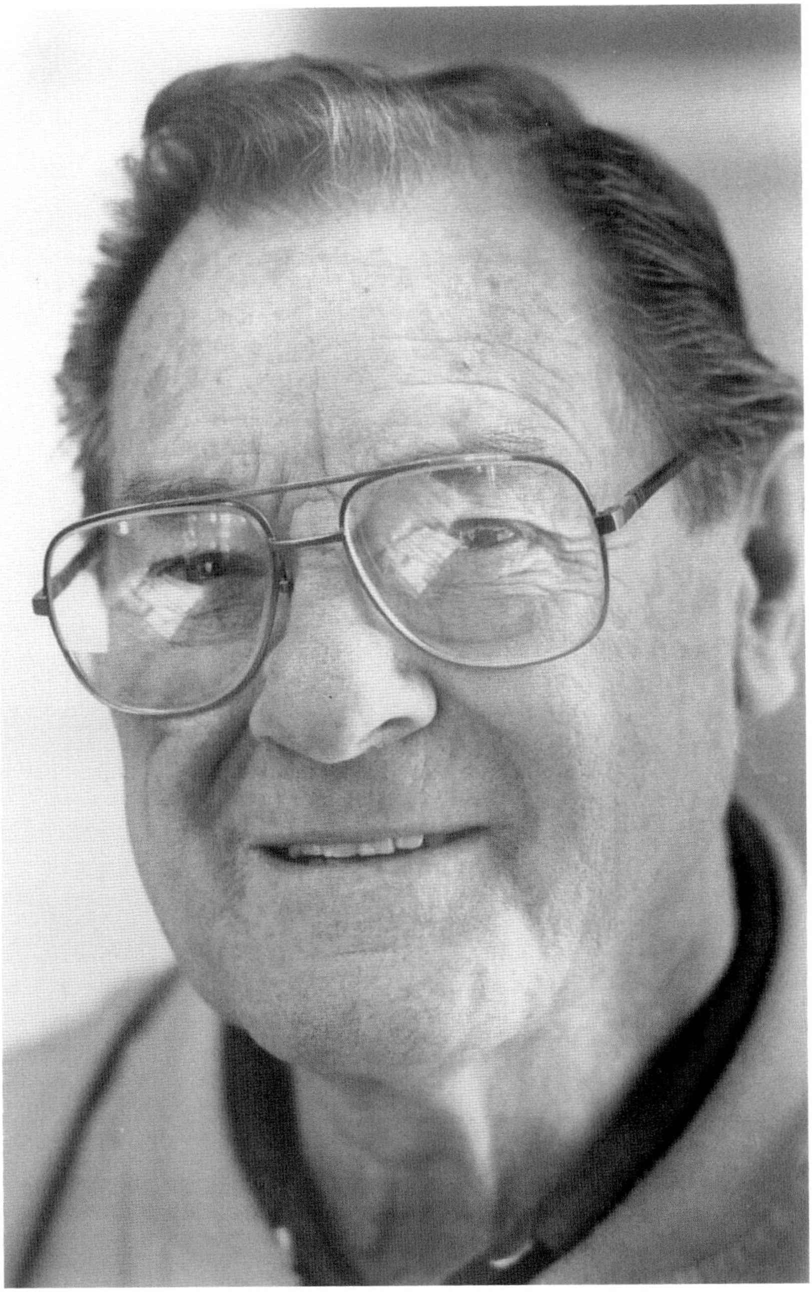

Devoted to Sports

During Ernie Craner's 22 years as Idaho Falls Parks and Recreation director, the city's number of parks doubled and a second golf course, Sand Creek, was added. In his lifetime, he was inducted into the Idaho Softball Hall of Fame, the Idaho High School Activities Association Hall of Fame, and the University of Idaho Hall of Fame. Craner refereed hundreds of basketball, football, and softball games, from the junior high level all the way to collegiate competition. He served on the Community Hospital board that donated 34 acres for Community Park along with $100,000 to develop it. Craner retired in 1984 and died in 1997. (Courtesy of the Idaho Falls *Post Register.*)

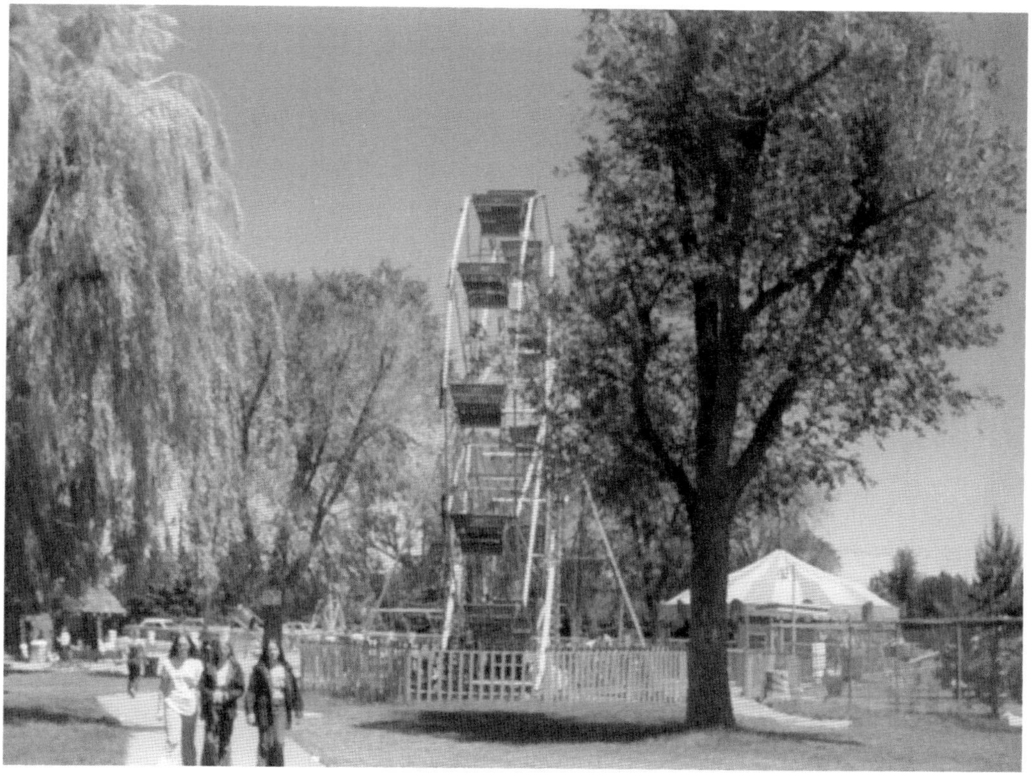

Destination Fun

Leo Larsen was an accountant at Utoco Oil in 1950 when four businessmen who owned the carousel at Tautphaus Park asked whether he could figure out what was making it squeak. Larsen and some coworkers took the merry-go-round apart and rebuilt it. He ended up buying the carousel and the amusement park that went with it, adding rides like the Ferris wheel and Octopus. Larsen retired in 2000. (Courtesy of the Idaho Falls *Post Register.*)

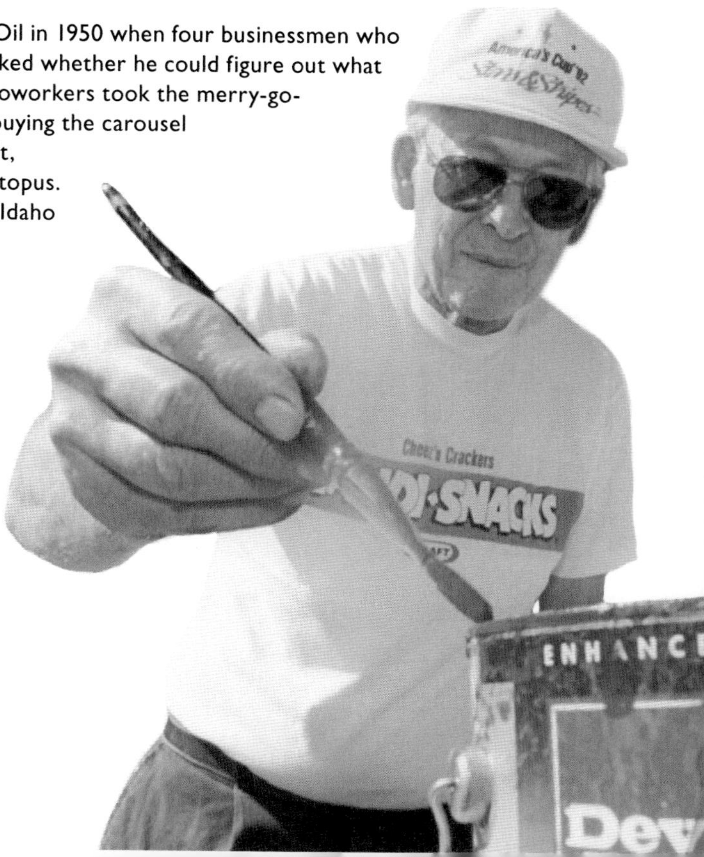

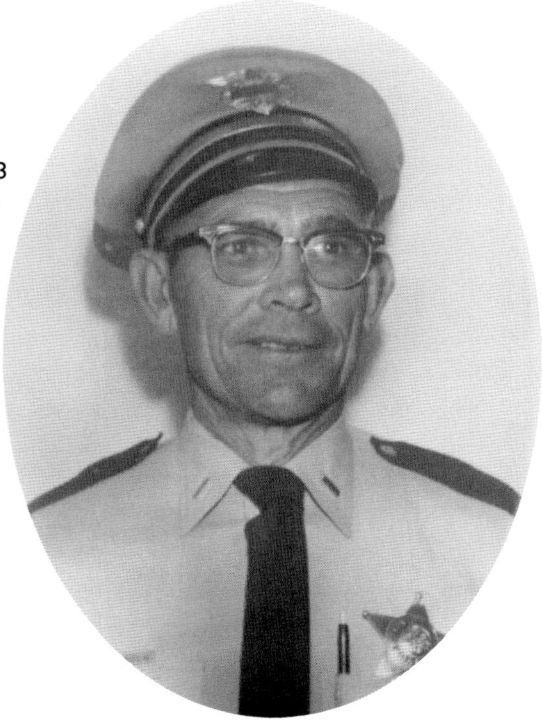

Hobo to Hero

Scyril "Tex" Hamberlin first came west in 1933 as a boxcar-hopping hobo. Five years later, he came back for good and became an Idaho Falls police officer in 1949. His most notable day was in June 1965, when a young boy fell into the Snake River. Hamberlin, who had grown up swimming in the Brazos River, swam to the boy and brought him to the riverbank. The boy could not be revived, but Hamberlin received a commendation for his effort. "It was my duty to do what it was my ability to do," he said. (Courtesy of the Hamberlin family.)

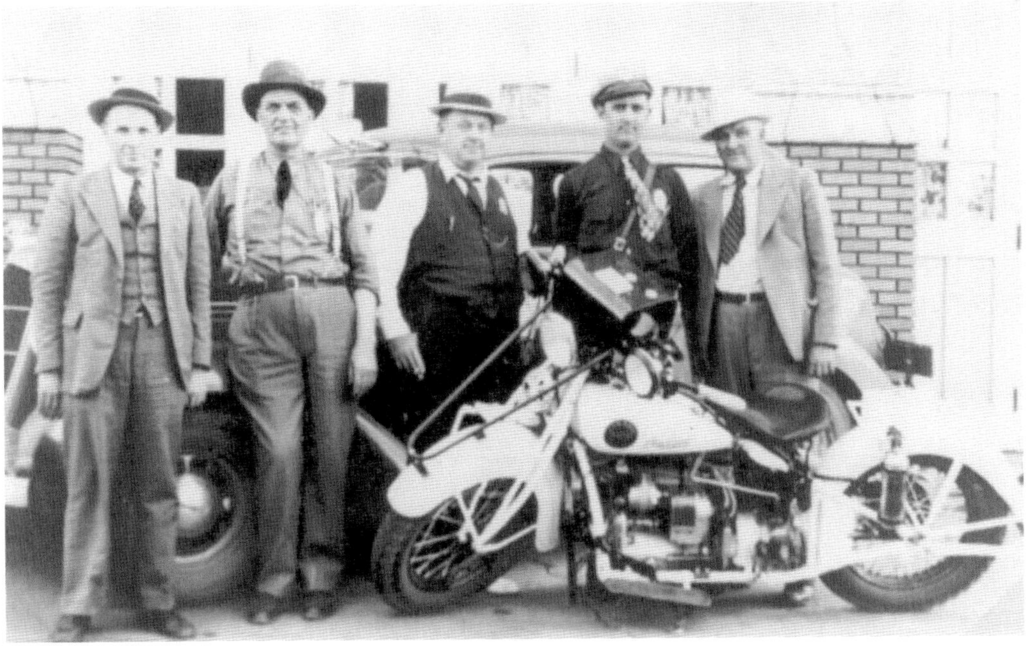

Gift for Gadgetry

Paul Crowder rode a motorcycle north from California in 1933 and became the Idaho Falls Police Department's first motorcycle officer. With an aptitude for electronics and gadgetry, Crowder set about updating the department's communications, and Idaho Falls became the first department in the state to have a radio communication system. (Courtesy of Idaho Falls Police Department.)

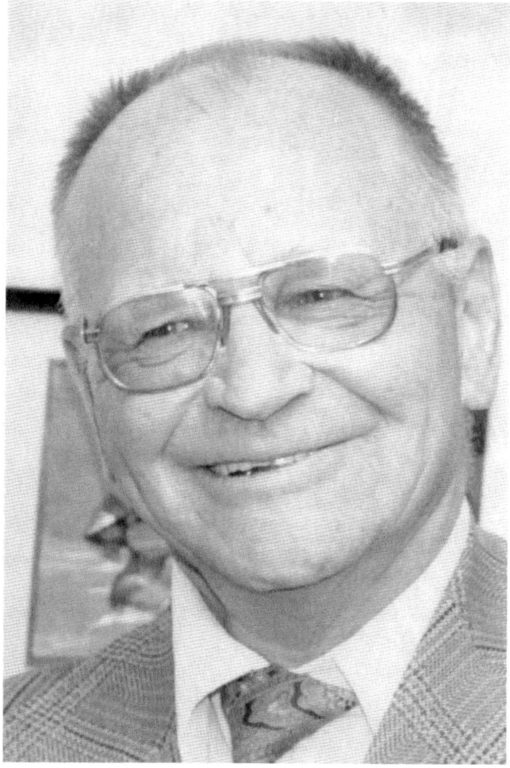

A Department in Transition
No Idaho Falls police chief held the job longer than Robert Pollock, who led the department from 1964 to 1987. Pollock joined the department in 1946. At that time, when someone called the police, an officer would push a button that turned on one of four lights around the city. The officer who saw the light would find a pay phone, call headquarters, and ask where help was needed. Pollock oversaw the modernization of the police department and its move into the Law Enforcement Building in 1978. (Courtesy of the Idaho Falls *Post Register.*)

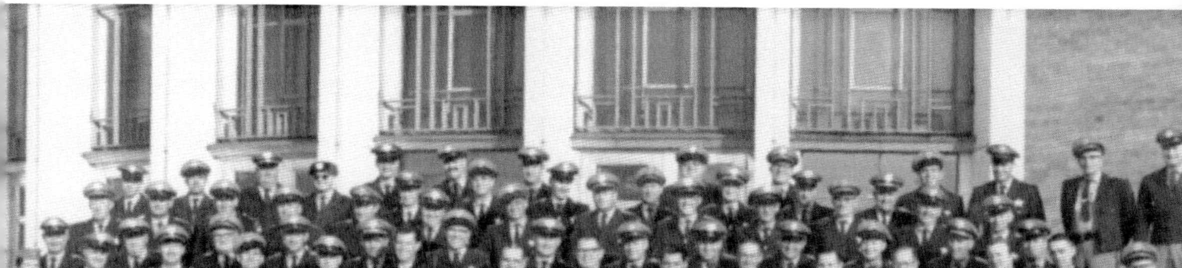

First Female Officer
At the far left in this photograph from 1966 is Doris Evans, the Idaho Falls Police Department's first female officer. The department had decided in 1964 it needed a woman to work with juvenile offenders, particularly young girls. Evans was with the department for 12 years before she moved to Boise. (Courtesy of Idaho Falls Police Department.)

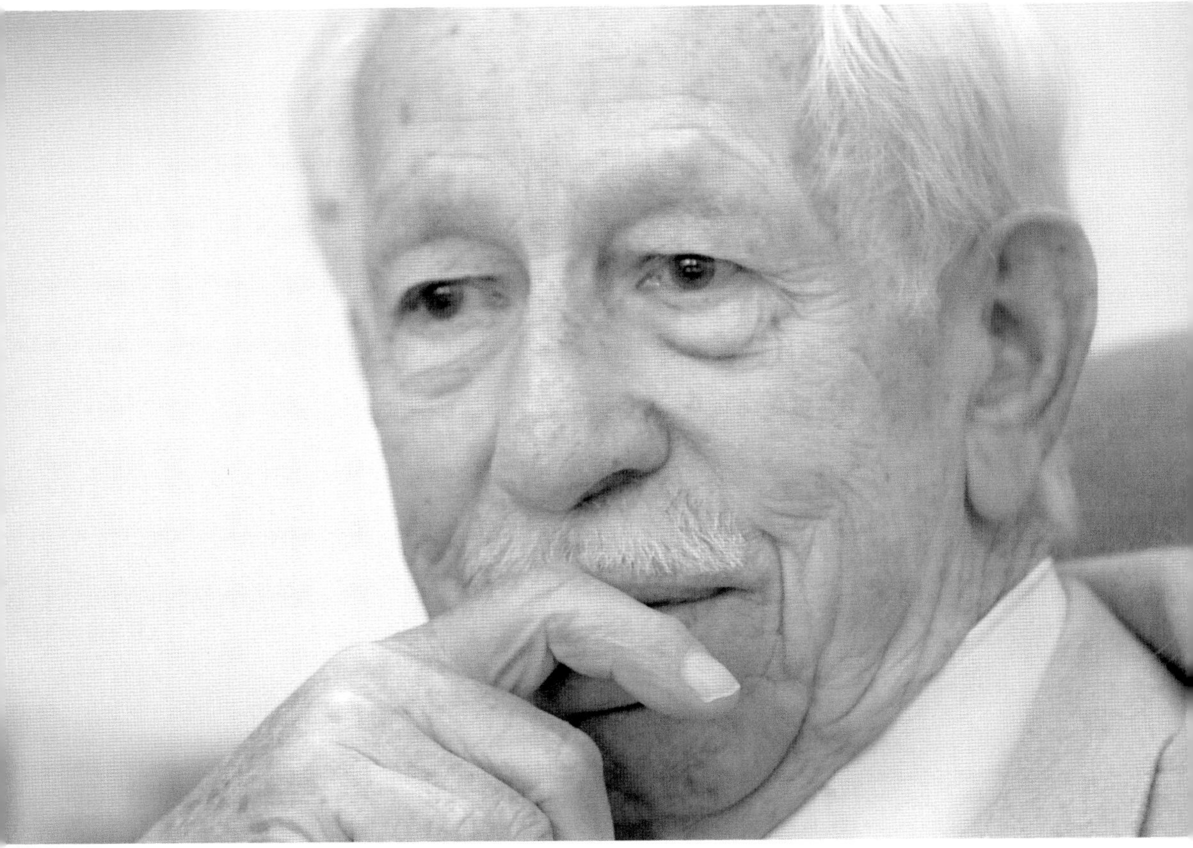

Old School Attorney

While establishing his practice in the early 1950s, Edward "Ted" Pike played drums in Jack Jaegar's orchestra, which had a steady gig at the Elks Club and paid union scale wages. He was elected county attorney in 1954, and in 1957, took the lead in prosecuting a group of Idaho Falls police officers who had been stealing from unlocked homes and businesses. Six were sent to prison, but Pike went back to private practice. "I alienated all the people in 20 or 30 families," he said. "You don't get reelected when you do that." He died in 2009. (Courtesy of the Idaho Falls *Post Register*.)

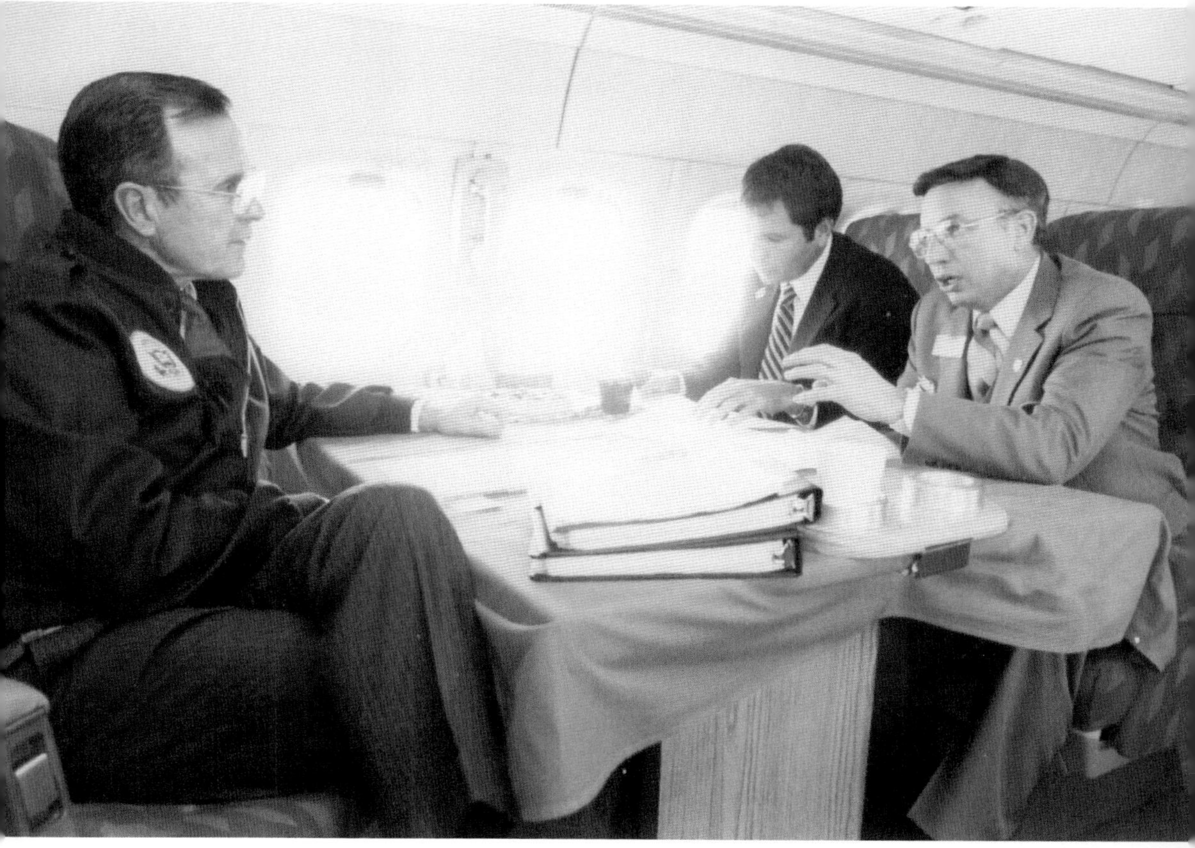

Passion for Politics

Attorney Dennis Olsen, Vice Pres. George H.W. Bush and Sen. Steve Symms are pictured here aboard Air Force Two in 1982. Olsen directed the Republican Party in Bonneville County in the 1970s and 1980s, a time when it rose to dominance in local politics. A Goldwater/Reagan supporter to the core, Olsen, who died in 1985, took a broader, less partisan view at the local level, according to his widow, Sheila. He died in 1985. (Courtesy of Sheila Olsen.)

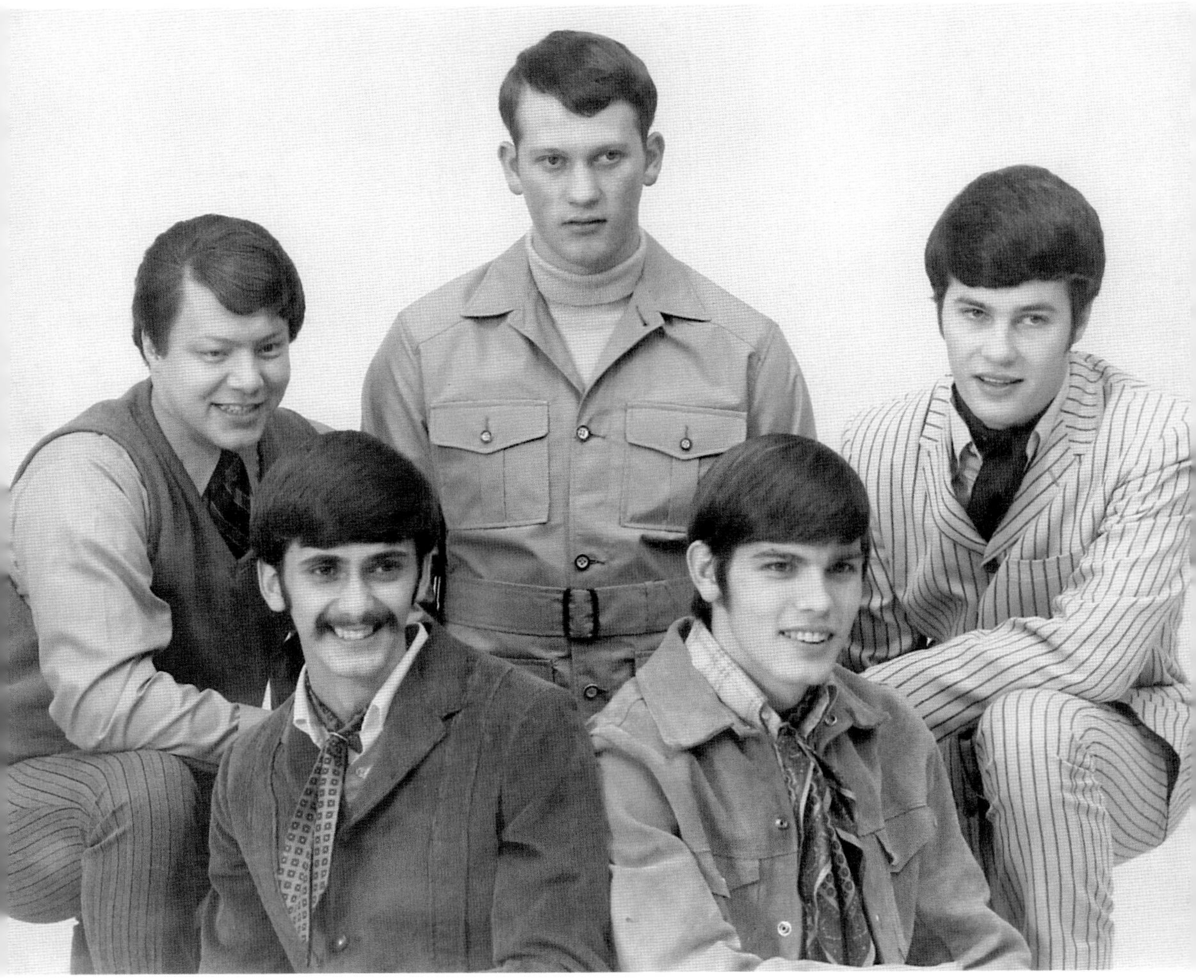

Eastern Idaho's "Fab Five"

In the explosion of groups in the 1960s that followed the Beatles, eastern Idaho's entry was the Affection Collection: Hal Rowberry (vocals), Don Christensen (vocals, keyboards), Mike Doggett (guitar), Ray Hassell (bass), and Tim Comeau (drums, percussion). The group recorded in Clovis, New Mexico, with famed Buddy Holly producer Norman Petty. Their first single, a cover of the Andrews Sisters' "Apple Blossom Time," was picked up by United Artists. Other singles and a self-titled album followed before members split to pursue college and careers. In recent years, members have played at reunions and public events in Idaho Falls. (Courtesy of Mike Doggett.)

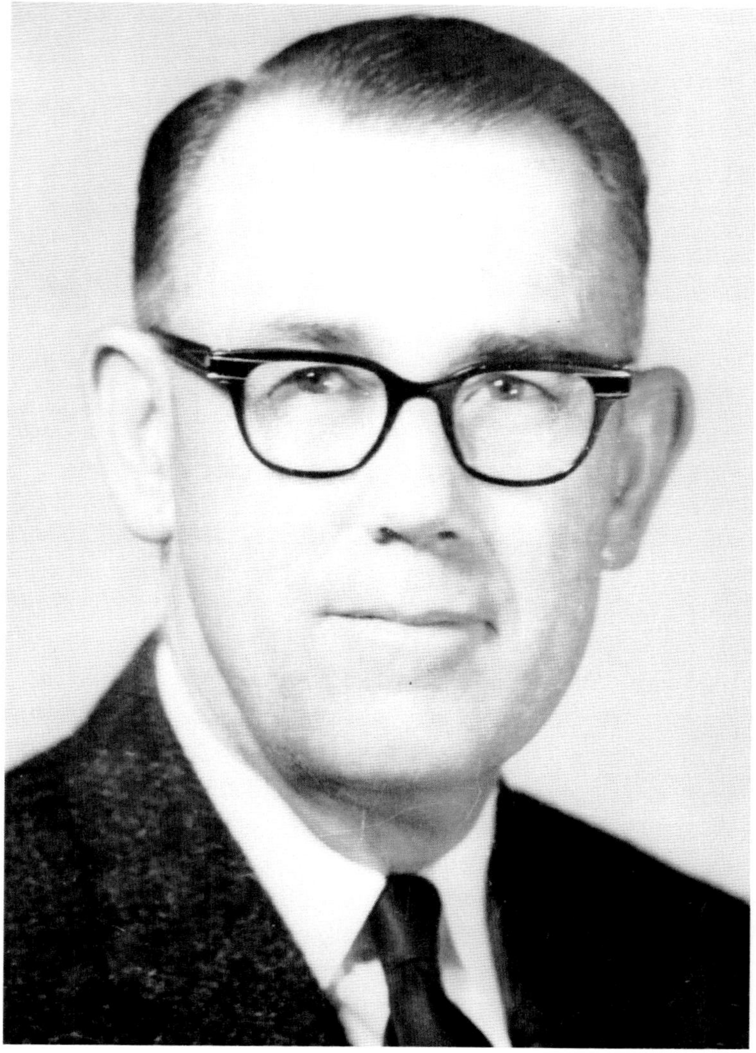

Willingness to Volunteer

Alex D. Creek came to Idaho Falls in 1948 as a distributor for Texaco Oil Co. With a strong sense of community service, he volunteered extensively, and when he retired, his involvement became even more pronounced. He was president or chairman of Toastmasters, 20-30 Club, Idaho Falls Chamber of Commerce, Pacific Northwest Travel Association, Shrine Club, Idaho Falls Kiwanis Club, and Community Chest. He was also involved with the Idaho Division of Tourism and Industrial Development, Idaho Department of Commerce, the Salvation Army Advisory Board, Eastern Idaho Vocational-Technical School (now Eastern Idaho Technical College, where there is a building named after him), Bonneville County Economic Development Committee, and the Bonneville County Waterways Commission. He was on the Idaho Falls city council from 1959 to 1963, serving one year as council president. He was particularly proud of his part in the city's purchase of land that became Sandy Downs Golf Course and Rodeo Grounds. He was appointed to committees by five different governors of Idaho: Idaho Division of Economic and Community Affairs, State Rural Development Council, and Idaho Private Industry Council. He served as board president of Development Workshop and a member of the advisory council for Sacred Heart Hospital. He was involved in the Elks Lodge and was associated for 50 years with the Masonic Lodges. He died in 2006. (Courtesy of Greater Idaho Falls Chamber of Commerce.)

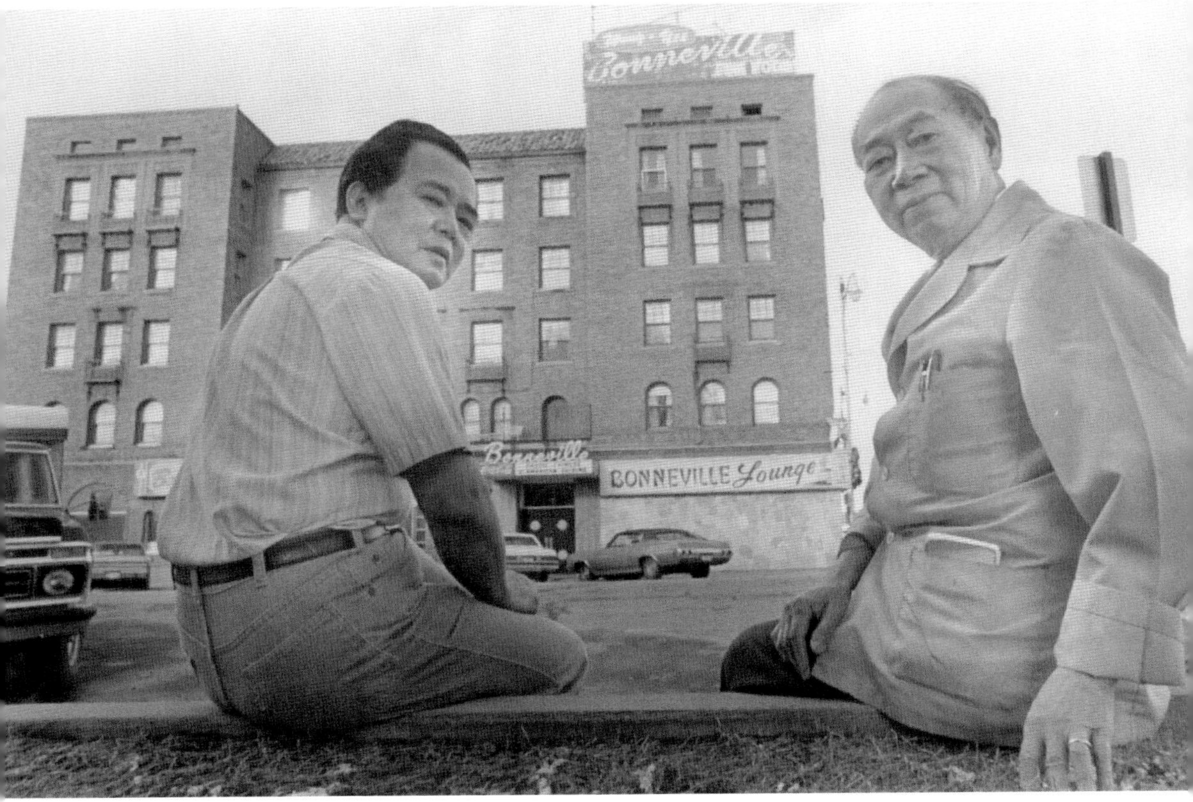

Cuisine of the East

For Chinese food in the 1960s, 1970s, and 1980s, there were a few choices: Ada's Cafe, the Paris, and the Bonneville Restaurant and Lounge, where Sam D. Wong (right) started cooking in 1967. Wong's first partner was Harry Yee, renowned for his style of pouring tea. When he died in 1986, Wally Gee (left) came on the next year. The restaurant was situated on the ground floor of the historical Bonneville Hotel, built in 1927. In the 1970s and 1980s, the restaurant was where judges, lawyers, and reporters would gather almost daily for lunch. (Courtesy of the Idaho Falls *Post Register*.)

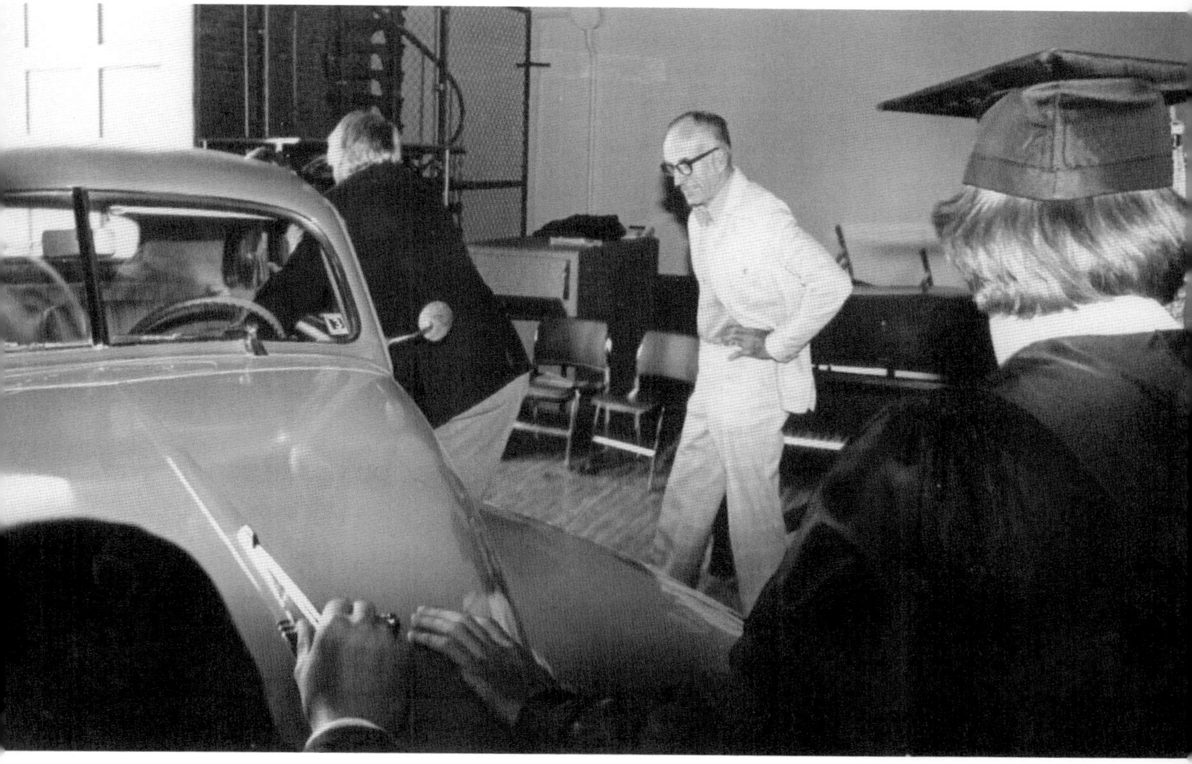

Pranking the Principal

Longtime Idaho Falls High School principal Glenn Manion got a surprise at a May 1978 student awards assembly when the 1948 Chevrolet sedan he had reported stolen the previous week showed up onstage with new upholstery and a fresh paint job. Manion, principal for 22 years, was visibly moved, but admitted he had suspected that something was up. The car had been in rough shape, and its use was limited to fishing trips because of its high clearance. Manion died in 2012 at age 96. (Courtesy of the Idaho Falls *Post Register.*)

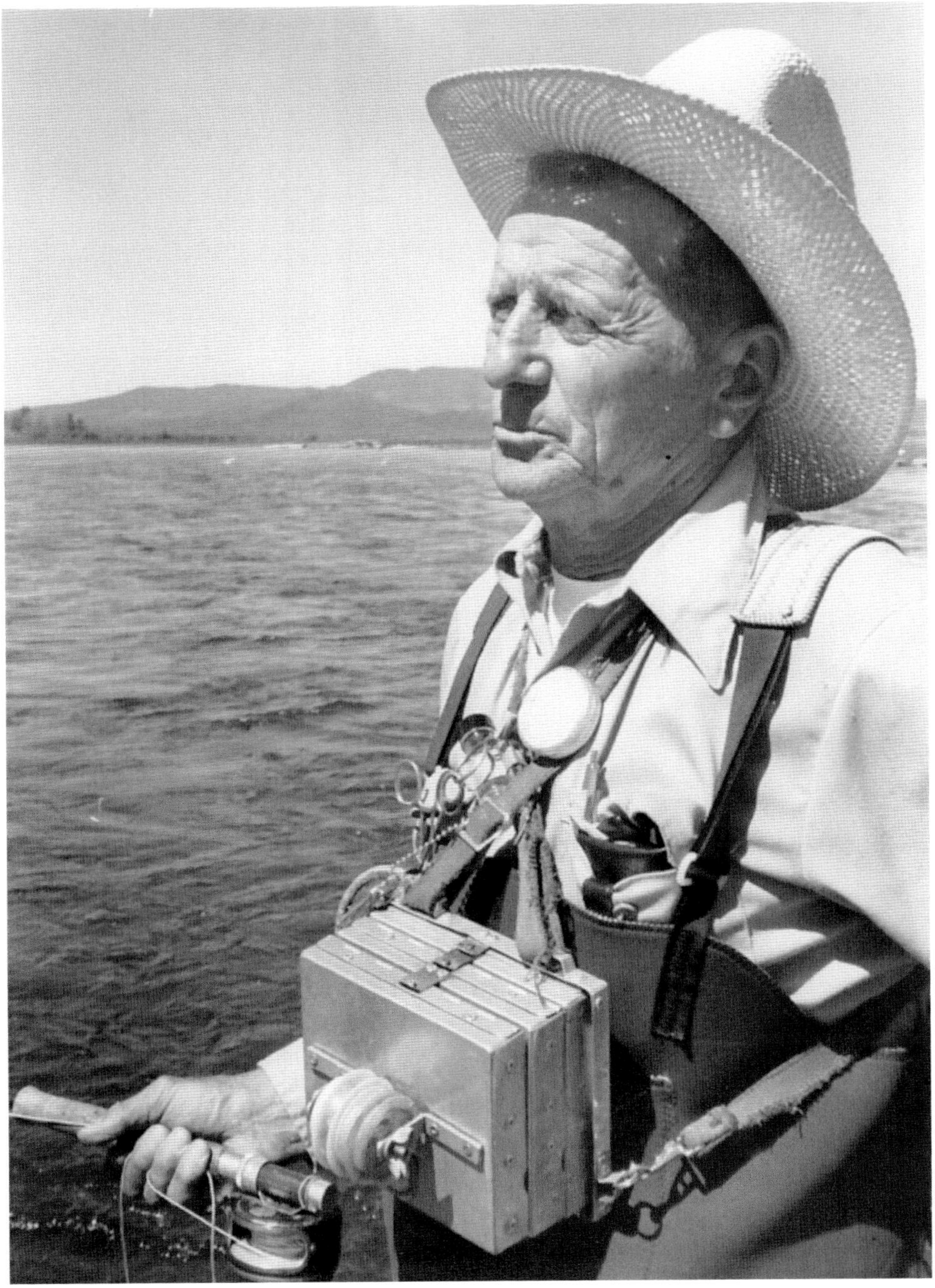

Lord of the Flies

Bing Lempke returned to Idaho Falls from California in 1957 to take a pipefitting job, but it was the fish in the rivers that were calling him home. Renowned for his fly-fishing and fly-tying abilities, Lempke said the Green Drake hatch cost him three good jobs, as he couldn't stay away from the Henry's Fork in June. In 1991, at age 74, he won the Federation of Fly Fishers Buz Buszek award for his contributions to the sport. Today, the Western Rocky Mountain Federation of Fly Fishers gives an award to young anglers annually in his name. (Courtesy of the Idaho Falls *Post Register.*)

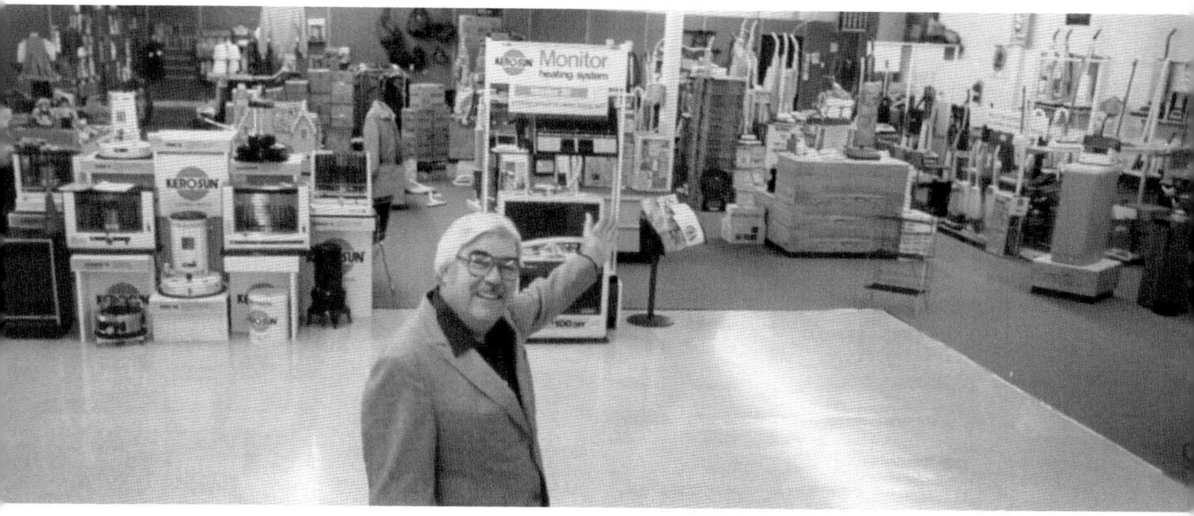

Appliances in Action

Cliff Brady started out in 1965 with a 400-square-foot vacuum cleaner store in Idaho Falls. He moved to a bigger location two years later, adding water softeners and sewing machines. The store moved again in 1971, then again in 1984 (to the store on Woodruff Avenue, pictured here), and finally in 2001 to its 36,000-square-foot superstore on Lincoln Road. Other locations have opened in Pocatello and Twin Falls. The stores are now run by his sons, but Brady remains active in civic affairs and the Greater Idaho Falls Chamber of Commerce. (Courtesy of the Idaho Falls *Post Register.*)

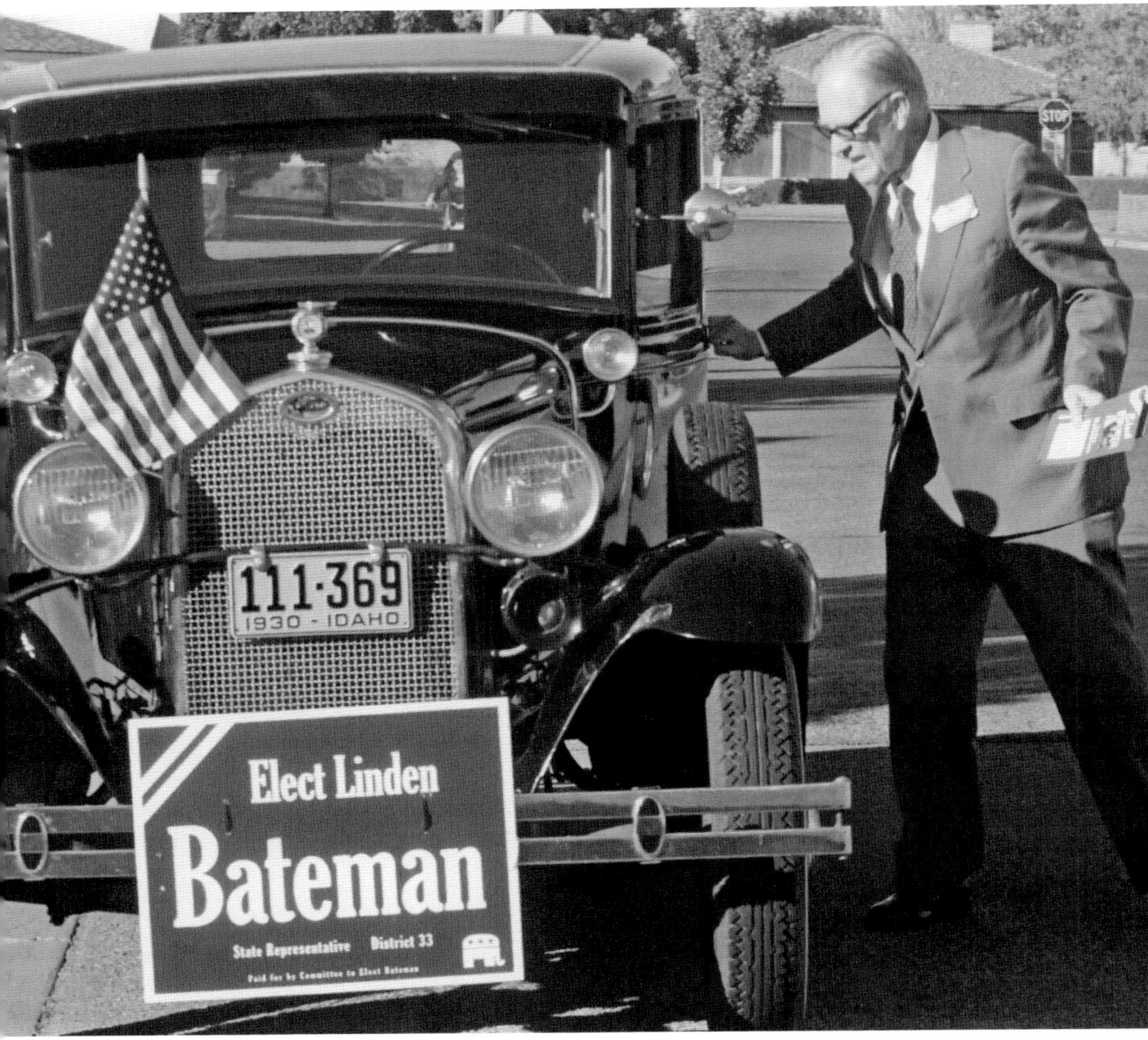

Civic Ideals

A longtime teacher of history and civics, Linden Bateman served in the Idaho House of Representatives from 1977 to 1986 and again from 2010 to the present. His most recent claim to fame was a bill he introduced in the 2013 session to make cursive handwriting a mandatory subject in elementary schools. His main concern was that if cursive was not taught, people would soon be unable to read it, limiting future generations' understanding of important historical letters and documents. The bill failed, but Bateman remains a staunch advocate of traditional ideals. (Courtesy of the Idaho Falls *Post Register.*)

CHAPTER FOUR

Quality of Life

By the early 1980s, Idaho Falls's population had grown to near 40,000. The growth of the AEC years was over, and while employment at the Idaho National Engineering Laboratory continued to grow, there was widespread awareness that something new would be needed.

With the end of the Cold War, the awareness turned to alarm as the Department of Energy made it clear that the peace dividend was going to bring job reductions to the site.

Was Idaho Falls in for a crash landing?

What surprised many was that as employment at the national laboratory shrank by 42 percent between 1993 and 2006, Idaho Falls's economy continued to grow at a modest if not spectacular rate. Much as they had been since the beginning of the 20th century, agriculture, retail trade, and medical services continue to provide an underpinning.

Two major projects shifted growth in Idaho Falls in a southern direction, rather than north and west as had been anticipated. The first, the Grand Teton Mall, opened in August 1984. The mall refocused commercial attention and brought heavy traffic to 17th Street and Hitt Road, previously two-lane country roads.

Two years after the mall came Eastern Idaho Regional Medical Center (EIRMC), immediately to the southwest. Built to replace the city's two aging facilities, EIRMC became the nucleus of a wide swath of medical offices and facilities, including a second hospital, the privately owned Mountain View.

According to the 2010 census, the Idaho Falls Metropolitan Statistical Area—Bonneville and Jefferson Counties—had a population of 130,374. As a retail-trading center, however, Idaho Falls continues to act like a magnet over a very large geographical area. A study done for the Idaho Falls Regional Airport in 2008 estimated there are 294,557 people within 60 minutes' drive time of Idaho Falls. Within two hours, that number expands to 665,359.

For the past 30 or so years, the people of Idaho Falls have been focused on maintaining prosperity and attracting new people. The quality of life is a major selling point. Crime and unemployment are low, as is the cost of living and buying a home. The city is located close to some of the best skiing, hunting, and fishing in the world. Millions have been spent on developing the Greenbelt around the Snake River into a place where people can walk, ride bicycles, or gather at public events. With new, independently owned shops and restaurants, the downtown business district has bounced back from its low in the 1980s, when two major retailers, JC Penney and the Bon Marche, migrated to the mall.

As Idaho Falls looks toward the second half of its second century, it can look to the people who made it the place it is: public servants and private business people who shared strong ideas and provided opportunities for the community.

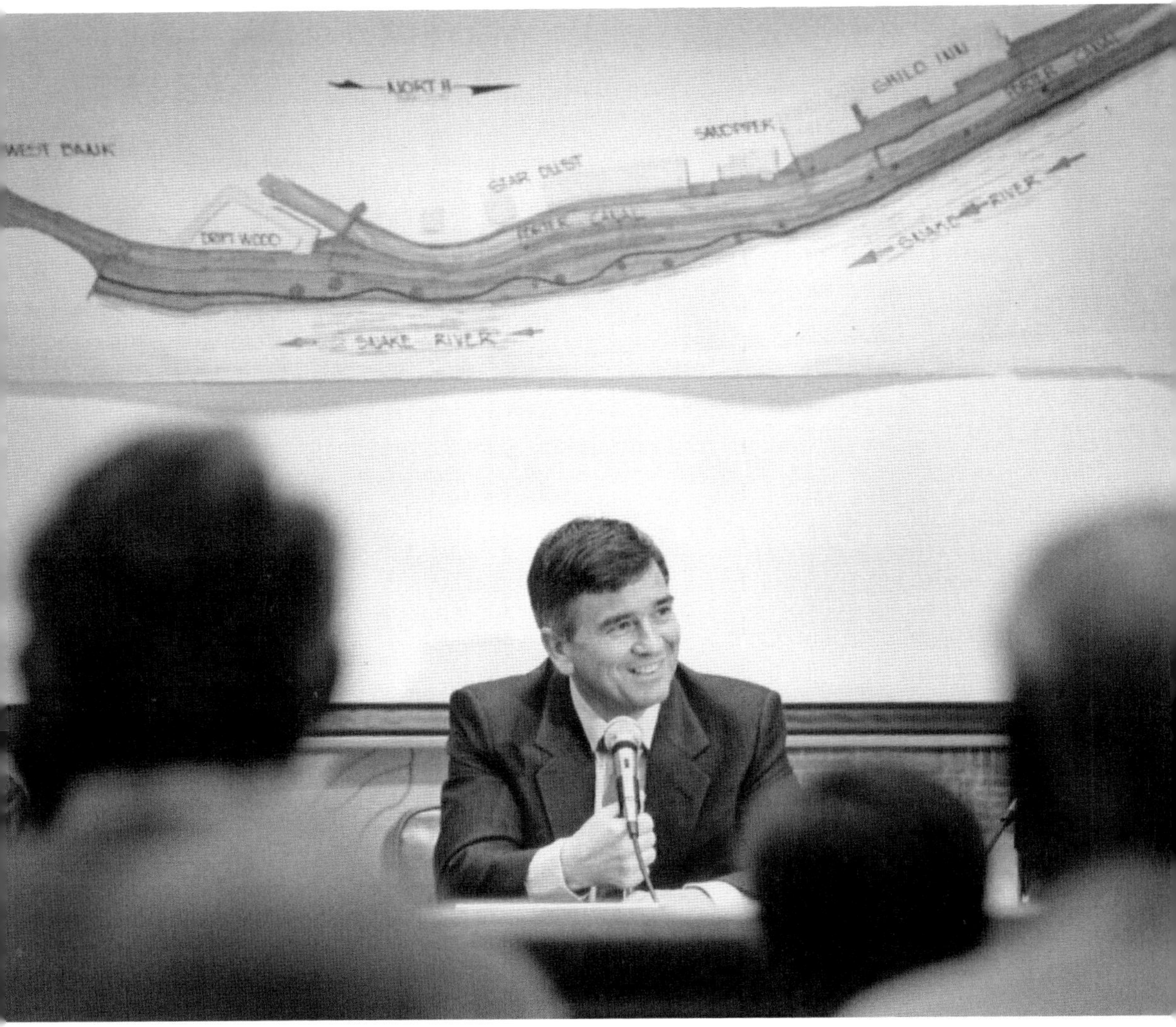

The Greenbelt Mayor

Mayor from 1978 to 1993, Thomas C. Campbell succeeded S. Eddie Pedersen and continued his predecessor's ambitious building goals for the city. Projects on his watch included the Bulb Turbine and the Gem State Hydroelectric Dam, the Sand Creek and Sage Lakes golf courses, and the Idaho Falls Greenbelt. Here, Campbell smiles at the city council's vote in 1989 to approve the River Parkway Greenbelt improvements. A teacher before he was mayor, Campbell became superintendent of Bonneville School District 93 after he left city hall. (Courtesy of the Idaho Falls *Post Register.*)

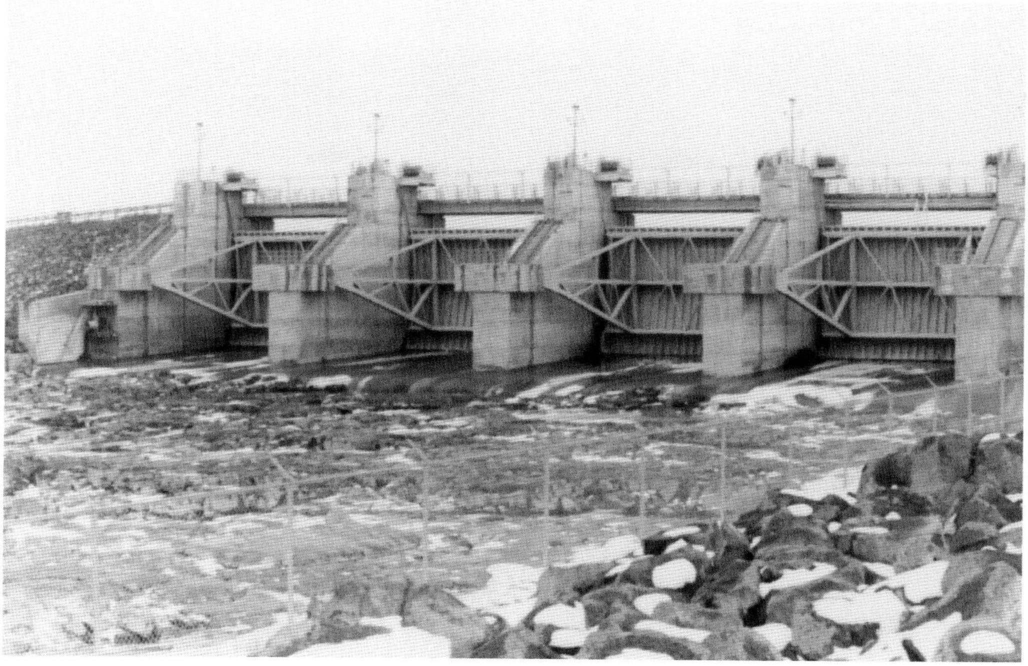

Big Projects

Above is the Gem State Hydroelectric Project south of Idaho Falls, completed in 1988, the last of the city of Idaho Falls's hydropower generation works. Below is the Idaho Falls Greenbelt as it appears today, continuing a public-private partnership. (Above, courtesy of Idaho Falls Power; below, author photograph.)

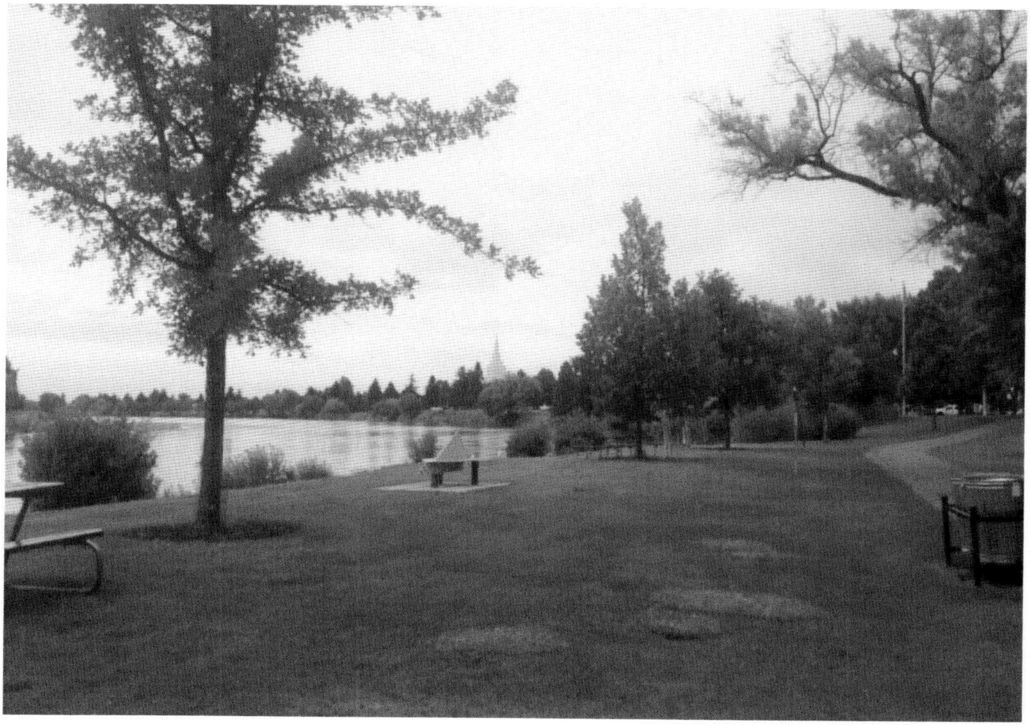

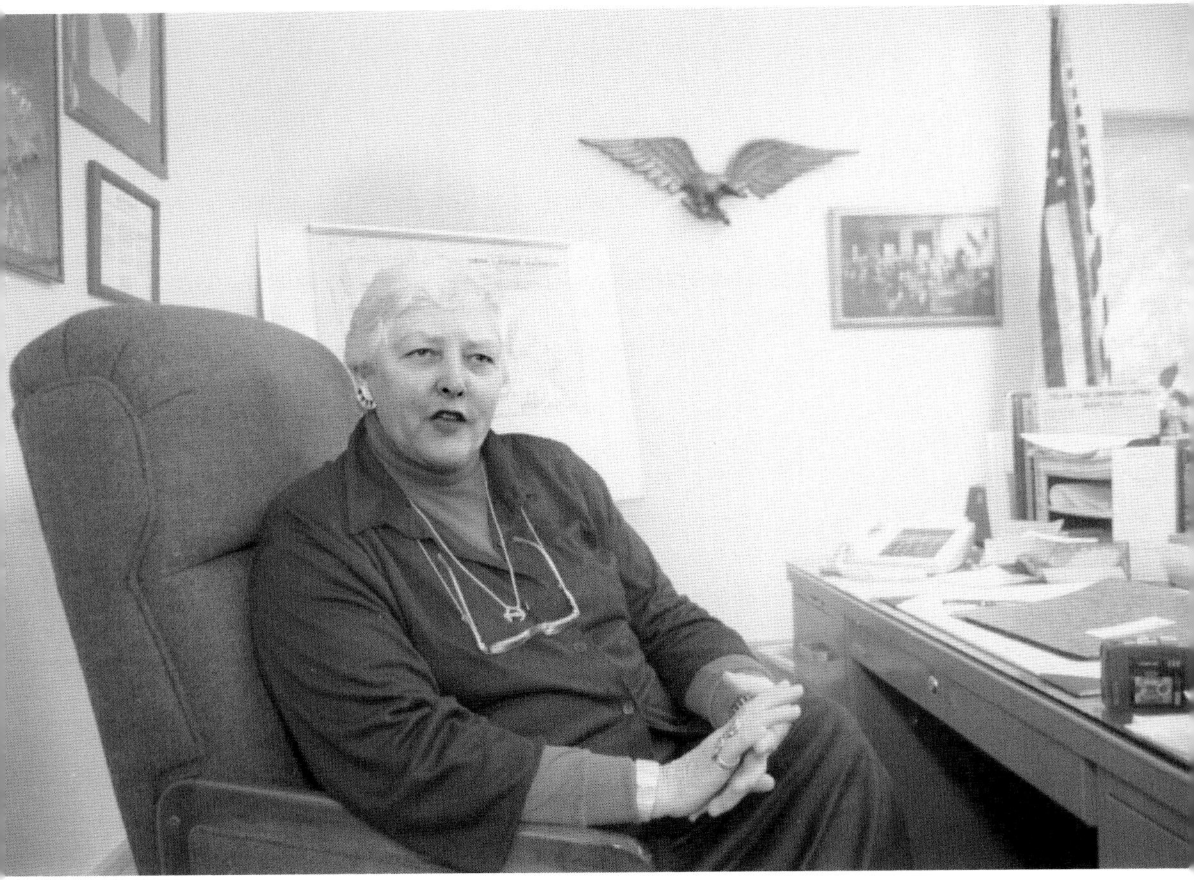

Horse Sense
Horses and politics have distinguished Edith Stanger's career. She was the first woman to serve on the Bonneville County Commission, and with her husband, Dick, she created the Double Arrow Ranch, the world's largest registered herd of Appaloosa horses. She was a founding member of the Idaho State Horse Council in 1975, president of the Intermountain Appaloosa Club, and secretary of the Snake River Valley Horse Show. As a lobbyist, she pushed legislation aimed at aiding the racing industry. Her equine expertise earned her a spot on a study tour of the light horse industries in Europe. (Courtesy of the Idaho Falls *Post Register.*)

A Steady Hand

Idaho Falls's first female mayor, Linda Milam, took office in 1993 at a time of great anxiety over imminent job cuts at the Idaho National Engineering Laboratory. She stressed the need for the city to build up its reserves, and when she left office in 2006, the city had constructed a new fire station without incurring debt, improved flood control, widened busy streets, and lowered the tax levy. While employment at the lab declined 42 percent during her three terms in office, the local economy grew at an annual rate of 2 percent. (Courtesy of the City of Idaho Falls.)

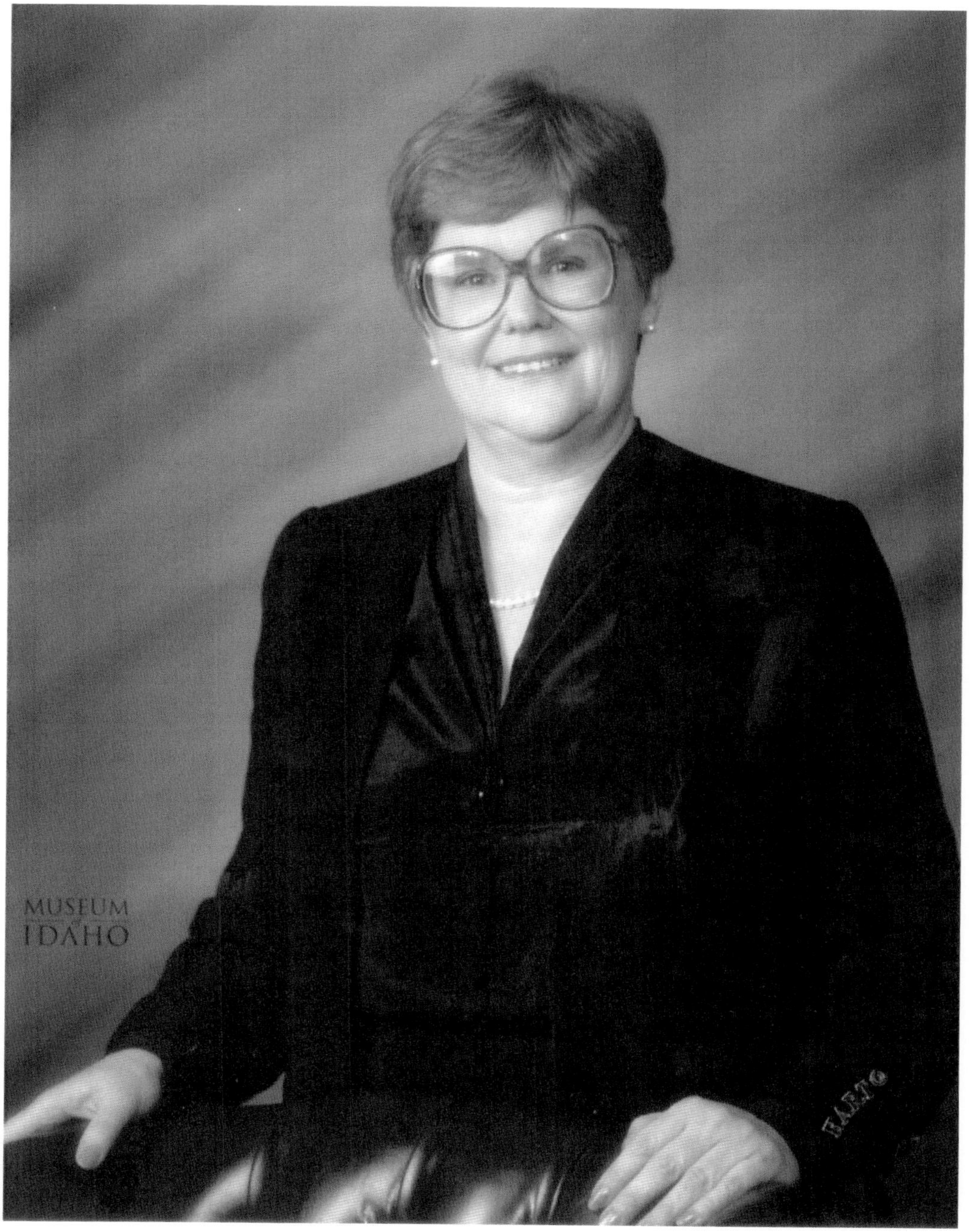

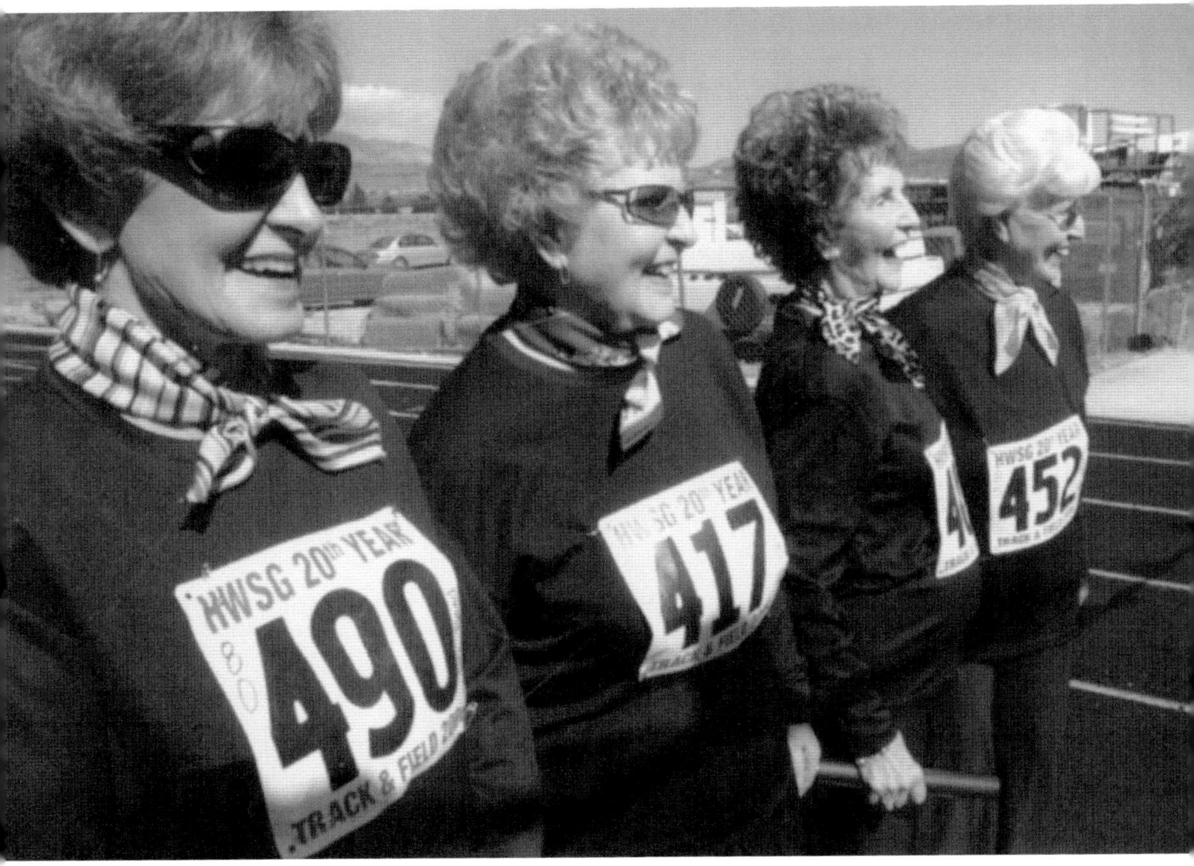

Energy and Enterprise

Verla Ball was a driving force and partner in several eastern Idaho businesses, including King B Jerky, Beauty for All Seasons, and Melaleuca. She owned and operated the Hebgen Lake Lodge in Montana and a restaurant in Rexburg called the Queen Bee. At age 87, when most would be retired peacefully, she began participating in the Senior Olympic Games. When she learned in 2006 that they could be in the record books, Ball, then 90, persuaded her three sisters, Ava Hessing (85), Ruby Call (83), and Nelda Reed (80), to enter the Huntsman World Senior Games in St. George, Utah. That October they became the oldest female team to finish the 4-by-100 relay. "Our mother taught us that exercise was good for the body. Staying active helps us feel alive and energetic," Ball said. The team was sponsored by Melaleuca, the company that she and her sons, Allen and Roger, started in the 1980s. (Courtesy of the Idaho Falls *Post Register*.)

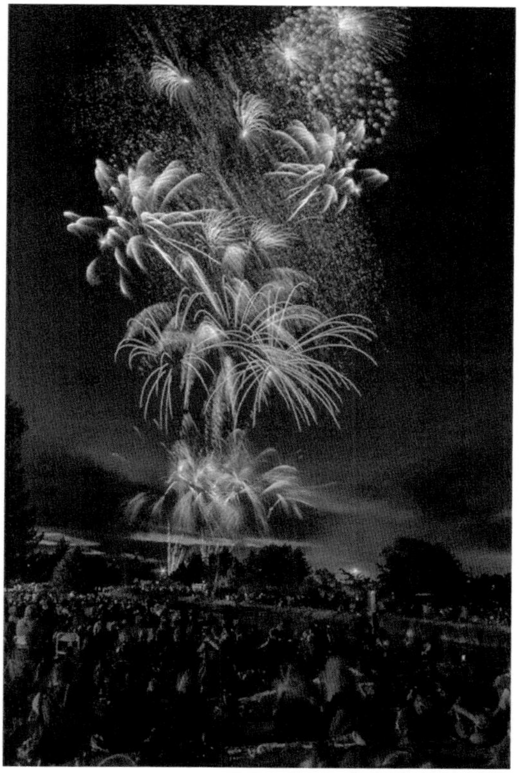

Fantastic Fireworks
Every Fourth of July, the Melaleuca Freedom Celebration is one of the biggest fireworks shows in the West. (Courtesy of Melaleuca Inc.)

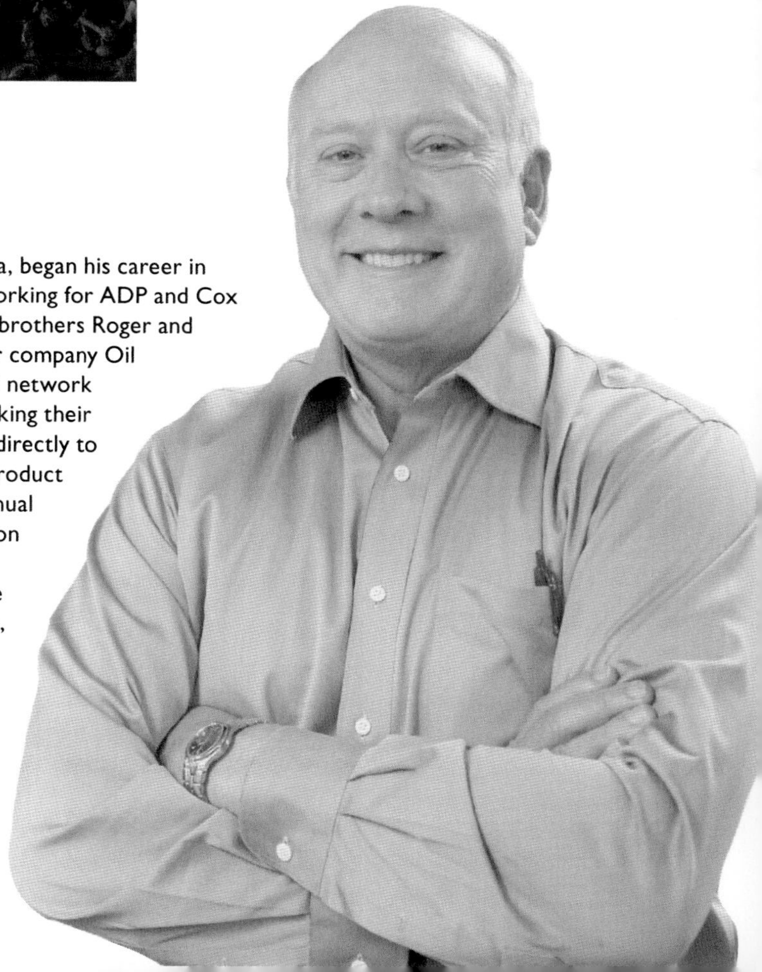

Business Builder
Frank VanderSloot, CEO of Melaleuca, began his career in marketing selling beef jerky before working for ADP and Cox Communications. In the early 1980s, brothers Roger and Allen Ball hired him to help with their company Oil of Melaleuca. Adopting a home-based network sales system that relies on people making their commissions by referring customers directly to the company rather than serving as product distributors, Melaleuca now posts annual sales worldwide of more than $1 billion and employs nearly 2,000 people in eastern Idaho. VanderSloot is also the owner of Riverbend Communications, which operates several radio stations, and the Riverbend Ranch, which breeds prize-winning cattle. (Courtesy of the Idaho Falls *Post Register*.)

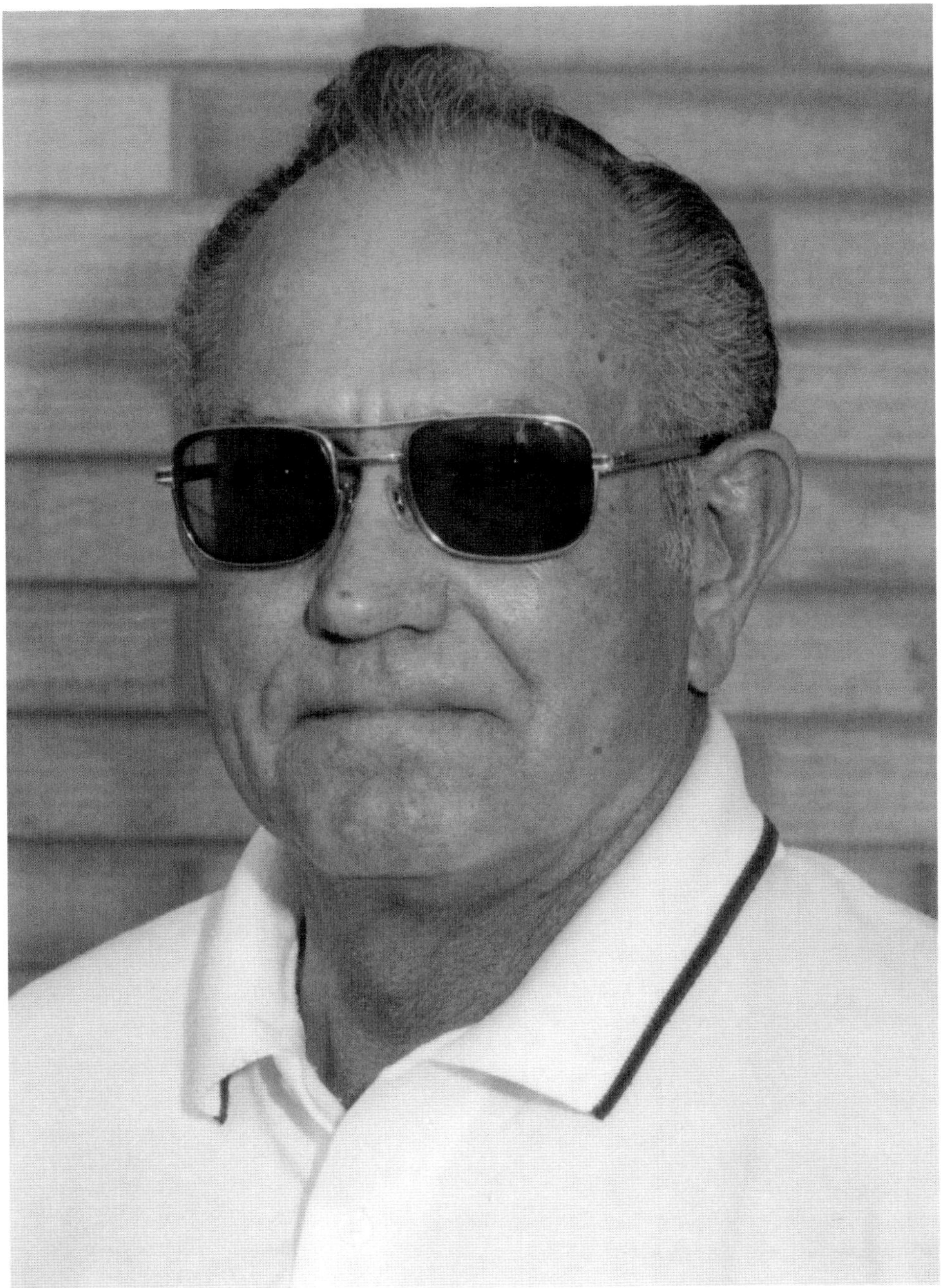

"Coach Ras"

There was no tougher coach on the local high school sporting scene than Mahlon N. Rasmuson, "Coach Ras" to his players at Skyline High School. Anyone who played football against his teams could be sure they were going to get roughed up by his defense. "The kids would play like heck for him just to satisfy him," said longtime radio sports announcer Jim Garchow. Rasmuson retired in 1985, after taking the Grizzlies to their first state championship. He was later a charter inductee into the Idaho High School Hall of Fame. He died in 2007 at age 84. (Courtesy of Skyline High School.)

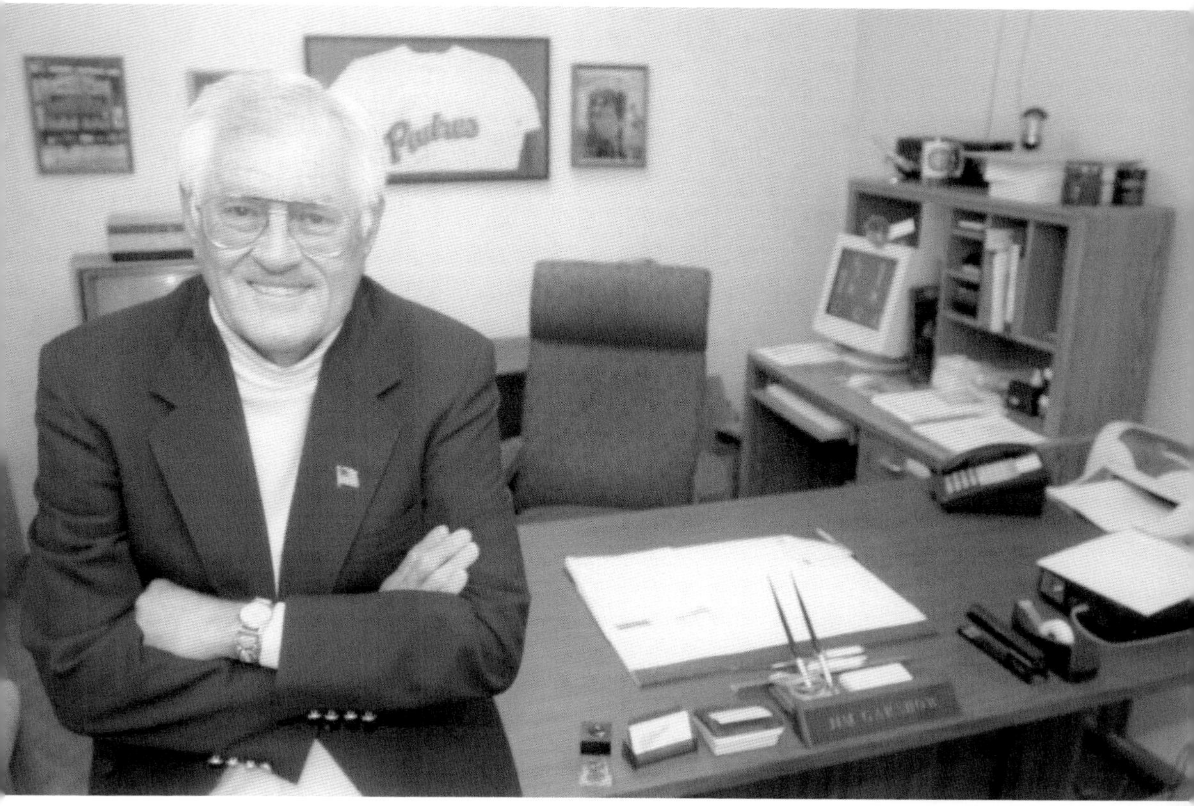

Play by Play

Chicago had Harry Carey and New York had Red Barber, but in Idaho Falls, Jim Garchow was the sportscaster to listen to, spending 39 seasons on the air. Garchow (pronounced "gar-show") came to Idaho Falls in 1969 to manage KUPI Radio, which he changed to a country music format. The next year he started calling baseball games on the air, and at the time of his death in 2009, he had called minor league baseball with the same club longer than any other broadcaster in America. In 1976, he became the voice of Skyline High School, broadcasting all football and basketball games. Away from the microphone, he supported individual athletes in need by buying them shoes, gear, or uniforms. "When you are young, it's kind of hard to realize what people can mean to you," said Yo Murphy, an Idaho Falls High School graduate who went all the way to the NFL. "It's great to have people genuinely care and want you to do well. I wasn't just some story to him." Garchow was also a heart transplant recipient, receiving one in 1987, and frequently spoke on behalf of organ donation. At the time of his passing, he was the longest living heart transplant recipient from the University of Utah program. (Courtesy of the Idaho Falls *Post Register.*)

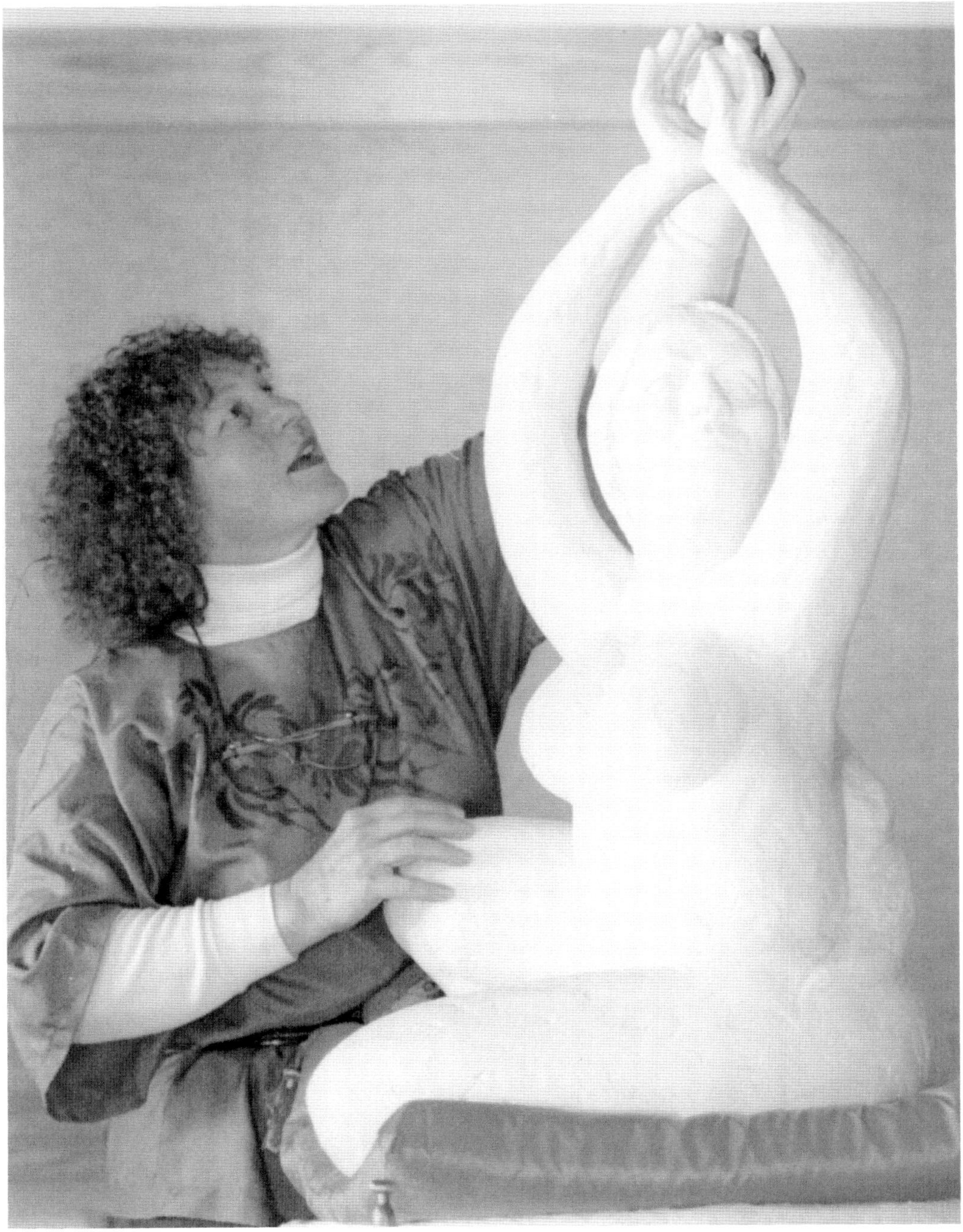

Sculpting Marvels

Born and raised on Rainbow Ranch near Taylor Mountain, Marilyn Hoff-Hansen and her husband, Reed Hansen, raised five children on their family farm. During that time, she converted a former dairy barn into a two-story studio that has become a local art center. Working in a broad range of media—metal sculpture, oils, acrylics, and ink brush—her commissions include the Boise State University "Bronco" sculpture. As a member of Idaho's snow sculpture team, she placed first in nationals and then in the top 10 at the 1988 Olympic Snow Sculpture event in Calgary, Canada. (Courtesy of the Idaho Falls *Post Register*.)

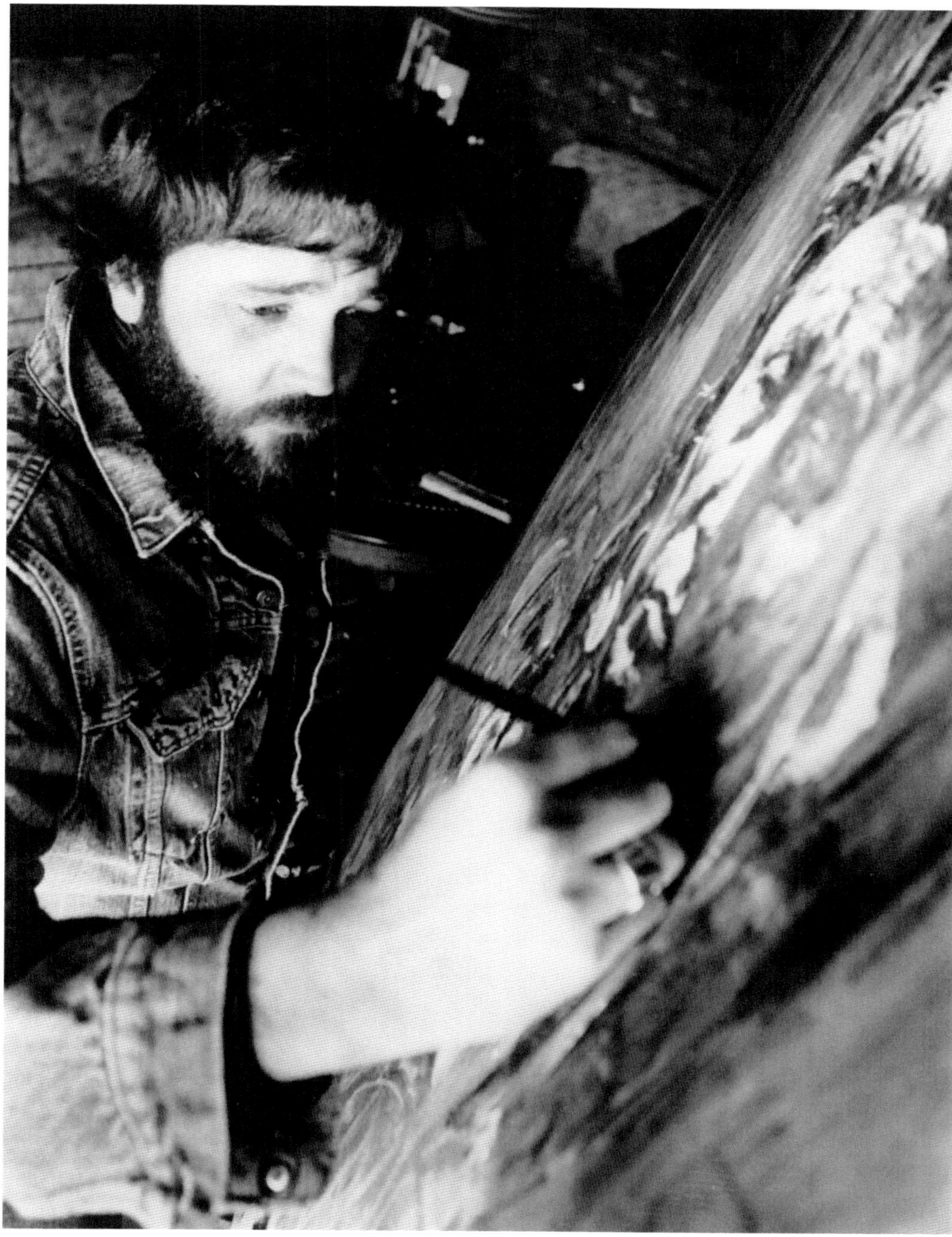

An Artist's Life

After bumming around in Alaska and California, painter Roy Reynolds came home to Idaho Falls to set up his studio. He has works in galleries throughout the United States, Europe, and Australia, and has done album covers for his close friend singer-songwriter Carole King. Reynolds picked up drawing as a young child but didn't start painting seriously until he took a class in high school from Helen Hoff Aupperle. "She taught me to appreciate beauty and have an interest in common things," he said. "I can find something beautiful from whatever is happening in front of me." (Courtesy of the Idaho Falls *Post Register*.)

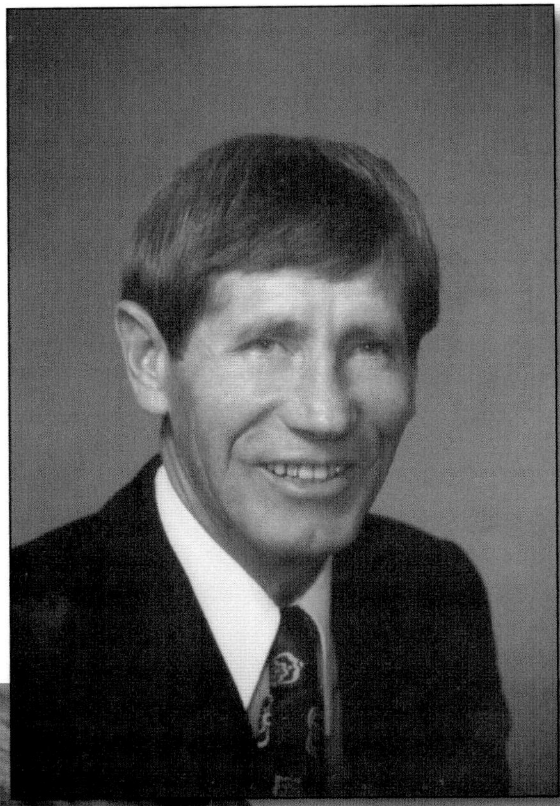

Civic Pride and Outdoor Fun

Born in 1923 in Bonners Ferry, Wes Deist served in World War II, completed his education on the GI Bill, and moved his family to Idaho Falls in the early 1950s. He taught and coached at Kelly Canyon Ski Resort until he was over 80 years old, and was also an instructor for the KIFI Ski School, where he is shown second from left in the picture below taken at Pine Basin. In the three terms he served on the Idaho Falls city council, Deist helped establish the city's Greenbelt and Community Park, and the aquatic center built while he was on the council was renamed in his honor after he left office. He passed away in January 2008. (Both, courtesy of the Deist family.)

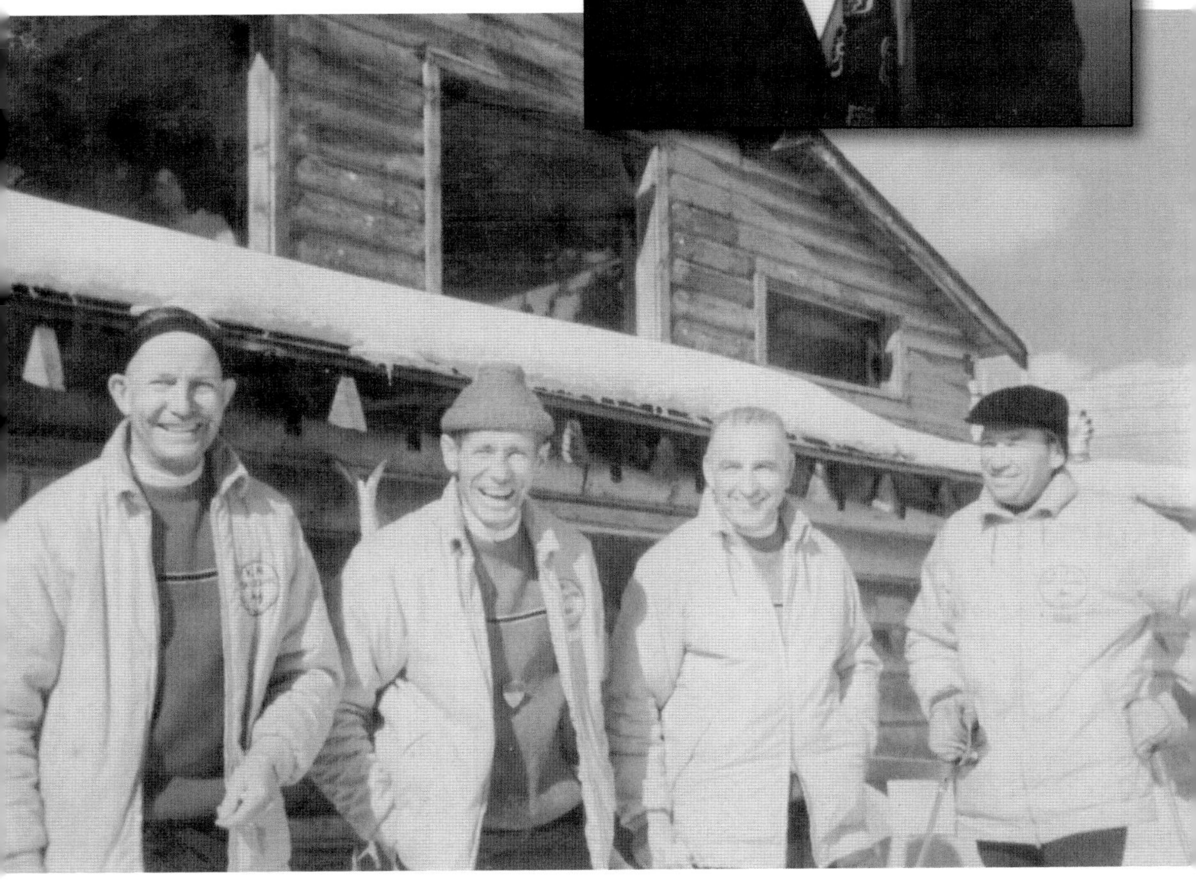

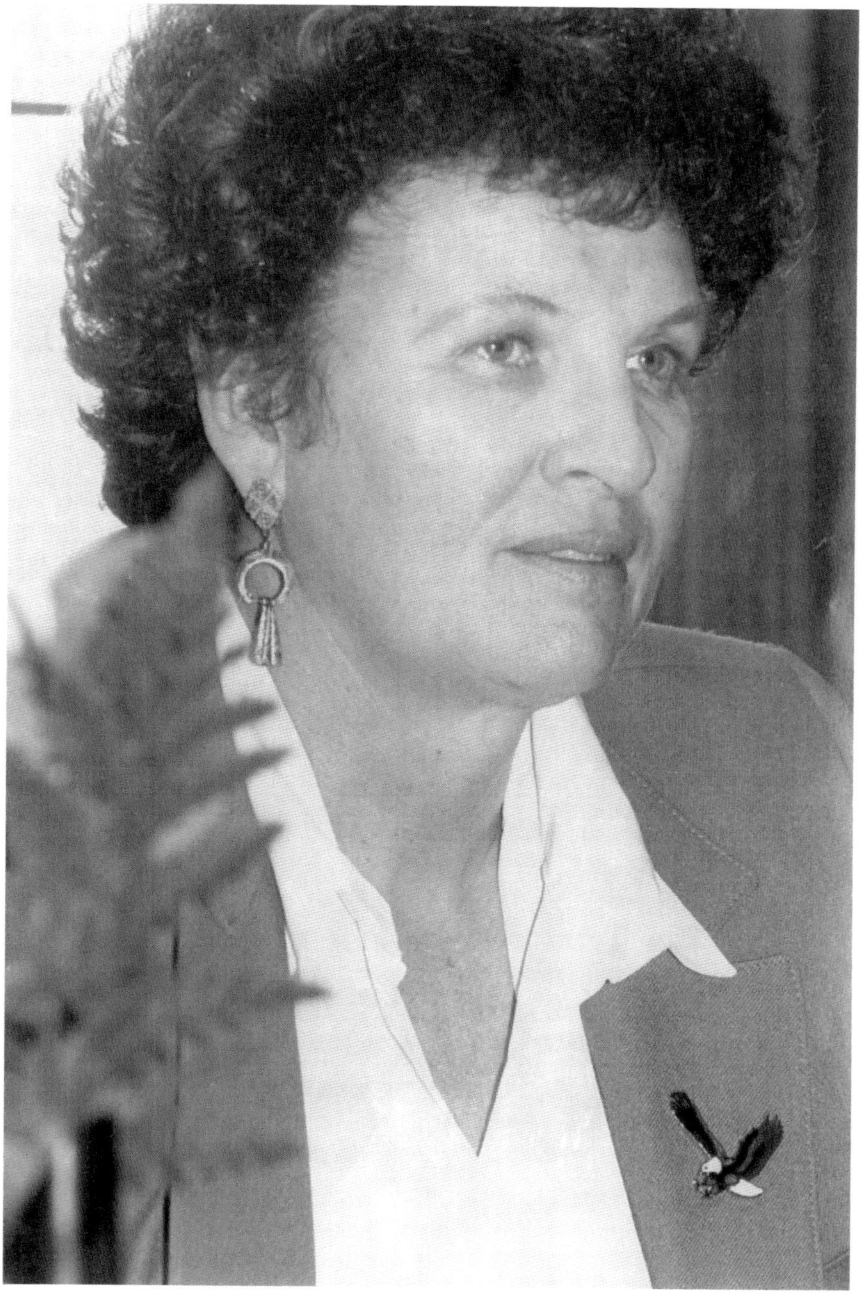

"Most Congenial"
Beverly Branson started as secretary to Idaho Falls mayor S. Eddie Pedersen and held the position through the administration of his successor, Tom Campbell. During that time, she was actively establishing Idaho Falls's Sister Cities program with Tokai, Ibaraki, Japan. Elected to the city council in 1993, Branson was both the city's institutional memory and its friendliest face. "You could have 100 people in a room, and Bev wanted to make all those 100 people happy," said fellow council member Larry Carlson. Branson died in 2000 at age 68, after a battle with cancer that lasted nearly five years. (Courtesy of the Idaho Falls *Post Register.*)

On the Bench

Few who came before Magistrate Judge William Black ever forgot his gruff demeanor and talent for stern admonition, particularly on "Father's Day," when men delinquent with their child support payments were brought before the bench. Yet those who knew him say he was actually a very genial man who enjoyed a good laugh. This photograph was taken at a roast in 1989, the year he retired from his position as trial court administrator. (Courtesy of the Idaho Falls *Post Register.*)

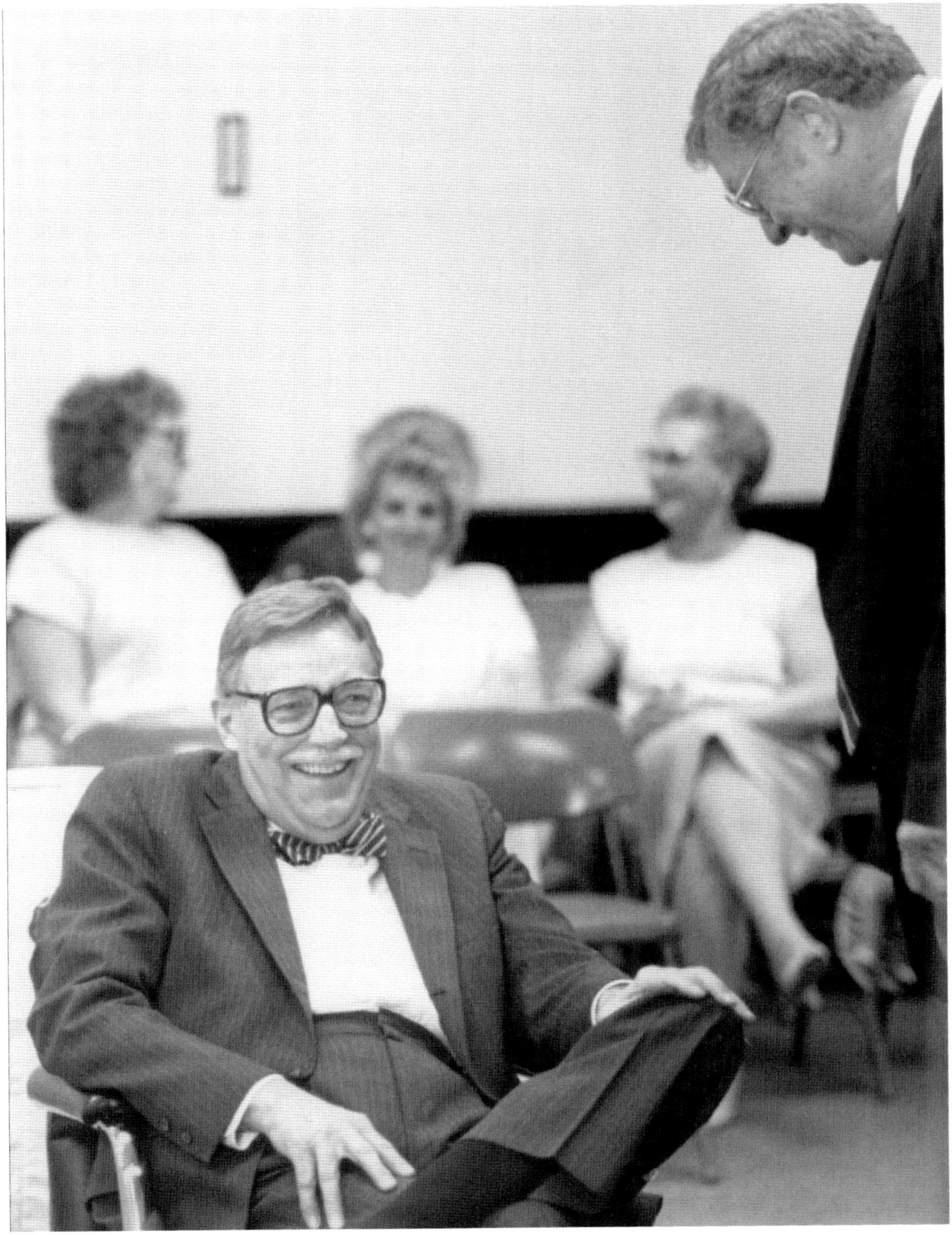

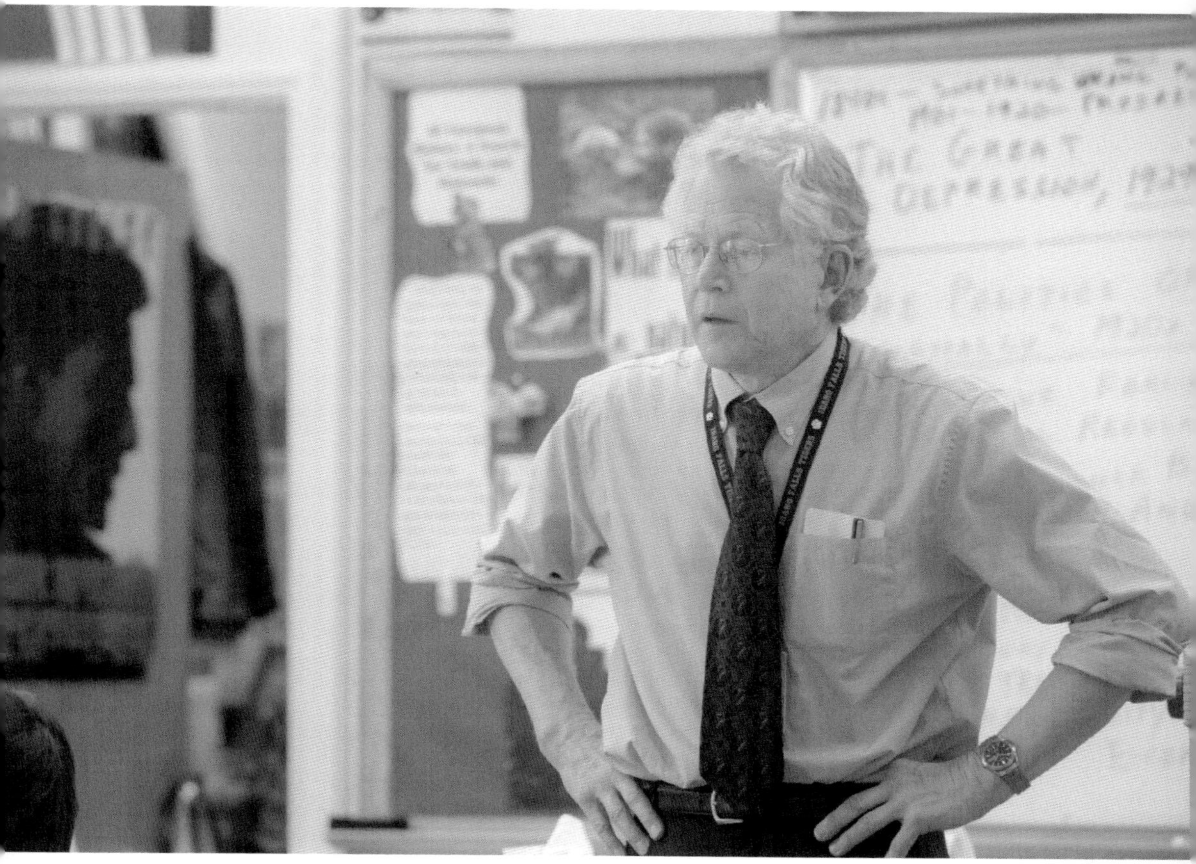

Making Them Think

A teacher in the Idaho Falls school district for 34 years, 23 of which were spent at Idaho Falls High School, Jim Francis gained a reputation for teaching the old-fashioned way: making his students think. In 2011, the year he was honored by the Idaho Humanities Council (and announced his retirement), Francis conceded his teaching approach didn't always mesh with a system focused on standardized testing, but offered no apologies. "I did not want it to become just a test prep course," he said about his Advanced Placement European history course. "I wanted it to become a philosophical course." (Courtesy of the Idaho Falls *Post Register.*)

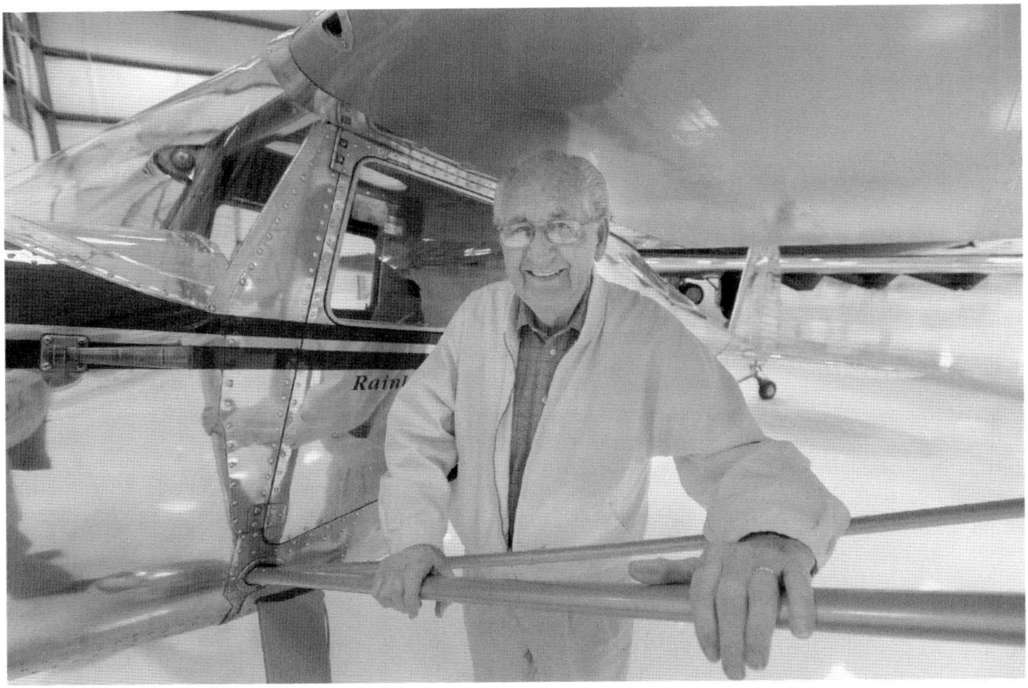

Han Solo's Flight Instructor
Bob Jones's first time in an airplane cockpit was in 1944 after enlisting in the Army Air Corp. The war ended before the Rexburg native saw active duty, but his military training qualified him for a commercial pilot's license. After getting a college degree on the GI Bill, Jones started giving flying lessons at Fanning Field (now Idaho Falls Regional Airport). In the decades that followed, he taught more than 1,000 people to fly, including Harrison Ford. Jones let his instructor's license expire in 2013 at age 88, but he has kept flying for his own enjoyment. (Courtesy of the Idaho Falls *Post Register.*)

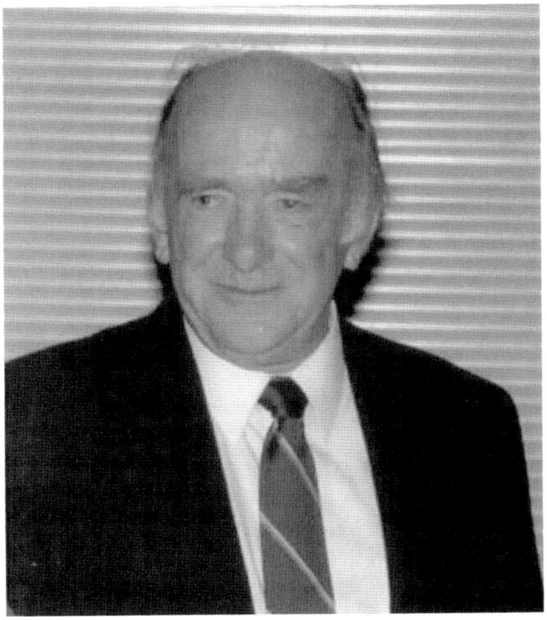

Serving the Poor
Jack Viggers, an Episcopal priest, was one of a group of people who got together in 1968 to administer $35,000 in federal funds to help older people in need. Today, Eastern Idaho Community Action Partnership (EICAP) is a multi-million dollar service organization that manages a food warehouse and homeless shelter, and helps with affordable housing, Head Start centers, and energy assistance for people who can't afford to heat their homes. "The prevailing attitude about seniors was that everybody was doing fine and that anybody who needed help could get it from the church," said Viggers, who died in 2009. "We proved right away that wasn't so." (Courtesy of EICAP.)

CHAPTER FIVE

Greener Pastures

There's a common lament in small town America: "There's nothing to keep kids here once they're done with school," and while it may be true, there is something else to be considered. Some people cannot wait to engage with the wider world. Idaho Falls has produced its fair share of innovators and free-thinkers who have found acclaim and fortune far from their hometown.

"[I] spent seventeen years there in an ice cavern, drawing, doing dumb little plays I wrote, and making flip books. Everything I learned to do then, I make money doing now," said Dame Darcy, an alternative cartoonist and musician who grew up Darcy Stanger, daughter of sign painter and musician Mike Stanger and granddaughter of former county commissioner Edith Stanger.

Her friend on the same block, Jared Gold, occupied himself as a teenager by printing silkscreen t-shirts and selling them, publishing an info-zine called *Aqualung*, and organizing raves in Idaho Falls and Rexburg.

"It gave me a lot of confidence, and when I moved to a bigger city I was ready," said Gold, who became a fashion designer and has appeared as a judge on *America's Next Top Model.*

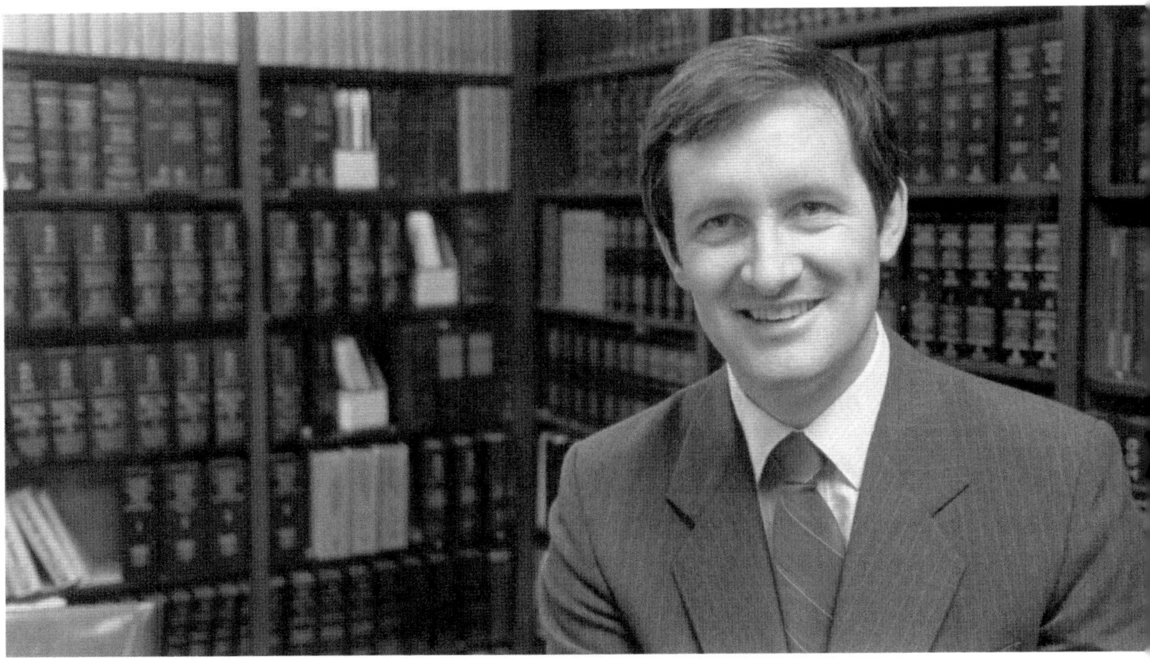

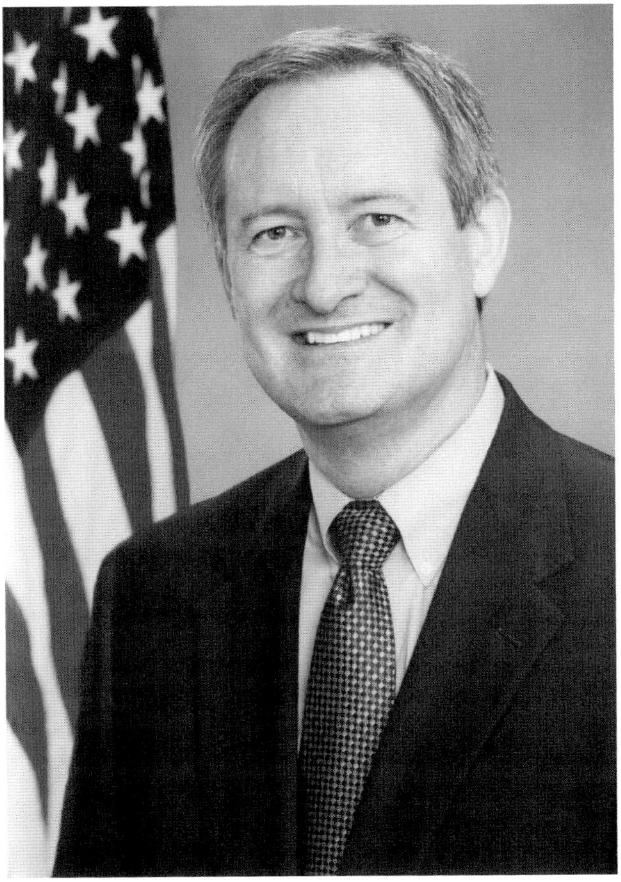

Favorite Son in Washington
Idaho Falls has no greater connection to Congress than Sen. Mike Crapo, who went to Washington, DC, in 1993 and has served since then. Born in 1951, he graduated from Idaho Falls High School before going on to Brigham Young University and Harvard Law School. He became active in Republican Party politics in the 1980s, gaining election to the Idaho State Senate in 1984. He was elected to the House of Representatives in 1992 and served three terms before running for Senate in 1998. In 2004, he was the only US Senate candidate to run unopposed, and was elected with 99 percent of the vote. (Courtesy of the Idaho Falls *Post Register.*)

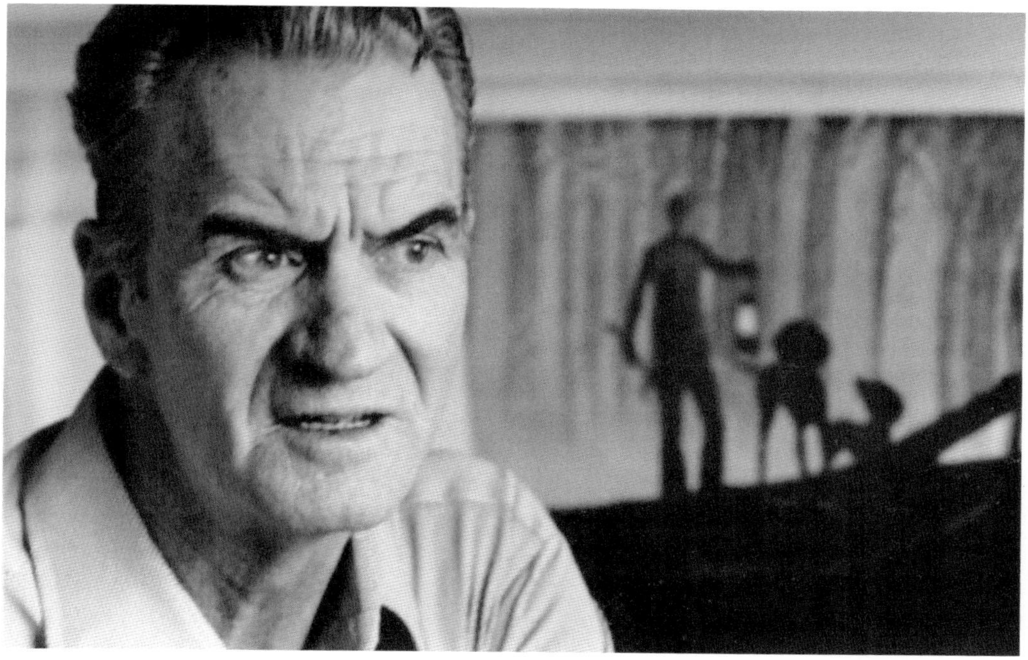

Literary Legend

An Oklahoma native, Wilson Rawls came to eastern Idaho in the late 1950s to work on a construction job for the Atomic Energy Commission. He met his wife, Sophie Ann, an AEC budget analyst, and the two settled into domestic life in Idaho Falls. An aspiring writer with little confidence in himself, one day in frustration he burned his early manuscripts. It was at his wife's urging that he rewrote from memory the story he'd sketched out about a boy in the Ozarks and his dogs. This story was first serialized in the Saturday Evening Post as *The Hounds of Youth*, but when Doubleday picked it up it was given a new title, *Where the Red Fern Grows*. The book languished in obscurity for six years and almost went out of print until a Doubleday editor sent Rawls to speak to more than 5,000 teachers and librarians at a conference in Salt Lake City. Copies were made available, and the orders started coming in a trickle that turned into a raging torrent. It has been adapted to film three times. Locally, Rawls was honored as grand marshal of the Idaho Falls Fourth of July parade in 1974. A sculpture by Marilyn Hoff-Hansen depicting the main characters of the novel adorns the front lawn of the Idaho Falls Public Library. (Courtesy of the Idaho Falls *Post Register*.)

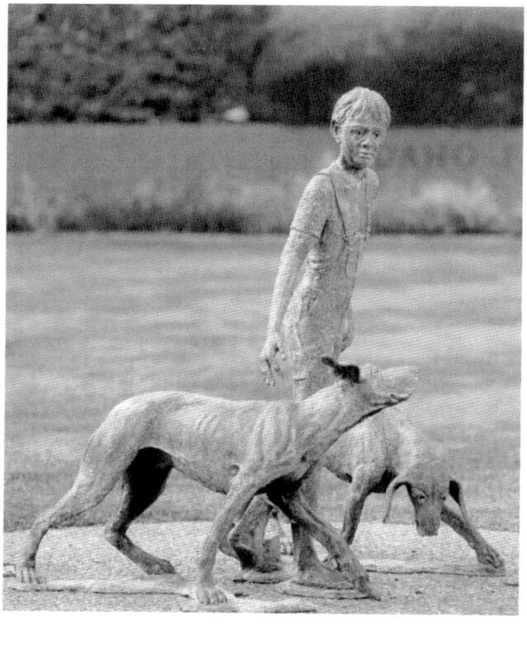

Old Dan and Little Ann

This statue at the Idaho Falls Public Library, entitled *Dreams Can Come True*, was created by Marilyn Hoff-Hansen honoring *Where the Red Fern Grows* and Wilson Rawls's lasting impact on children's literature. (Courtesy of the Museum of Idaho.)

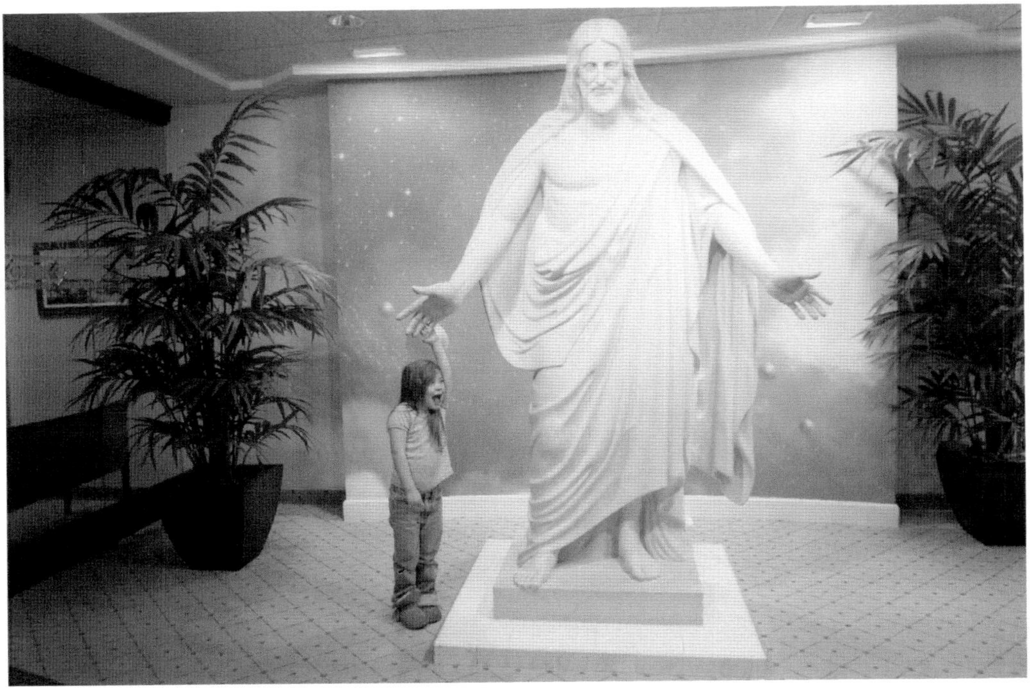

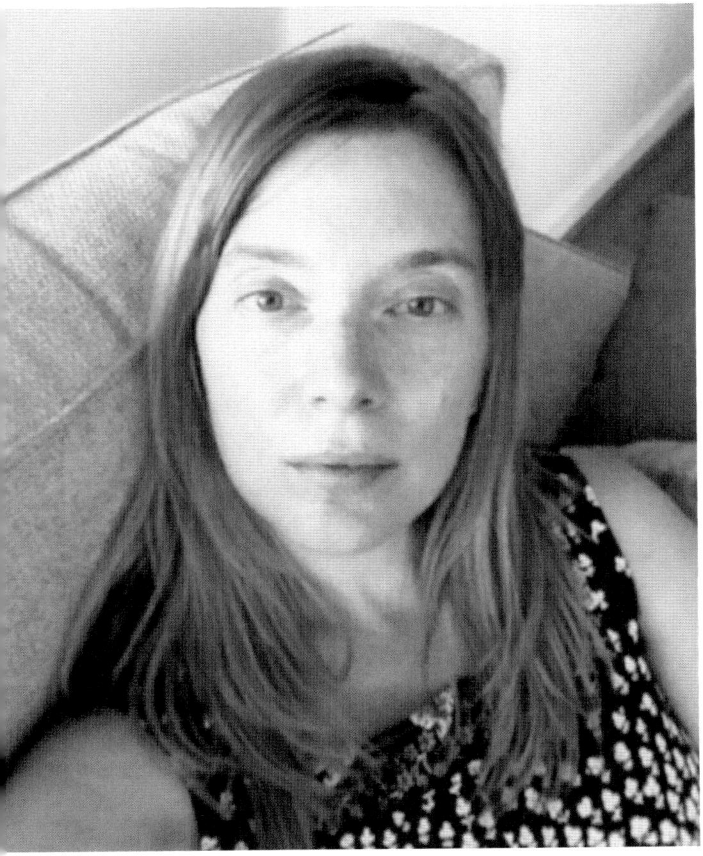

Globetrotting Photojournalist
Natalie Behring left Idaho Falls to make her mark in the world of photojournalism, first for Reuters News Ltd., covering Pres. Bill Clinton's visit to China, the government crackdown on Falun Gong, and the Palestinian Intifada. She spent 12 years in China, during which she worked as a freelancer for Greenpeace, Nike, the *New York Times*, and others. She currently lives in Portland, Oregon, and is well known for distinctive images like the one above. (Both, courtesy of Natalie Behring.)

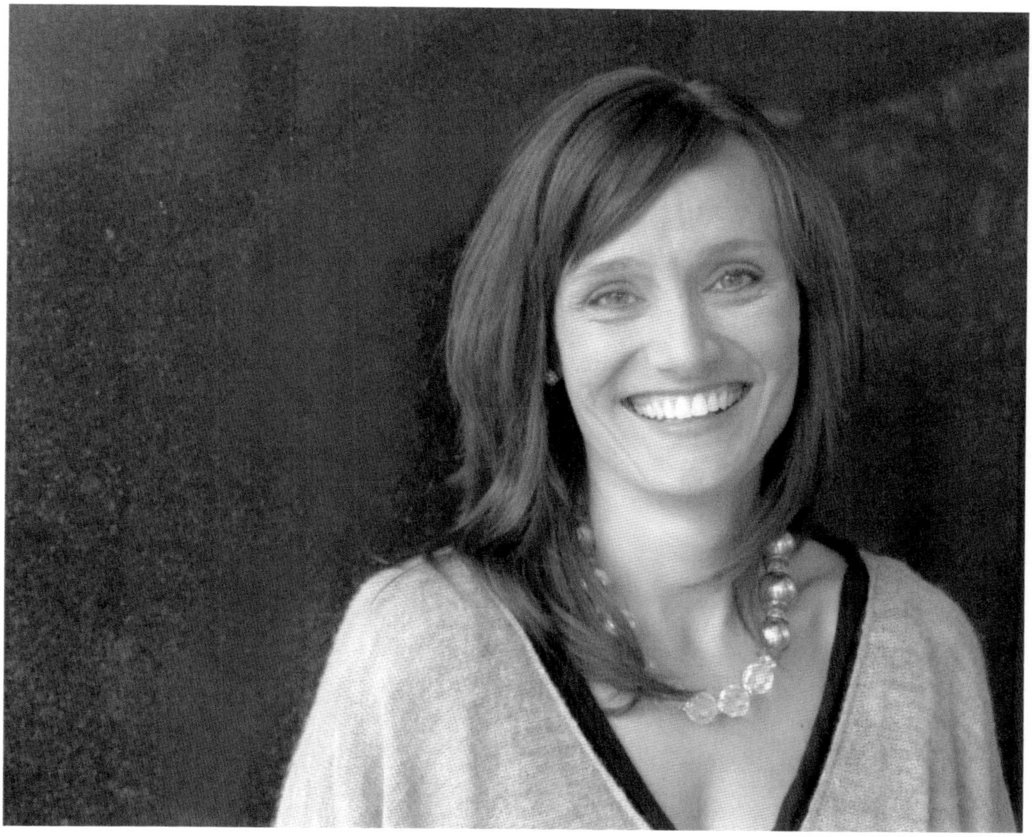

Weekend Commentator

Host of National Public Radio's *Weekend Edition Sunday*, Idaho Falls native Rachel Martin started as a producer and reporter in San Francisco at KQED. She has reported widely from Afghanistan, on politics and government, women's issues, and the US-NATO fight against the insurgency. She covered US military operations in Iraq and the strategic alliance between Sunni sheiks and the US military in Anbar province (below). After a stint with ABC News in 2008, she returned to NPR in 2010. (Both, courtesy of National Public Radio.)

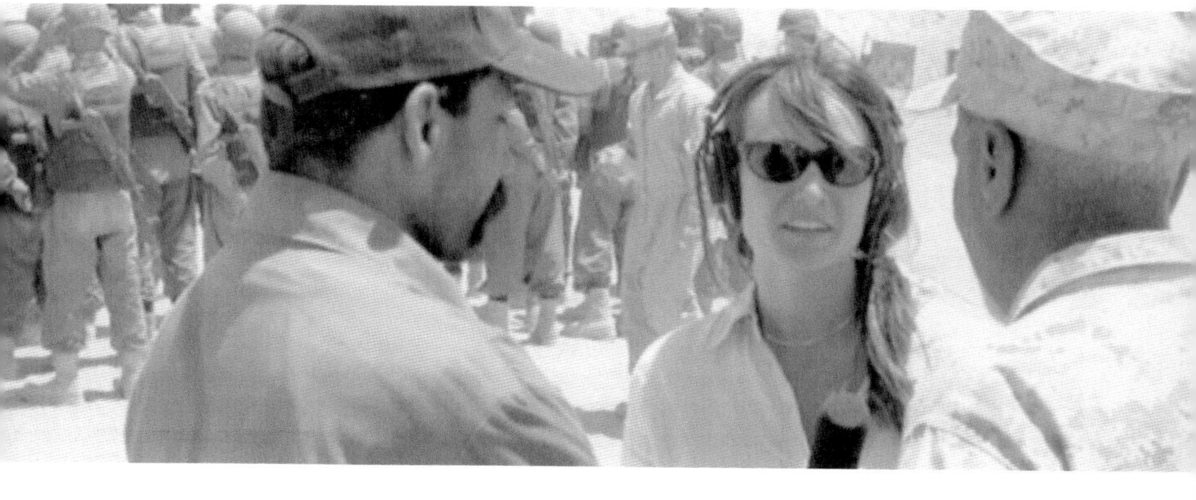

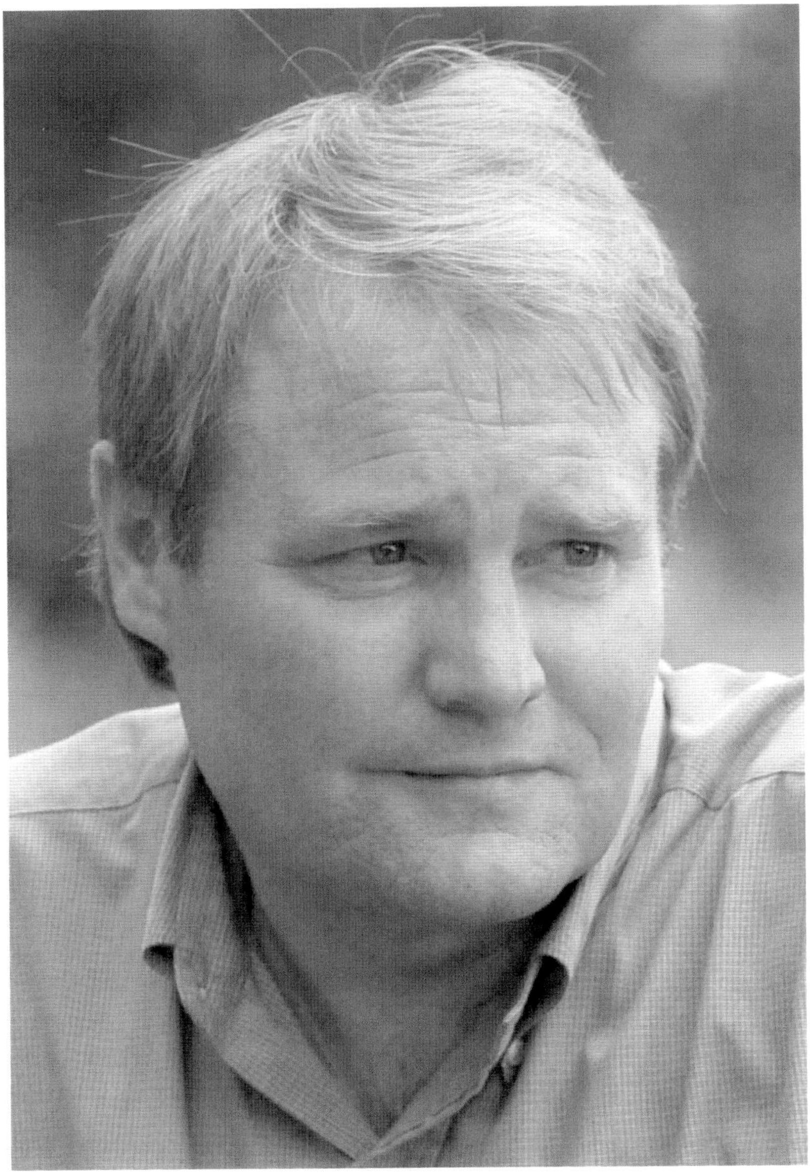

Human Rights Philanthropist

In the 1980s, Greg Carr co-founded Boston Technology, one of the earliest firms to sell voicemail systems to telephone companies. From 1996 to 1998, he was chairman of Prodigy, an early global Internet service provider, and co-founded Africa Online, serving as its chairman until 1998 when he left business and dedicated himself to humanitarian activities. He formed the Carr Center for Human Rights Policy at Harvard in 1999 and the Gregory C. Carr Foundation. Through the foundation, he has been involved in restoring Gorongosa National Park in central Mozambique. The team has reintroduced species to the ecosystem, planted millions of trees in the rainforest, boosted ecotourism, and provided health and education programs to people living near the park's borders. In his hometown, Carr helped finance the expansion of the Bonneville Museum into the Museum of Idaho. In 2001, after it was seized by court order, he bought the Aryan Nation's compound near Hayden Lake and donated the land to North Idaho College. It is now a peace park. (Courtesy of the Carr Foundation.)

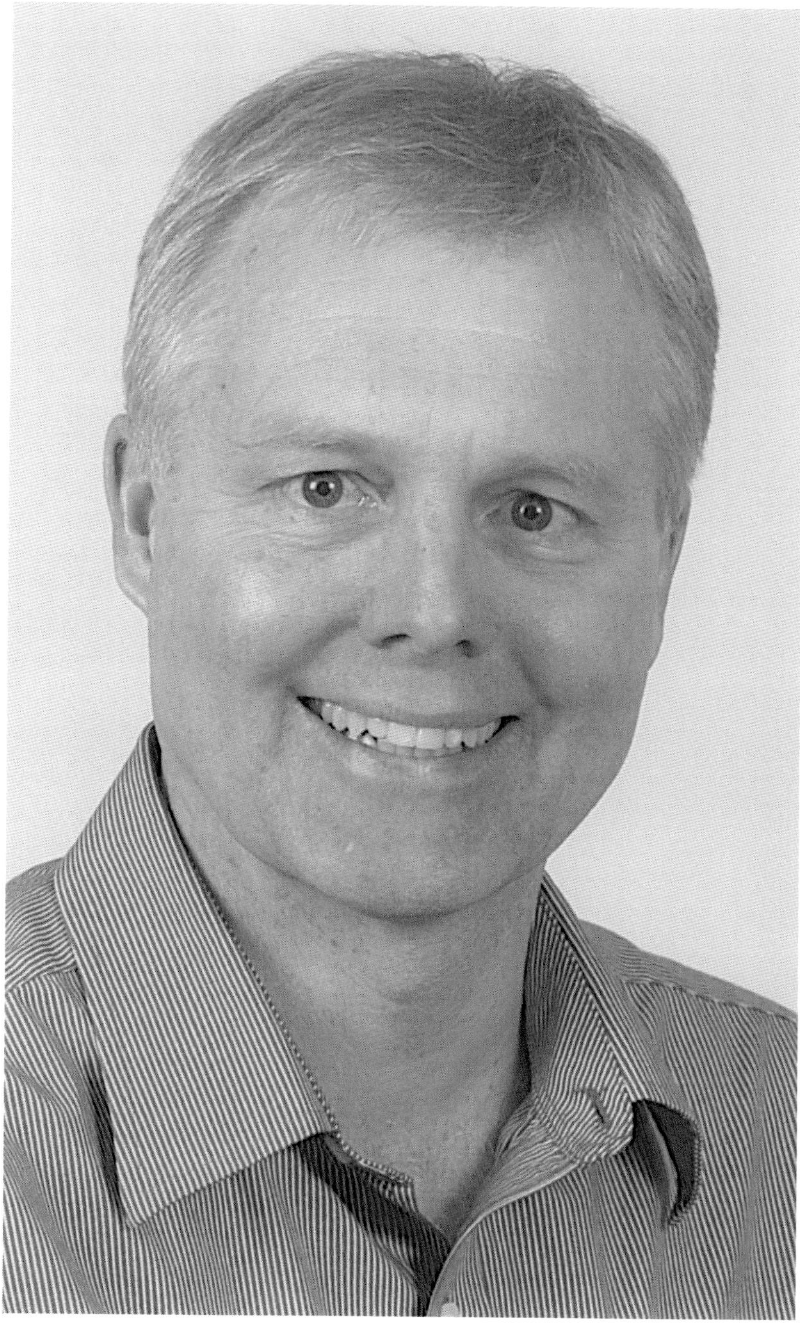

International Service

An Idaho Falls attorney, developer, and social activist, Steven E. Carr is also the first and only American ever elected to the Standing Commission of the International Red Cross and Red Crescent Movement, and was named its vice-chair in 2011. Carr served on the board of governors of the American Red Cross from 2002 to 2008 and chaired the International Services Committee. He also sits on the board of Refugees International. Locally, he writes for the *Post Register* and *Idaho Falls Magazine*. He and his brother Greg are two of the sons of Dr. Taylor and Betty Carr. (Courtesy of the Idaho Falls *Post Register*.)

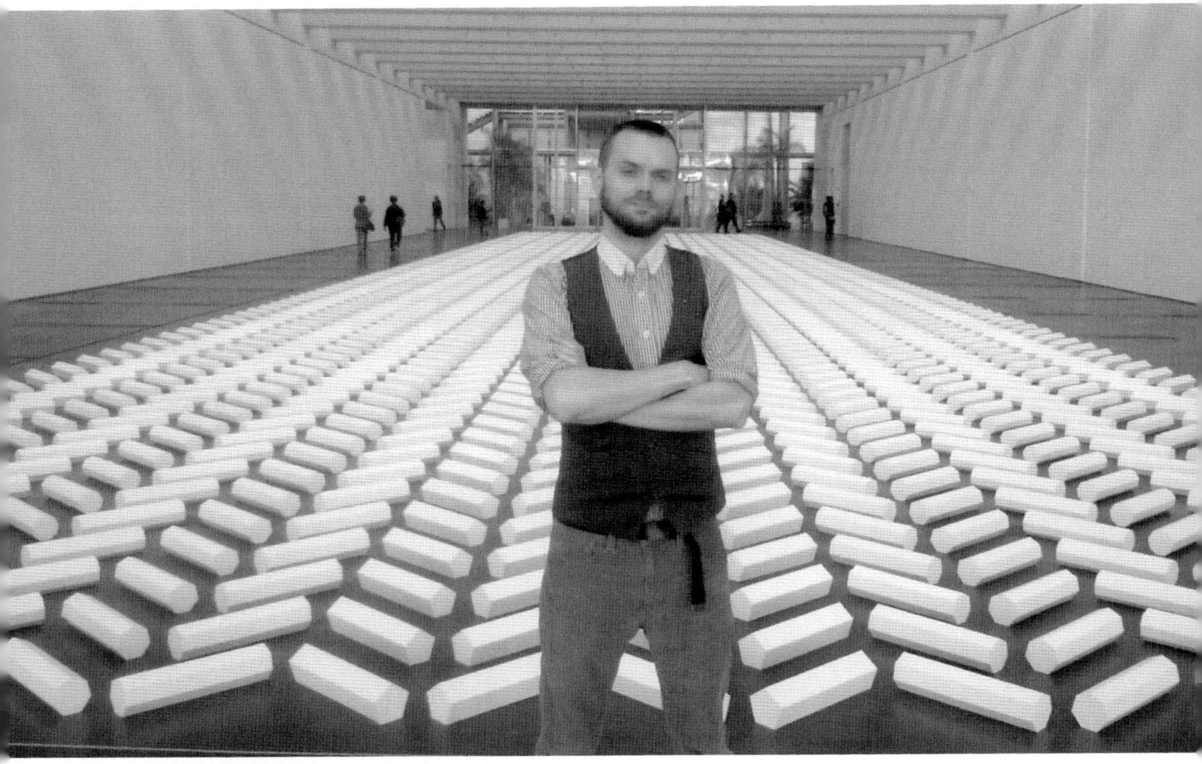

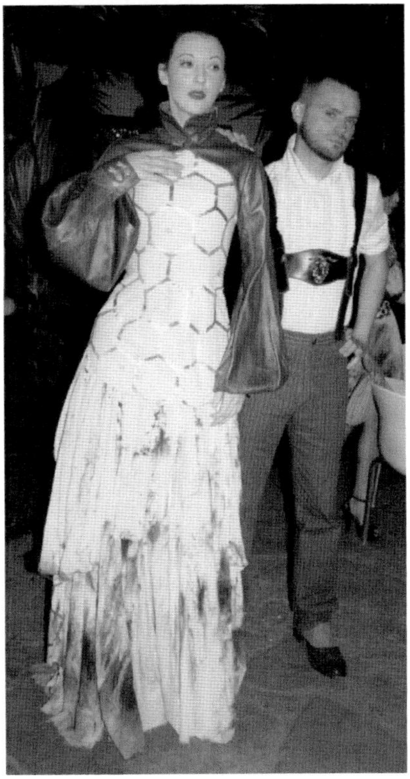

Fashion Forward

A piano prodigy in his youth, Jared Gold was as interested in the runway as he was in the conservatory. In high school, he occupied himself by selling silkscreened T-shirts, publishing an info-zine, and organizing raves. He moved to Salt Lake City, then to Los Angeles, where he studied at Otis Parson's School of Design. He has been creating fashion since 1992 and appeared as a guest judge on *America's Next Top Model* in 2006 on an episode that featured his "roachbrooch" jewelry. He is now a creative director at Woodbury University in Los Angeles. (Both, courtesy of Jared Gold.)

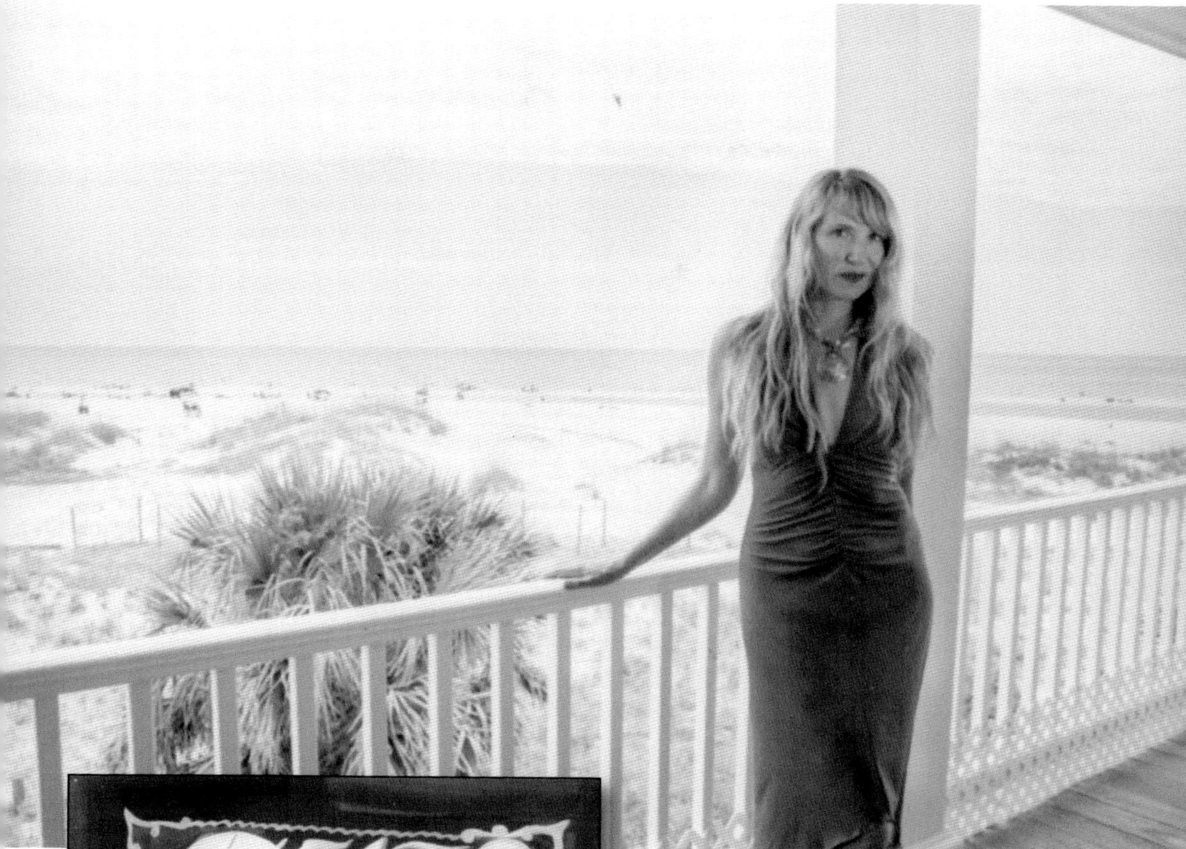

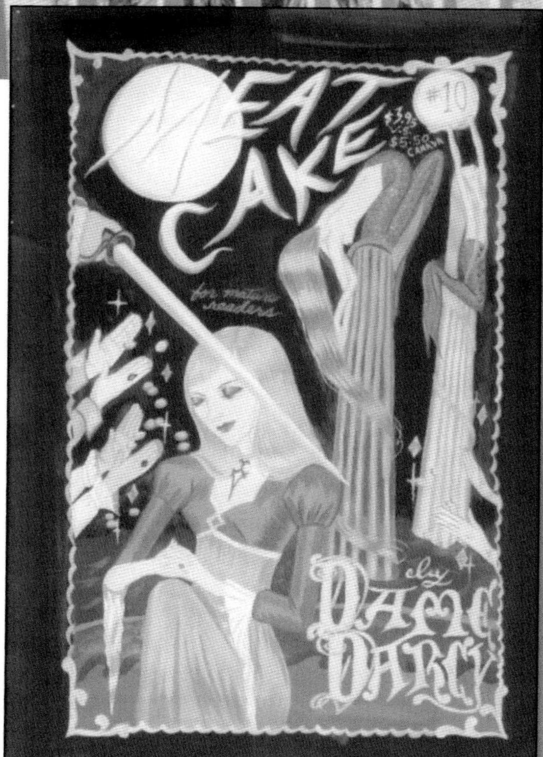

Edgy Artist
Born Darcy Meghan Stanger in 1971, Dame Darcy has made a name for herself as an alternative cartoonist and graphic novelist. She studied at the San Francisco Art Institute, and her comic book *Meat Cake* has been published by Fantagraphics since 1993. The scope of her interests also includes music, and she has been in several bands, singing and playing autoharp, bass, banjo, and singing saw. She has painted murals and designed stained glass for celebrity homes and window displays for Forbidden Planet in New York City. She now lives in Savannah, Georgia. (Both, courtesy of Dame Darcy.)

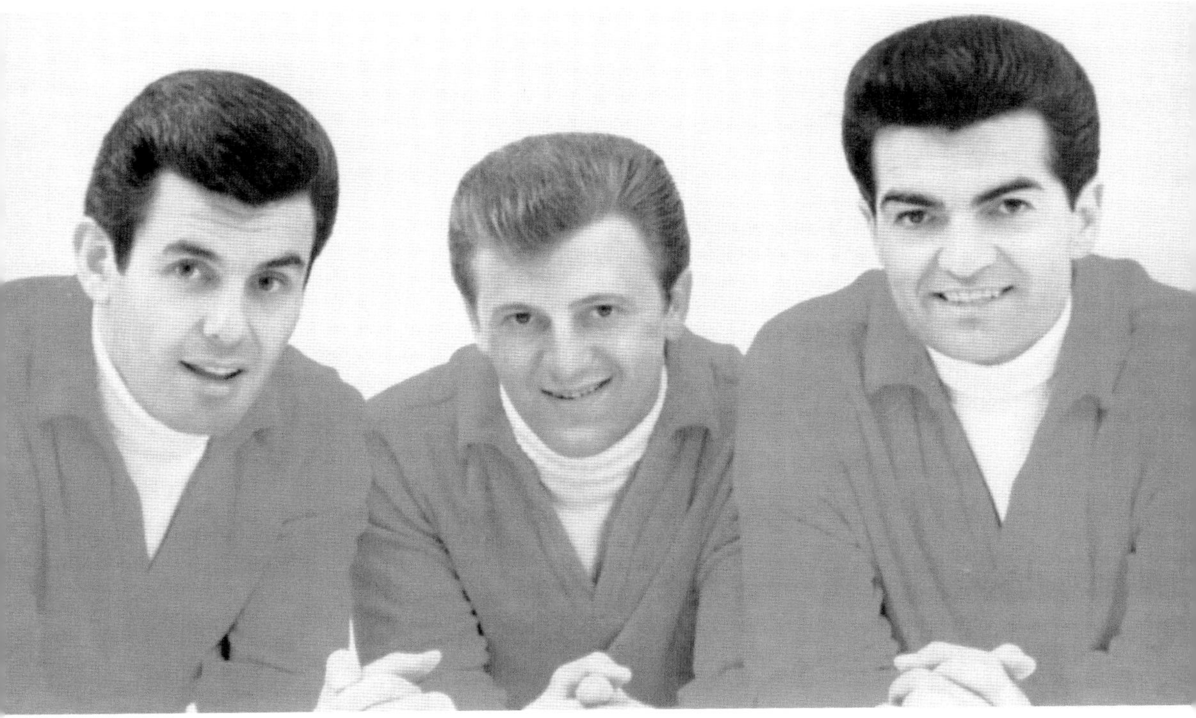

Jim Pike (The Lettermen)
A star athlete at Idaho Falls High School in the 1950s, Jim Pike (center) teamed up with Tony Butala and Jim Engemann in 1960 to sing as The Lettermen, a group that posted 16 top-10 singles. In 1967 when Engemann left to spend more time with his family, he was replaced by Pike's younger brother, Gary. Pike left the group in 1974 due to vocal problems, but with past Lettermen, he formed Reunion in 1983. When NASA decided to leave a recording representing American popular music in a time capsule on the moon, one of the songs chosen was "Love," The Lettermen's last chart hit, a solo sung by Pike. (Courtesy of Capitol Records.)

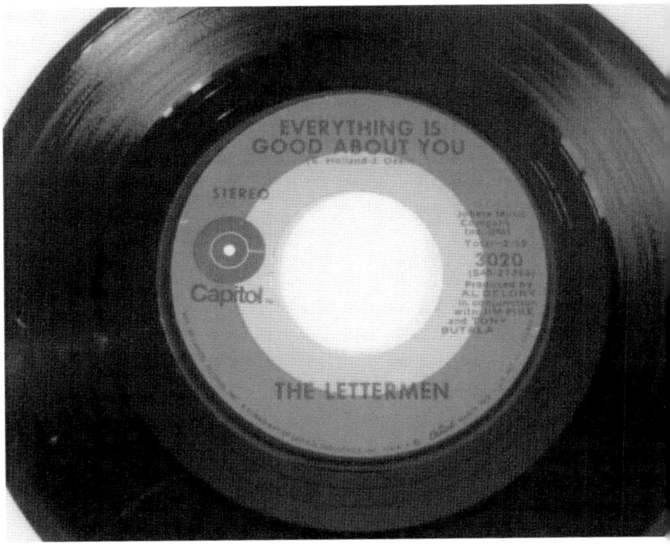

Iconic Label
Shown is one of The Lettermen's big hits in the 1960s. (Courtesy of Capitol Records.)

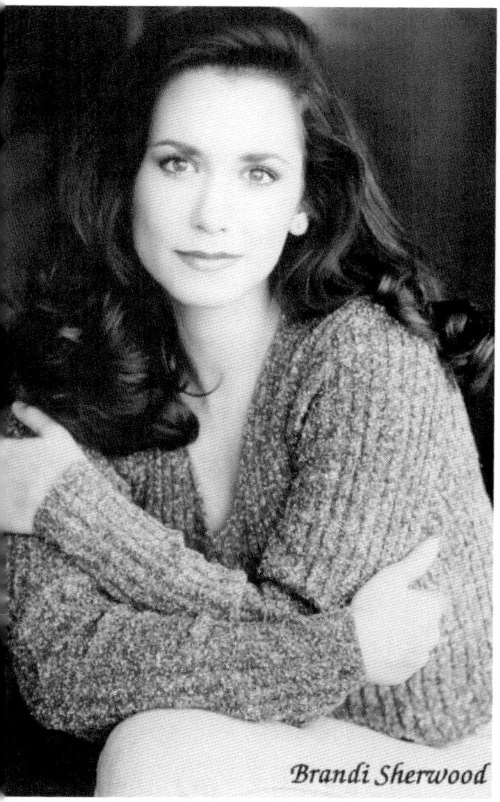

From Pageants to *The Price is Right*

Born in Idaho Falls in 1971, Brandi Sherwood was named Miss Teen USA in 1989 and Miss USA in 1997, the only woman to have held both titles. She went on to work in show business, appearing in commercials and the 2003 feature *Shark Zone*. Between 2002 and 2009, she appeared in millions of homes as a hostess on the daytime television game show *The Price Is Right*. During her reign as Miss USA, Sherwood worked with the Special Olympics. (Courtesy of the Idaho Falls *Post Register.*)

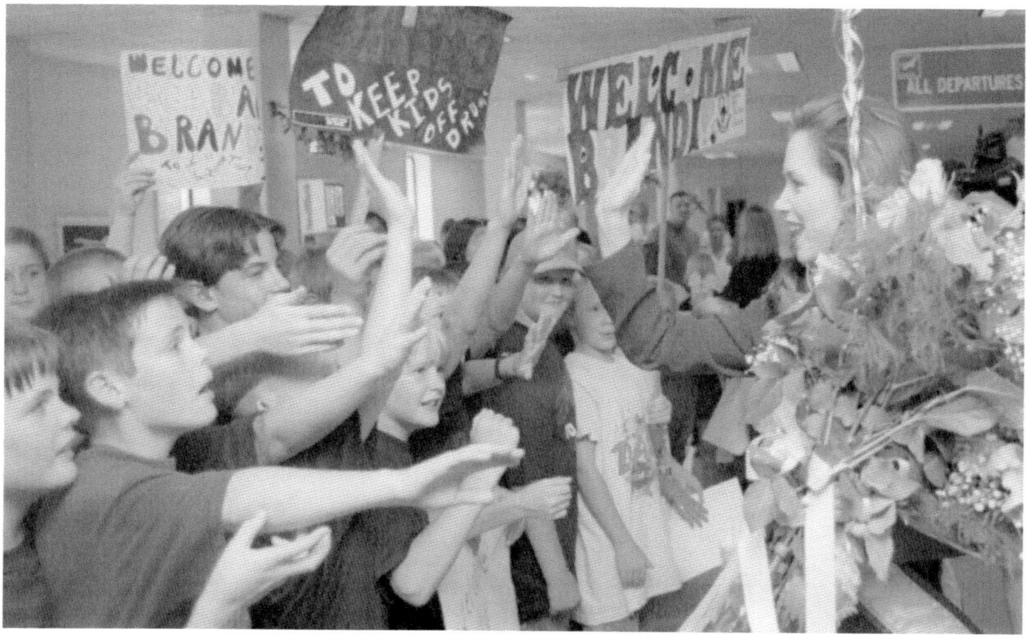

DARE Advocate

Making an appearance on behalf of the DARE program, Brandi Sherwood greets students at the Idaho Falls Regional Airport (Courtesy of the Idaho Falls *Post Register.*)

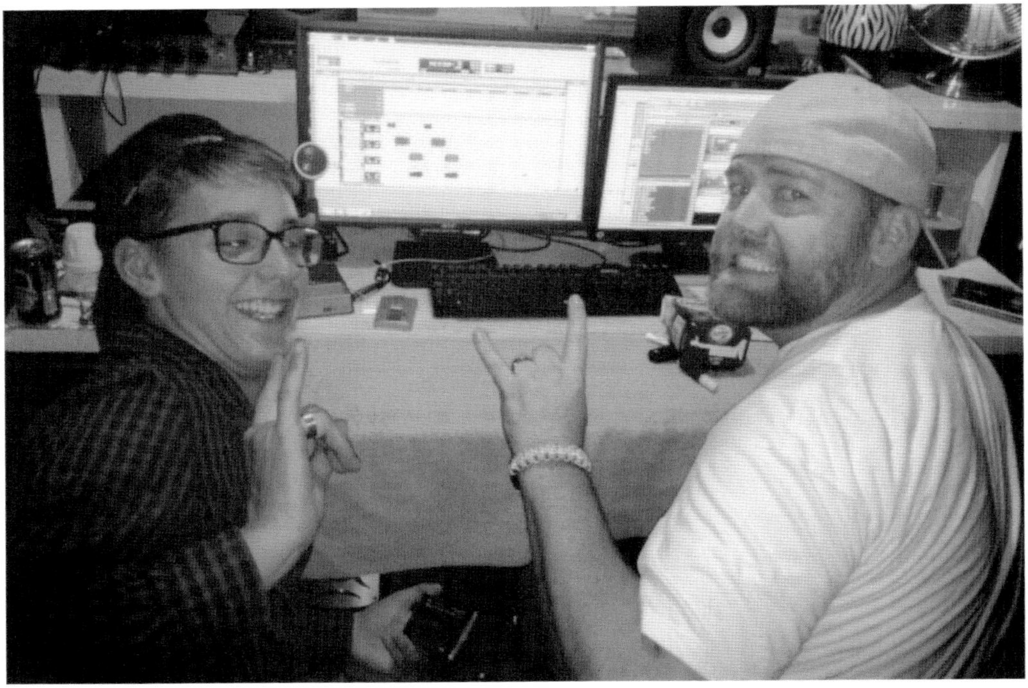

Studio Stalwart

Gregg Hale grew up in Idaho Falls, but it was in Liverpool in 1997 that he met members of the multi-platinum band Spiritualized (below) and joined them on tour after the release of *Ladies and Gentlemen We Are Floating in Space*, named Record of the Year by New Musical Express. He moved back to Utah the next year to start his label Handsome Rob Records and Lincoln Street Sound Studio in Midvale. He has also done extensive recording work for Fox and Fox Soccer Channel, and reviews music for LDS music blog *Linescratchers*. (Both, courtesy of Gregg Hale.)

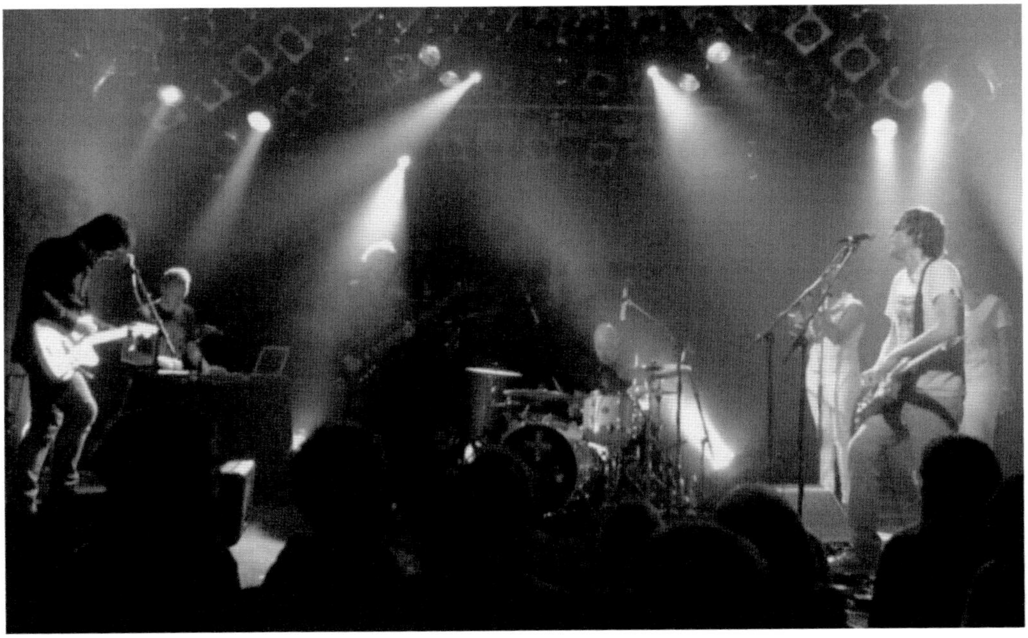

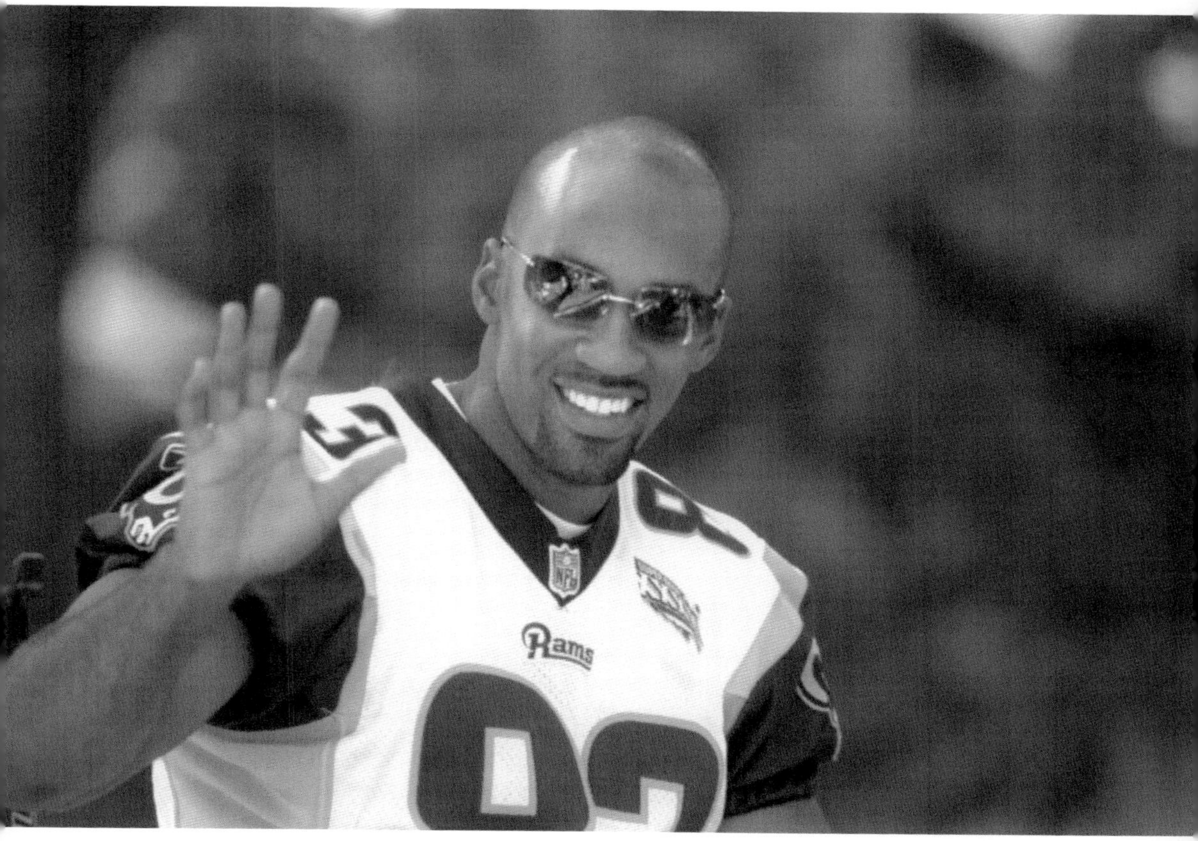

Emotion Bowl to Super Bowl

Llewllyn "Yo" Murphy took Idaho Falls High School to a state championship before attending the University of Idaho. In 1992, he was chosen first-team All American by three publications, coming in second in the NCAA with 68 receptions for 1,156 yards and nine touchdowns. After college, he played with the BC Lions in Vancouver, then with the NFL Europe's Scottish Claymores, and was named World Bowl MVP in 1996. He returned stateside in 1999 to play for the Tampa Bay Buccaneers, Minnesota Vikings, Kansas City Chiefs, and St. Louis Rams, with whom he went to the Super Bowl in 2001. He now works as a coach and fitness trainer in Florida. (Courtesy of the Idaho Falls *Post Register.*)

INDEX

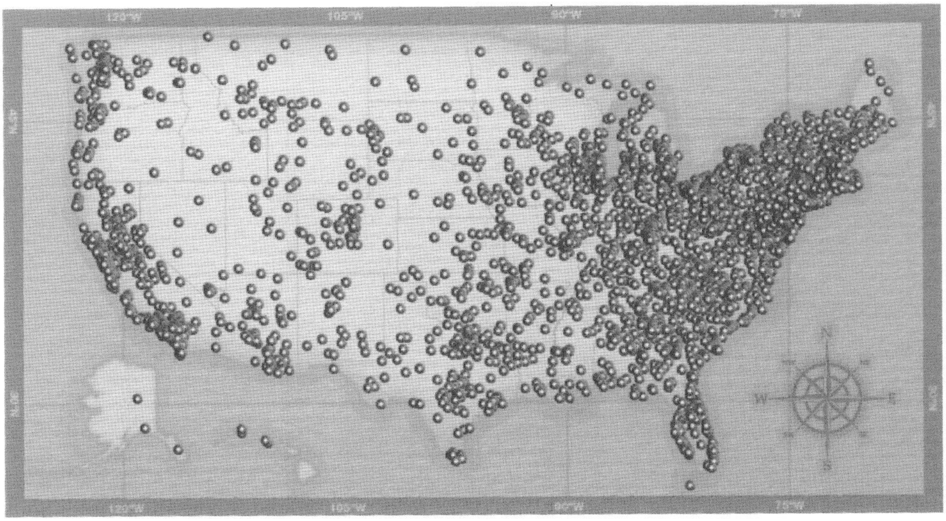